from Sally

Christmas '08

Curmudgeons, Drunkards, and Outright Fools

Courts-Martial of Civil War Union Colonels

THOMAS P. LOWRY

Foreword by William C. Davis

University of Nebraska Press
Lincoln and London

Originally published as *Tarnished Eagles: The Courts-Martial of Fifty Union Colonels and Lieutenant Colonels* (Stackpole Books, 1997).

Library of Congress Cataloging-in-Publication Data
Lowry, Thomas P. (Thomas Power), 1932–
[Tarnished eagles]
Curmudgeons, drunkards, and outright fools: courts-martial of Civil War Union
colonels / Thomas P. Lowry; foreword by William C. Davis.
p.   cm.
Originally published: Tarnished eagles. Mechanicsburg, PA: Stackpole Books, 1997.
"Bison Books."
Includes bibliographical references and index.
ISBN 0-8032-8024-6 (pbk.: alk. paper)
1. Courts-martial and courts of inquiry—United States—History—19th century.
2. Trials (Military offenses)—United States—History—19th century.   3. United States.
Army—Officers.   I. Title.
KF7641.L69   2003
343.73′0143—dc21
2003044799

DEDICATED TO THE MEMORY OF

Group Captain J. F. W. Pembridge, AFC, RAF

One of the good colonels

CONTENTS

PART FIVE A MISCELLANY

ACKNOWLEDGMENTS

First and foremost, I wish to express my gratitude to Beverly A. Lowry, my wife, who not only found half of these colonels in our perusal of National Archives records, but also rendered my indecipherable scrawl into a finished manuscript.

To my editor, William C. "Jack" Davis, I owe much to his ability to crystallize, in a few words, the issues that could raise this compilation from a scrapbook into a book.

The medical histories of these men are largely the work of Jack D. Welsh, M.D., while the background information on the New York colonels came from Benedict R. Maryniak.

No serious work on the Union army can be done without the help of Michael P. Musick of the National Archives, and this book is no exception. DeAnne Blanton, too, pointed the way to many useful files. At the U.S. Army Military Institute, Michael J. Winey and Randy W. Hackenburg introduced us to their wonderful collection of photographs, and David C. Cole at the U.S. Army Center of Military History added valuable insights.

Mary Beth Linné and her staff in the National Archives reading room were invaluable in keeping track of documents and maintaining order among a milling throng of researchers.

Finally, I wish to acknowledge my debt to those unsung heroes, the compilers, whose reference works we often take for granted: Frederick H. Dyer, William Frayne Amann, Ezra J. Warner, and the anonymous authors of the *Official Army Register*.

As always, the author bears sole responsibility for interpretations, errors, and omissions.

THE SOURCE MATERIAL

The Union court-martial records in the National Archives are handwritten records, varying in length from two to a thousand pages. The paper may be white or blue and is usually about eight-by-fourteen inches, but might be almost any size, depending on local availability during the war. Most trials were written on both sides of the sheet, and the completed records were usually tightly bound with red ribbon, paste, or steel clips (now rusted). Most of the courts-martial were not page numbered, and in the past 130 years, some have been disassembled, producing a "paper salad," with pages out of order. Occasionally, a scribe would carefully number the pages, but this is rare.

The trials are filed in numbered manila folders with labels such as LL854. Each numbered folder in Record Group 153 might contain one court-martial or dozens. For these reasons, it is possible to cite the folder number and nothing more. A researcher wishing to read the original text would need to search the folder, find the correct trial, and read its contents page by page in order to locate the exact location and context of any particular quoted section of a trial.

FOREWORD

"Boys will be boys." The expression is so common it has become a cliché, and like so many idioms, it has little real meaning when carefully examined. For a start, it is almost always applied not to "boys," but to men. For another, it seems to imply that there is some standard or measure that can be applied to explain the behavior of men in general, whereas the male of the species is, if anything, just as complex and varied in instincts, moods, and behavior as the female.

In the main, this aphorism appears whenever men misbehave, and there perhaps it has some validity, as men seem to be more prone to misconduct than women. If the expression had been coined by the 1860s, it certainly would have seen a lot of use when nearly three million American men went to war, for, along with their bravery and innocence, they took with them their penchant to break free from the traces of rules and propriety from time to time.

What startles us, however, just as it surprised them at the time, was how prone their commanders were to the same misbehavior. These were the men expected to set examples for the rest, and yet we find now that these officers and gentlemen were constantly embroiled in legal troubles for offenses great and petty. Thomas P. Lowry's *Tarnished Eagles* is the first systematic look at Civil War courts-martial, and focusing exclusively on Union colonels, it offers the surprising finding that officers, in fact, were in trouble more often than the enlisted men.

More than 100,000 men in the Union Army alone faced court-martial. And although the great bulk of Confederate records did not survive, there is no reason to suppose that Southerners were any less prone to misbehave or that their offenses would have been any different. Until now no one has gone through that mass of documentation to study in depth what happened when those "boys" were being "boys." Thomas and Beverly Lowry have been engaged for several years in a pioneering exploration of all of the surviving court-martial records. The ultimate result of their work is yet to be realized, as the research continues even now. But *Tarnished Eagles* is the first fruit of their work, and already promises to alter our view and understanding of the men who led.

With the exception of the few who were tried for cowardice, nothing emerges to challenge the courage of most of them on the battlefield. It is in their other responsibilities that we see human foibles and weaknesses manifest themselves.

Some were just inefficient. Others were insubordinate. A few were brutes. And many simply represented the clash of cultures and attitudes when nonprofessional volunteer officers came up against career army officers as superiors. In a way, they symbolize the age-old struggle in America between the minuteman tradition and the professional military. The Civil War, especially in the Union, crystallized the conflict as the scale of warfare, and of America's role in the world, escalated far beyond the abilities of the then traditionally tiny peacetime army. These *Tarnished Eagles* are evidence of growing pains as the American military and the attitudes of American citizenry toward an army began to mature. In no future war would such a stunning proportion of American officers go before courts.

A few of them are inevitably engaging. Who is there who has ever served in uniform who did not at least once dream of cursing some annoying officer to his face? "All of you are damned fools," complained one miscreant in these pages. "Am I to be annoyed to death by old soldiers?" A few of them filled their idle hours with drink. A couple of them kept distinctly unregulation mistresses. Some simply seemed to make a profession of being unpleasant, while others were just naturally contentious. Not surprisingly, more than a few had been attorneys in civil life, and did not grasp that entering the military put them in a realm that did not welcome adversarial discourse.

Lowry lets their court-martial records speak for themselves, wisely reserving judgment on the individuals for the most part, while drawing some far-reaching conclusions from their experience as a whole. An army is a dynamic creature, subject continually to internal stresses and turmoils not evident to those outside, and the Union army was no different. *Tarnished Eagles* does not remove the glitter from the brass and bullion of these officers; they did that to themselves. But it does lift a cloak to reveal the often discordant "corporate culture" of an army of the people whose officers did not always seem to realize that the foe was on the other side of the battleline.

—**WILLIAM C. DAVIS**

INTRODUCTION:
THE REFINER'S FIRE

War is a crucible, a glowing furnace where the hot blue flame of responsibility sears the human amalgam of vice and virtue, blasting away imperfection in a fiery shower of sparks, leaving behind only the glowing substrate, the noble elements which endure.

Danger, death, and duty are the lot of every soldier, but the colonel's situation is unique: His span of control is large enough to make a difference, yet small enough so that he is known at sight by all his men. The Civil War, with its enormous scope, its impassioned issues, and its preponderance of locally raised regiments, may well have been the ultimate test of American colonels, and this national conflagration, this orgy of destruction, this locomotive of history which disarranged and transformed every facet of American life, brought to the fore two vital issues—how men handle command, and the relationship between citizen-soldiers and career military men. Both these issues retained their vitality and their relevance from Fort Sumter to Appomattox.

The prewar army was small, while, at its peak of the Civil War, nearly two million men wore Union blue. Most were volunteers—a more reassuring word than amateur. There were more than 2,500 regiments in the Union army, with no possibility of the old professional army providing 2,500 colonels to command these regiments. Most of the volunteer officers came to colonelcy by one of three routes: raising their own regiments, receiving a state governor's appointment, or being elected by their own men. Whatever the route, most had one thing in common—little or no military experience.

Above colonels were the generals: brigadier generals, major generals, and, rarely, a lieutenant general. These posts were filled largely by old army men, the only ones whose training had equipped them for such a role. This set the stage for conflict between amateur colonels and professional generals. In the chain of command downward, there were, too often, jealous majors and lieutenant colonels, anxious to displace their leader and see silver eagles upon their own shoulders. While these tensions usually led to ill will and inefficiency, a number of them were severe enough to generate a general court-martial, the military equivalent of a civilian jury trial for a felony offense.

1

In the first eighteen months of the war, ninety colonels and fifty-one lieu-tenant colonels were the subject of a general court-martial or, more rarely, a court of inquiry or a military commission. In these tribunals, both the great issues—how to exercise command and professional versus amateur—were writ large. It would be an error, however, to expect the same procedures and assump-tions as might be seen in a civil trial. To understand the origins of the difference, we need to go back 2,000 years.

THE HISTORY OF COURTS-MARTIAL

The Western origin of both civilian and military jurisprudence traces directly from ancient Rome. Since Roman history, in all its many aspects—kingdom, republic, empire—spans nearly 1,000 years, and many records have been lost, only a partial view is possible, but even that will show startling parallels with more recent codes and regulations.[1]

Two crucial factors governed Roman military discipline. The first was the traditional role of a Roman father. Both the law and custom gave him literal life and death powers over his own household: his wife, his children, his servants, even his sons- and daughters-in-law, as well as his grand- and great grand-chil-dren. The direct transference of this principle into martial jurisprudence may be seen in the following event from the life of the consul Manlius Torquatus. His son, Titus, a cavalry commander, was on reconnaissance, ordered to observe and report, but to avoid battle. Titus encountered an enemy chief, engaged in single combat, killed the chief and brought home the armor of the vanquished. The father, far from pleased, publicly noted Titus's disobedience of orders to avoid combat, had his son tied to a stake and beheaded before the entire command.[2]

Titus's fate illustrates the second point, as well: the purpose of military courts is not justice, but maintenance of order and the enforcement of obedience. The Roman procedures for night sentries further illustrate these points. Each sentry on each shift received a numbered tablet. These were collected when the cavalry patrols made their night rounds. A sentry asleep or away from his post would have no tablet to present. At dawn, any missing tablets would instantly identify the cul-prit, who was then beaten to death with clubs that same morning. Polybius remarked, "The night watches of the Roman army are most scrupulously kept."[3]

While no unified, organized code of Roman military law exists, various compilations such as Justinian's *Digest* and the *Laws of Ruffus* do give a basis for comparison with later codes and regulations. Ruffus (380 A.D.) writes, "If any legionary dare resist his superior officer, he shall suffer the supreme penalty," while the articles promulgated under James II (1688 A.D.) state, "If any soldier shall presume to resist his Superior Officer, he shall suffer death." Ruffus noted that failure to follow a command would be punished with death, while James II merely required "punishment." Both Ruffus and James prescribed death for *unauthorized* looting, as spoils were to be divided fairly, and premature looting opened the army to counterattack.[4]

The Romans executed soldiers who spoke ill of the emperor, while in 1688, a soldier who used "traitorous words" against the "Sacred Person of the King's Most Excellent Majesty" would also die.[5] (There are courts-martial of many Union men who spoke ill of Abraham Lincoln, but conviction usually led to prison, not to the firing squad.)[6]

Justinian's *Digest* states, "Every disorder to the prejudice of common discipline, such as laziness, insolence or idleness, is a military offense," a phrase so broad as to be applicable to almost any sort of disruptive behavior.[7] This concept of an all-purpose law seems to be a useful one, since it has endured for more than 2,000 years. In the 1775 Articles of War, approved by the Continental Congress for use by the fledgling American army (and largely lifted verbatim from the British Army regulations), we see in Article 50 the same concept, in which "all disorders and neglects which are to the prejudice of good order and military discipline" may be punished.

Leaping ahead eighty years, we find in the regulations used during the Civil War, in Article 99, the words forbidding "conduct prejudicial to good order and military discipline." The concept is the same; nearly any offense could be described under such a rubric. And was. In the 1920s, Billy Mitchell, the visionary Army Air Service pioneer, was tried and convicted under the "conduct prejudicial" clause of the regulations then in force.[8] In 1950, Congress enacted the Uniform Code of Military Justice, in an attempt to more closely match military justice to its civilian equivalent, but we see in today's Article 134, almost unchanged from the words of Justinian, the proscription of all "disorder and neglects to the prejudice of good order and discipline." The past is ever close to us.[9]

In Rome, soldiers who committed rape had their noses cut off. The theft of a sword was punished with "severe" flogging, while the theft of a mule was punished by the loss of both hands. Malingerers were executed, a procedure which certainly must have simplified sick call.[10]

As the Roman era faded into the confusion of the Dark Ages, it might seem that military codes would be absent, but such was not the case. The chivalric codes (based largely upon church ethics) were often unwritten, but widely known, and governed much of military behavior, especially in regards to terms of surrender, granting of quarter, setting of ransom, and the treatment of prisoners. Shakespeare addressed this in *Henry V,* in which Henry, in direct violation of the chivalric code, killed thousands of French knights who had surrendered and stood swordless and helmetless, as defenseless as tortoises. Later, Henry defended himself on grounds of "military necessity," but it was ever a blot.[11]

The chivalric codes themselves were eclipsed by four later events: the Crusades, where non-Christians were butchered; the final Crusade in which the victims were Byzantine Christians; the invention of firearms (a bullet gave no time for negotiated surrender or chivalric behavior); and the rise of Protestantism, in which Christians began killing other Christians with increasing frenzy and impassioned self-justification.

As the chivalric tradition faded, specific military codes took its place. The British Articles of War of 1685 defined two types of courts-martial: general, which heard only capital cases; and regimental courts-martial which, in theory, tried only misdemeanors. In actual practice, the regimental courts-martial frequently exceeded their bounds, and imposed punishment severe even by the standards of that day. General courts-martial were required to have a sworn clerk, who made a summary, but the records of the regimental proceedings were often scanty. Further, regimental courts-martial sentences were not subject to royal review. The result was abuse. Floggings exceeding one hundred lashes were common, and the wooden horse, with weights hung from the soldier's legs, would dislocate the hip joints, a barbaric punishment tending to reduce the man's usefulness as a soldier. In 1722, the Judge Advocate General under George I inveighed against such brutality, but without success, and the regimental courts-martial continued essentially unrestrained.[12]

As general courts-martial came increasingly under Parliamentary and crown control, the procedures of indictment, hearing, and trial were regularized, and prolonged pretrial confinement was reduced. Civil trials required two witnesses for conviction, but British military law required only one.[13] This appeared severe, but was less so than the French requirements in the same era, in which torture was recommended if evidence for conviction was lacking.[14]

In 1715, British general courts-martial began to require an oath of all witnesses and of the members of the court. In 1753, the Mutiny Act entitled a soldier to a copy of his trial transcript, something unknown before. Beginning in 1774, a defendant could request a postponement to prepare his case and became entitled to cross-examine witnesses.[15]

The concept that ignorance of the law might constitute a defense was early recognized, and in 1718, new regulations prohibited the death sentence for men who had never been read the Articles of War. (It was quite reasonably assumed that enlisted men would be illiterate.) In order to remedy this loophole, in 1718, it was required that the Articles of War be read to every regiment every two months. (The defense of not having heard the Articles of War was still widely used in the American Civil War.)

These improved procedural safeguards did not make much change in the ferocious nature of the sentences. In 1642, in the British Army, twenty-one different crimes called for the death penalty, and it was not until 1718 that a few were dropped from the list, including "destruction of corn fields," which had previously been punished by hanging. In 1722, the courts were given further discretionary power, in many cases, to commute a death sentence to flogging or to transportation to a distant post.[16]

Flogging was not abolished in the British Army until 1881, and until 1817, the civil courts were still ordering stripes and lashes for women. In the early 1700s, a British army deserter might receive as many as 3,000 lashes, which invariably required hospitalization afterward, at which point the regimental surgeon was held responsible if the victim died. In 1740, as a reform(!), the number of lashes was set at a maximum of 1,000.[17]

In the 1700s, critics of the system of discipline noted that a penalty disproportionate to the crime might be harmful to morale, and suggestions were made that good soldiers be rewarded, as well as bad ones punished. In 1812, as a concession to this reform movement, regimental courts-martial were restricted to sentences of 300 lashes or less. Many diarists noted the role of punishments in the lives of British soldiers. Alexander Alexander, writing in 1801, described watching a man die after 229 lashes and noted many men receiving up to 700 strokes of the whip. Rifleman Harris described General Crauford who, when retreating through the snow in 1808, stopped the regiment long enough for one man to receive 300 lashes for grumbling. Corporal Ryder, serving in India in the 1840s, recalled an epidemic of men striking their superiors, a condition soon cured by two public executions by firing squad.[18]

Col. George Croghan, an American hero of the War of 1812, was inspector general of the U.S. Army from 1826 to 1845, and made annual visits to the western forts. In 1836, he was asked to comment on the effects of the recent but temporary abolition of flogging. He noted—a century and a half earlier than today's behavioral scientists—that certainty of punishment rather than severity, is the best deterrent of crime. The thin supply of officers in the western forts meant that many months would be required to assemble a general court-martial, months in which the laggard relaxed in the guard house while his well-behaved companions labored at building fortifications. This unnecessarily comforted the wicked and annoyed the virtuous. Croghan recommended that immediate regimental courts-martial of deserters be held, that the malefactor receive the full number of authorized lashes, be put to hard labor in chains for the term of his enlistment, and upon his departure from the army be branded on the shoulder to warn future recruiters against reenlistment.[19]

More encouragingly, Croghan noted the posts where morale and efficiency were good. He attributed this to enlightened commanders, who rewarded good soldiers and punished bad ones.

AMERICANS AND DISCIPLINE

Even before America was a nation, its army had Articles of War, sixty-nine of them, which covered everything from dueling to church behavior. The rules are clear, straightforward and logical, a model of concise and coherent prose. The principal surprise for modern readers is the distinction drawn between line and artillery officers, a difference no longer relevant with changed training and technology. What do these articles and their application tell us about the Revolutionary War?[20]

Today, there is a certain cachet attached to being a descendant of a soldier of that war, a gloss exceeded only by finding an ancestor who stepped ashore from the *Mayflower.* While many men fought with forbearance and distinction, even a limited survey of the regimental orderly books reveals more than 3,000 courts-martial, with malefactors and punishments that might surprise readers today. Consider Lt. Col. James Abrams of a Massachusetts regiment, who received seventy-five lashes for killing a cow and some geese. The list of defendants runs literally from A to Z: Pvt. William Aams, of Colonel Wisson's regiment, absent without leave, was given thirty lashes; Sgt. William Zimmerman, who robbed a New Jersey home, was reduced to the rank of private. It is not recorded whether Zimmerman then survived his hundred lashes. In their Revolutionary War application the Articles of War seem harsh and cruel, rife with bleeding backs and a far cry from the genteel images of powdered wigs, Washington praying in the snow, and Martha on the porch of Mount Vernon—illustrations commissioned to soften the jagged contours of real history.[21]

In 1861, as our next great conflict opened, the Articles of War and the Army Regulations represented the culmination of 2,000 years of evolution. They were a consensus as to the correct balance between strictness and leniency, with an intent of removing caprice and brutality. Still, their purpose remained unchanged—discipline, rather than any concept of individual liberty or justice. The Articles existed to preserve the army as an obedient and predictable fighting force, not to encourage individualism or personal agendas.[22]

The very nature of military discipline, of course, runs across the grain of most Americans. Studies done of American soldiers in 1944 showed almost unanimous resentment of the social distance maintained by the officers, with their better food, luxurious clubs, and freedom from physical labor. Almost universally, the enlisted men deeply resented the caste system that underlay these officer benefits. The same studies showed that the exercise of authority and the use of rigid discipline were approved only by higher ranking officers, while the enlisted men and many junior officers rejected and disliked the ego-humbling aspects of rigid requirements for obedience. In general, Americans in 1944 placed little value on impersonal authority, unquestioning obedience, or orderliness. However, efficiency, as opposed to orderliness, was highly prized. Americans like to "get things done," but see little reason for rigid procedures in accomplishing a task. (The German soldiers studied at the same time felt just the opposite.)[23]

The trait most highly prized by American soldiers was that of group solidarity, but even this would be abandoned if the group began to disintegrate. The final common denominator of American soldiers in 1944 was self-interest, the placement of the individual above the needs of the group.

There is little to suggest that this was different in 1861, when central authority was weak and less evident. Though Union soldiers were not fighting for states' rights, their very designation as state regiments, often with names reflecting hometown origin, gave a different focus to their feelings, as opposed to being national troops. The individual, the neighborhood, and the small town all played major roles, reinforcing the traditional posture of disregard for central authority, discipline, and unwarranted restrictions, which, of course, are the very bases for a modern army.

The conflict between authority and freedom was ever present in the Civil War. A coordinated attack by 50,000 men required that the men involved be where they were supposed to be at the designated time and do what they were ordered to do in the designated manner. Personal danger and inconvenience were secondary considerations.

A command is an order, not a suggestion or the basis for discussion. But unquestioning obedience to a command is not a common trait in Americans. The regular-army men had some familiarity with obedience and authority and, though influenced by the same national traits as the volunteers, had at least the habit of obedience.

The volunteer colonel, on the other hand, faced challenges from below, from within, and from above. Below him were roughly 900 enlisted men and junior officers, whose obedience he needed and to whose needs he must attend. Within, he had his own ambivalence about authority, mixed with various wishes for glory and admiration. Above him, he had commanders whose orders might or might not suit him.

Thus Americans, both Union and Confederate, passionate about individual, community, and states' rights were men ill suited to constitute great and cohesive fighting machines. Yet they set about to create just those entities, trying to grasp and resolve the paradox—so familiar in religion and philosophy—that perfect freedom is perfect obedience.

As a means of studying these phenomena in action, we have selected the courts-martial and courts of inquiry of fifty colonels and lieutenant colonels. They were discovered in the course of a larger project, still under way: the indexing of all 100,000 Union general courts-martial, beginning with the outbreak of the war. In the months following the siege of Fort Sumter, these fifty men were the first Union men of their ranks to be subject to such legal procedures. The only criterion for inclusion was that they be colonels or lieutenant colonels. The trial records, the compiled service records, and the pension records of each man, wherever discoverable, form the bases for the stories presented here.

The underlying theme of the offenses studied fall into five principal groups and are presented here under those headings. The first is that of "insubordination." A colonel, like anyone else in the military, must obey those above him. From the American traits already discussed, it would not be surprising to find insubordination.

The second grouping is "conduct unbecoming an officer and a gentleman." This represents a failure to set an example of good behavior. An officer must show his men how to conduct themselves, not merely tell them. *Webster's* defines a gentleman as "a man of good breeding, kindness, courtesy and honor, with worthy ideals and refinement of thought." Whether any man achieves that ideal is an open question, but many of our colonels fell far short of it.

8

The third category of shortcomings is "failure of leadership." A colonel, like any leader, must be both firm and considerate. He must govern with consistency, not by caprice or fits of temper. He must not abuse his men, either to degrade them emotionally or to break them down physically. He must generate respect and loyalty by his leadership, and create a climate where men will follow where he leads.

The fourth failing reflects the ultimate purpose of an army: success in battle, and such success requires bravery, the willingness to face real physical danger without collapse; in brief, he must not show "cowardice."

The fifth and final group of trials is a miscellany, "outliers," who do not fall neatly into the four prior groupings. Instead they reflect the myriad possibilities inherent in something as large and as complex as a modern army and its tasks. The outliers include possible chloroform addiction, a refusal to let enlisted men freeze to death, and a man who was too popular with his soldiers—hardly a common thread among them.

These five categories are not airtight. Both the complexities of life and the tendency to file multiple charges and specifications in a single trial mean that there inevitably will be some degree of unavoidable overlap among the five categories. Furthermore, a particular theme does not mean that a defendant necessarily was guilty of a certain act, only that he had been accused of it. Thus, though the theme may have been cowardice, it does not necessarily mean that the testimony will confirm the charge.

Beyond the exploration of these five categories, there is another purpose, perhaps a metapurpose—that of presenting stories which, by their very nature, are interesting and worthy of our attention. They inform us of the human condition in all its permutations. Cravenness and bravery, nobility and pettiness, sobriety and drunkenness, the flames of ethnic passions, the collision of titanic egos—all these are here. They show us, once again, that war is not just cheering and banners, not just blue and gray arrows on a map, but rather a tumultuous stream of conflicting agendas and forceful personalities, all part of the vast cavalcade of midcentury America.

In brief, the purpose of this study is to examine two themes: how men handle command responsibility and how the unavoidable conflict between authority and freedom was addressed in the Civil War.

A further analysis explores the relative frequencies of trials of colonels, lieutenant colonels, and privates, and considers the intriguing question: why was the rate of court-martial so much higher for colonels than privates? Two states produced a disproportionate share of Union courts-martial. This finding, too, will be explored.

Finally, this study of military discipline opens a whole new avenue into our understanding of that great war, which still burns in the hearts of many men and women today, four generations after the guns fell silent.

PART ONE

Insubordination

Chapter One

Flames at Buckroe Farm

COL. WILLIAM H. ALLEN

Colonel William H. Allen of the 1st New York Volunteers may be unique in that at his own court-martial he conducted a hostile cross-examination of his own commanding general, Maj. Gen. Benjamin Butler. The general, an experienced politician, a successful lawyer in civilian life, and not one to suffer fools gladly, was more than equal to the task.[1]

The case, heard in July 1861, involved six charges against the colonel. First, he had disobeyed orders by sending his command past a line clearly delineated by the commanding general. Second, his conduct was prejudicial to good order in that he had arrested three civilians who carried safe-conduct passes issued by General Butler. Third, it was charged that Colonel Allen had, without authorization, burned twenty-five acres of ready-for-harvest wheat. The next charge was that of conduct unbecoming an officer and a gentleman, in that he lied about having given the order for burning the wheat. The fifth charge related to breach of arrest; he had been confined, but went about as he pleased. The final charge was that of public drunkeness; the locale was General Butler's office.

In the trial, Colonel Allen may have established some sort of record in raising objections. He began by objecting to the composition of the court. Allen claimed that Col. J. Dimick, a regular army officer, was unqualified to sit in judgment of an officer commanding a *volunteer* regiment. The logic of this escaped the court, and the objection was overruled.

The charges and specifications were then read; Colonel Allen pled not guilty to all charges and requested permission to retain civilian counsel. Permission was granted, and Isaac Catlin, G. S. Melville, and C. M. Martin were recognized as Allen's legal advisors. Allen then requested a continuance in order to confer with his attorneys. The request was denied, and the court turned to some of the charges: Allen had sent a contingent of his troops to Buckroe Farm, beyond the limits clearly delineated by orders, and those troops, under Allen's orders, had burned twenty-eight acres of shooked wheat.

The first witness called, Capt. C. B. Rich, testified that he had heard the colonel say, "I did not order the wheat to be burned, but if it got afire acci-

Col. William H. Allen tried to convince Maj. Gen. Benjamin Butler that he was sober. Allen failed. MASSACHUSETTS COMMANDERY MILITARY ORDER OF THE LOYAL LEGION, U.S. ARMY MILITARY HISTORY INSTITUTE.

dentally, I shouldn't care." The court then adjourned, ending the first day.

The second day of the trial began with Allen's request that reporters be excluded from the trial. The request was denied. Allen then presented a long written report, which he believed proved "insufficiency" in the charges; his request, to dismiss all the charges on technical grounds, was denied.

The prosecution then introduced Brig. Gen. Byron Pierce as a witness. Pierce brought a copy of General Butler's Special Order No. 27, which defined the boundaries of Allen's jurisdiction. Pierce was adamant that Allen had *no* permission to pass those boundaries.

Allen promptly objected that the evidence (Special Order No. 27) had not been certified. The court arranged for certification. Allen then objected that no proof had been entered of General Butler's authority to issue such an order. The objection was overruled.

The next witness was Lt. A. Christensen of Allen's regiment. The lieutenant testified that he had been ordered to burn the wheat in question and to arrest all the white males at the home of a seccessionist named Thompson (this home was Buckroe Farm). The court then ordered that the men he arrested be brought in to testify. Allen objected to their appearance, but was overruled.

General Pierce was called again to testify, and stated that the only valid passes for civilians were ones signed by him, or by General Butler. According to Pierce, Colonel Allen had been issuing his own passes in violation of orders and had told his own officers that "Colonel Allen passes" were just as valid as those issued by Generals Pierce and Butler.

Allen then cross-examined Pierce, demanding to know by what authority he held a commission. Pierce, apparently alerted to Allen's style of defense, had brought with him his papers of appointment, including ones signed by Generals Winfield Scott and Benjamin Butler. Allen then cross-examined Pierce:

Q. Do you personally know of a complaint against me as an officer and a gentleman?
A. I do not.
Q. Was not the picket line in front of my area of jurisdiction complete?
A. No, it was not complete.
Q. Could there not be emergencies in which I must use my own discretion?

The court ruled the question was improper.

Q. If your own commission as a Brigader General was ruled invalid, am I not entitled to succeed you?

The court ruled that this question, too, was improper.

Allen and his attorneys then conferred and raised a host of legal objections that centered around the issue of who had preferred the charges against him. The court, after considerable internal discussion, concluded that it did not have proper jurisdiction to try Colonel Allen, and the first court-martial came to a halt.

A week later, a new court-martial was convened to try the same six charges against Colonel Allen. Once again, Allen requested his three attorneys and his request was granted. When asked if he objected to the presence of any members of the new board of officers, Allen replied strongly in the affirmative. He first objected to Col. Garrett Dyckman, citing personal enmity and the possibility of Dyckman benefitting by Allen's conviction. Dyckman was removed from the board.

Allen then objected to Col. A. Duryee, also on the grounds of enmity and animosity. The court sustained the objection, and Duryee withdrew. Allen's next objection was to Colonel Warren, on grounds of hostility, enmity *and* prejudice. Warren, too, withdrew.

Since Allen had no objections to the remaining officers, the court proceeded to the reading of the charges and specifications. When they were done, Allen moved for dismissal of all the charges on the grounds that the previous adjournment of the court was an admission of acquittal. In a lengthy and convoluted written statement, Allen argued that the principle of double jeopardy, which prohibits being tried twice for the same crime, was the operant point of law. As evidence of his innocence, Allen introduced into evidence the transcripts of the previous week's trial.

The court considered his arguments, and on the grounds that Allen had yet to be tried on any of the charges, refused to sustain his move for dismissal. Thus ended the first day of Allen's second trial.

The second day, the judge advocate was too sick to appear, and the case was continued. On the third day, Allen began by objecting to "the record of the court martial as it stands." This opening statement was followed by a prolonged obfuscation, which seemed to have little bearing on the matters before the court. After this objection, too, was overruled, the judge advocate announced that he had misjudged his medical recovery and had to go to bed. The case was continued once again.

From the fourth day onward, all the parties seemed to be in sufficient health to conduct the proceedings. The prosecution began by calling as witnesses the three white males who had been arrested at Buckroe Farm. The first to testify was Patrick Henry Hopkins:

> Soldiers from Col. Allen's came to Buckroe Farm and took several of my horses, without my permission. I went to Gen. Butler's headquarters and his Provost Marshal gave me a pass authorizing me to visit Col. Allen's camp. When I arrived, Col. Allen asked me if I'd like my horses returned. Of course, I replied that I would. He then said I could not have them. Then he had me arrested and put in the guardhouse. While I was there, I heard him tell a lieutenant to go and burn the shooked wheat at Buckroe Farm. After a few hours, General Pierce came to the guardhouse and ordered my release.

After Hopkin's testimony, the court called Lieutenant Christensen. Allen objected to this witness from his own regiment but was overruled.

The court asked Christensen if he had exchanged any written passes. Before the lieutenant could reply, Allen objected on grounds that if the passes themselves were not in evidence, then discussion of them was inadmissible. The objection was sustained, the lieutenant stepped down, and Hopkins returned to the witness chair, where Colonel Allen continued his cross-examination: "When you came to my camp, looking for your horses, were you not verbally abusive of me?" Hopkins denied having been abusive.

The next witness, also of Buckroe Farm, was William Clinton, who stated that Union soldiers came to the farm and said that they were going to burn the wheat. Here Colonel Allen objected, saying that any testimony about events at which he was not present, should be prohibited. Allen was overruled. Clinton continued: "The men said 'We burn by orders of Col. Allen.' After they burned 28 acres of wheat, they came to the house and asked for a drink. They said they were from the 1st Regiment of New York Volunteers."

The fifth day of the second trial began with Allen once more objecting to testimony about any event at which he was not personally present. He was again overruled. Richard Arrington, the third white male at Buckroe Farm, was called as a prosecution witness. He, too, testified that he had been arrested by Colonel Allen and released by General Pierce. On cross-examination, Colonel Allen queried the witness about his own military service. Arrington admitted that he had been in the U.S. Army infantry in Nebraska Territory, had been court-martialed, and had been drummed out of the service.

Allen then called as his witness, a Private Iverson of the 1st New York, who said, "I've been to Buckroe Farm and I have a poor opinion of the people living there. Three negroes told us that the wheat was going to the enemy that night. Those men wanted their horses back to carry the wheat to the enemy. The negroes helped us burn the wheat."

Lieutenant Christensen returned to the stand: "Col. Allen told me that these three men—Hopkins, Arrington and Clinton—had broken their parole and were aiding the enemy."

Then there was a prolonged discussion regarding a Robert Jackson and his "safeguard" (pass) which had been signed by General Butler. Allen objected that this was a replacement pass and that only the original pass should be allowed in evidence. Allen buttressed his objection by showing that Jackson could neither read nor write, so would have no idea what was written on the pass. The objection was sustained.

The next witness for the prosecution was General Butler himself. (Photographs of Butler in 1861 always show him as somewhat saturnine, his hooded, heavy-lidded eyes and immobile reptilian glance masking a mind as deadly and as swift as a poisoned rapier.) Colonel Allen began his cross-examination, speaking of himself in the third person, as was customary at that time.

Q. By whose authority do you hold your rank?
A. My authority is the President of the United States.
Q. Who ordered the arrest of Colonel Allen?
A. I ordered the arrest of Colonel Allen.
Q. How do you know that he breached his arrest?

A. I saw him outside the arrest limits with my own eyes.

Q. In what condition was he when he appeared at your office?

A. He appeared intoxicated, so much so that I did not continue my conversation with him.

Q. What is the basis of the charge of conduct unbecoming an officer and a gentleman?

A. He denied that he had ordered the burning of the wheat and blamed it on negroes. He so stated twice in my office. I have reason not to believe him.

Allen's cross-examination attempts to destroy Butler's testimony were brushed aside like annoying insects.

After Butler's departure, Colonel Allen called one final witness for the defense, a private of the 1st New York, who swore that he had seen "signal lights" at Buckroe Farm and that Allen was "fully sober" when he made his visit to General Butler's office.

Allen's final plea to the court was that he had been denied opportunity to call an adequate number of defense witnesses, and that if he had had such an opportunity, his innocence would have been manifest.

The court was unimpressed. Allen was found guilty on charges 1, 3, 4, and 5, and sentenced to be cashiered (dismissed from the service in disgrace).

Colonel Allen then filed sixteen pages of points and objections in rebuttal to his sentence, but they were in vain. His appeal went up through channels to the White House itself, then occupied by an attorney of long experience, Abraham Lincoln, who fully approved the sentence. Colonel Allen became citizen Allen.

Chapter Two

A Colonel Bucked and Gagged

COL. JOHN F. BALLIER

Painful and humiliating punishments were commonplace in Victorian armies. Loud, combative men were often "bucked and gagged": the wrists were bound together, the knees folded up, and the hands brought down over the shins. Then a stick was thrust behind the knees, locking the arms in place. A rag jammed into the mouth and tied into place completed the ensemble.

In a highly unusual incident, a future brigadier general was ordered to be bucked and gagged by a future major general. The ranking officer in this contretemps was Philip Kearney, a wealthy cavalryman who had entered the 1st Dragoons in 1837, served with the *Chasseurs d'Afrique* in Algiers, and lost his left arm at Churubusco in the Mexican War. Just before the American Civil War, he had served in Napoleon III's Imperial Guard, where he rode into battle with the reins in his teeth and his sabre in his remaining hand.

In the ill-fated Peninsular Campaign in Virginia, Kearney responded to George B. McClellan's orders to retreat with these ringing words, "I, Philip Kearney, an old soldier, enter my solemn protest against this order for retreat. We ought instead of retreating to follow up the enemy and take Richmond. And in full view of the responsibility of such a declaration, I say to you all, such an order can only be prompted by cowardice or treason."[1] If Kearney was not afraid of his commanding general, he would certainly not fear a subordinate.

Col. John F. Ballier began his Civil War career commanding the 21st Pennsylvania Volunteers, a three-month regiment mustered in at Philadelphia on April 20, 1861. They saw considerable service during their brief tenure, advancing down the Martinsburg Road in Virginia in June and on to Williamsport, Maryland. In July, they marched to Downsville, Maryland, back to Martinsburg, Virginia, and on to Harper's Ferry. After they were mustered out, Colonel Ballier assumed command of the newly organized 98th Pennsylvania Regiment, also from Philadelphia. The 98th was mostly volunteers of German origin. Their initial training was at Camp Ballier, in the city of Philadelphia. Ballier's new unit saw more extensive service, defending Washington, until March, 1862, then joining McClellan's invasion of the Peninsula.

The 98th fought at Yorktown, Williamsburg, Slatersville, Fair Oaks, Seven Pines, and the Seven Days. It was at Malvern Hill that Colonel Ballier and General Kearney met.[2]

The court-martial that marked their encounter was held at Rowland's House in eastern Henrico County, Virginia, on July 24, 1862. Presiding was Brig. Gen. William H. Emory. The charge was "misbehavior before the enemy." The specification was that on July 1, 1862, at the Battle of Malvern Hill, Colonel Ballier did

> without authority, retire with a portion of the regiment under his command, from his brigade, and on being afterwards ordered by Brigader General Albion Howe, Commanding Brigade, through Volunteer Aide de Camp Chaplain [Alexander] Steward, 102nd Pennsylvania Volunteers, and by Lieutenant J. B. Burt, Aide de Camp to Brigadier General Darius Couch, commanding the division, and by Brigadier General Philip Kearney, to join his brigade, did fail to do so until after the action.

To this charge, Colonel Ballier pleaded not guilty. With the following testimony, the story unfolded.

The 98th Pennsylvania had been fighting all day under the blazing sun of a Virginia July. The canteens were dry and no man had been able to fill his for twenty-four hours. But the men were plagued by more than thirst.

The regiment had been issued new patent cartridges that were seriously defective. Soon, more than half of the rifles of the 98th were malfunctioning, with balls jammed in the barrels. Fifty guns had the ramrods inextricably caught in the barrel. Further, more exploding shells were falling into the regiment, scattering the men. Colonel Ballier rallied his thirsty, weaponless men, who said to him, "Give us water and we will still fight, even with these useless rifles."

At this point, Chaplain Steward rode up and ordered the unit back into the line. The colonel spoke of the men's need for water. Next to arrive was Lieutenant Burt, aide-de-camp to General Couch. Burt was more forceful. Pointing a cocked revolver at the Colonel's head, Burt cursed him as "an old coward," and threatened to shoot any man who went for water. The men repeated their willingness to fight if they could only have water; Burt continued to wave his pistol and order them back into line. At this point, General Kearney arrived. His actions are revealed in his testimony.

"Colonel Ballier refused to obey my order to go forward. Since Colonel Ballier evidenced no fear, I could only conclude that it was intentional stubbornness . . . highly mutinous conduct." General Emory asked, "Did Colonel Ballier give you any explanation?" Kearney was disdainful of this line of inquiry: "I am under the impression that he gave no satisfactory explanation, nothing that had military bearing."

Col. John F. Ballier may have been the highest-ranking Union soldier to have been bucked and gagged, a painful punishment. MASSACHUSETTS COMMANDERY MILITARY ORDER OF THE LOYAL LEGION, U.S. ARMY MILITARY HISTORY INSTITUTE.

Ballier himself posed the next question: "Did I not explain my reasons?" The general loftily replied, "Some words passed, to which I paid less heed." Ballier persisted, "Did not one of my sergeants show you that his ramrod had run through his hand in attempting to load?"

The one-armed old cavalry general was not impressed. "Such things are so frequent that I would have dismissed it from my mind, or would have considered it as demoralization that he should pretend to leave the ranks."

Ballier turned then to his own considerations: "Did you order me bucked and gagged?" Kearney was vague. "I don't remember such an order, but at such a time I would have enforced my order in any shape. You exemplified perfect fearlessness, which gave me the idea that you did not know military discipline. The gagging I may have ordered, the bucking certainly not."

The next witness was Lt. F. Prurien. "I saw General Kearney ride up and say, 'Where is that damned old scoundrel! Arrest him, and buck and gag him.' We were in a bad way just then. Most of our guns had balls jammed halfway down the barrel." Capt. N. Voltaire added his observations, "The men were willing to obey Colonel Ballier's orders, but the falling and exploding shells were scattering them."

The court pondered all this testimony and found Ballier not guilty to both the charge and the specification. In a final comment, the court added these thoughts, "The Court feels called upon to notice the unusual punishment already inflicted on Colonel Ballier by confinement by the Provost Marshal, and they also feel constrained to censure the language used by the Aide of General Couch toward Colonel Ballier, when the latter tried to explain to the Aide the condition of his regiment."

Maj. Gen. Erasmus Keyes approved the proceedings of the court and ordered that "Colonel John F. Ballier, 98th Pennsylvania Volunteers, is released from arrest, will resume his sword, and return to duty."

Ballier did return to duty and continued his service to the Union. He was severely wounded in the foot at Salem Heights (near Fredericksburg, Virginia) on May 3, 1863, and was promoted to Brigader General in July 1863. He returned to civilian life on June 29, 1865.

Chapter Three

"Charge, Mes Enfants!"

LT. COL. JOSEPH A. VIGNEUR DE MONTEIL

The story of Joseph Antoine Vigneur de Monteil has it all: shipwrecks, documents in French, vicious dogs, riotous diners brandishing forks and throwing spoons, flamboyant heroism, and a three-year regiment that was disbanded two and a half years early for being a nuisance.[1]

The 53rd New York Volunteer Infantry (d'Epineuil's Zouaves) was organized in New York City in the autumn of 1861, and was mostly Frenchmen from all over the world, with the exception of one company of Tuscarora Indians. The colonel was Lionel Jobert d'Epineuil, who disappeared shortly before his own court-martial; he had claimed to be an experienced officer in the French Army, but was not. On August 8, 1861, d'Epineuil wrote to Vigneur de Monteil as follows:

> J'ai l'honneur de vous informer que sur l'examen des pièces constatant votre position du service de France, j'áccepte vos offres de service et vous confer provisoirment l'emploi du Lieutenant Colonel du régiment d'infantrie que je suis appelé à commander par lettre datié du 5 Août . . . du de la Secrétarie du Guerre à Washington.

Vigneur de Monteil accepted the offer and was enrolled as lieutenant colonel on August 16, 1861. It took him only three months to get court-martialed. The charges and specifications occupied many pages. The first charge was conduct prejudicial to good order and military discipline, in which he "used disrespectful and contemptuous words against his superior, Colonel d'Epineuil, saying, in the presence of two subordinate officers, that Colonel d'Epineuil was a gentleman but no officer, and knew nothing of military matters, and that he, the lieutenant colonel, took care of the men and made the regiment."

Furthermore, Colonel d'Epineuil had ordered that no liquor was to be sold by the sutler. Vigneur de Monteil went to the sutler and demanded brandy for himself and his party, and persisted in demanding brandy even when the sutler reminded him of the colonel's orders.

Lt. Col. Joseph Antoine Vigneur de Monteil demonstrated Gallic fortitude when his disgruntled men assaulted him with forks, spoons, and plates—he beat the regiment into submission with his cane. DIVISION OF MILITARY AND NAVAL AFFAIRS, NEW YORK STATE ADJUTANT GENERAL'S OFFICE, ALBANY, NEW YORK.

The second charge, that of conduct unbecoming an officer and a gentleman, included drinking in a saloon with enlisted men and being drunk on duty. The most dramatic specification was that his "vicious dog" had attacked a private, and when the victim tried to defend himself from the dog, Vigneur de Monteil beat the private "with great cruelty and violence . . . breaking a piece of board over his back." After reviewing the evidence, the court decided that this second charge, in its entirety, should be withdrawn.

The third charge noted that in August and September of 1861, when Vigneur de Monteil commanded the camp, he neglected to place guards at the exits from the camp, and that since most of the officers were away on recruiting duty and since "all military order and discipline had been lost," about 300 men simply walked away on the road to desertion.[2]

In the testimony and defense, it appeared that conditions at Camp Leslie were truly chaotic. Meals appeared without any regularity, producing riots and mutinous conduct among the men. During one riot, the men threw bread, spoons, and plates at the officers, and ignored their commands. In the words of his defense counsel, "Lieutenant Colonel de Monteil alone was able to stop them and establish order. It was only after the lieutenant colonel was struck three times that he was obliged to use his cane—the only weapon which he had. The Eighth Article of War, in fact, obliged him to quell the mutiny."

After many days of testimony, the court decided that there was some merit in the first charge ("The colonel is no military man"), but little to the rest of the charges, and concluded that overall, the charges were "not proven" and that he should return to duty.

The 53rd New York, having achieved some modicum of calm and organization, went to war. After a month's duty at Annapolis, they sailed with Ambrose Burnside's expedition to Hatteras Inlet at Roanoake Island, where the vessel carrying d'Epineuil's men was shipwrecked.

When the actual fighting came, only a few men of the 53rd New York were available, and they joined the 9th New York Infantry (Hawkins's Zouaves). There, on February 8, 1862, Vigneur de Monteil became the only officer of his regiment to be killed during the war. Col. Rush C. Hawkins wrote a letter of condolence to the widow.

It is with feelings of the greatest sadness that I am compelled to inform you of the death of your much-lamented husband. He had volunteered to go out with me to take part in the battle of the 8th instant. We were together when we entered the field and we were near each other until he fell. The last I saw of him alive, he was standing on a fallen tree, urging my men on to the charge. The last words I heard him utter were, "Charge, mes enfants, charge, zouaves." No soldier ever more gallantly acted or more nobly fell. He was the bravest of the brave and truly patriotic, and died in one of the best causes which man has ever fought for. Your husband had been on board of this ship with us since the expedition left Hatteras, and yet he had won all our hearts. His gentlemanly character was known and esteemed by us all. He dies deeply lamented by all of my officers and men who came in contact with him. If you wish me to do anything for you, I am yours to command. I shall do my utmost to have his remains sent to you for burial. I am, dear Madame, with great sympathy, most faithfully your friend.[3]

There were other communications also commending the fallen Frenchman. Brig. Gen. John Parke wrote, "He was killed instantly while urging his men to the charge. His bravery was as great as his patriotism was sincere." Burnside wrote, "Finding his regiment absent, he proffered his services as a volunteer and fought bravely until struck dead in the very moment of victory."

His widow's application for a pension gives a glimpse of their personal life. He had been an officer in the French Marine Artillery. Her maiden name was Marie Justine Soucher. They were married in England in 1852, when he was thirty-four and she was twenty-one. They had no children. Their home in New York City was at 166 East 33rd Street. She was awarded a pension of thirty dollars a month.

As for the regiment, it had established such a reputation as a brawling assembly of drunks, of little military use, that Maj. Gen. George B. McClellan ordered the men mustered out in March 1862. A few of the men transferred to other regiments, and that was the end of d'Epineuil's Zouaves. Vigneur de Monteil seems to have been the only spark of glory in their all too transient rise and fall.

Chapter Four

"An Oppressive and Insulting Act"

COL. WILLIAM HALSTEAD

The meteoric military career of William Halstead (also spelled Halsted) is notable for at least three factors: his advanced age, his being court-martialed twice in six months, and his capacity for quibbling. For the development of the latter trait, he enjoyed several advantages: he had been an attorney since 1816, had edited the seven volumes of *Halstead's Law Reports,* and had served twice in Congress. Zachary Taylor appointed him United States district attorney for New Jersey in 1849, a position he held for four years. His capacity for argument encompassed theology as well as commerce: he had been one of the chief prosecutors in the celebrated trial of Episcopal Bishop Doane.

When the war came, he raised Halstead's Cavalry, later the 1st Regiment of New Jersey Cavalry, and became its commander, assigned to the defense of Washington, D.C., until May 1862. He was age sixty-six. A month after he took command of his regiment, he was charged with violation of the 80th Article of War, in that he kept his own lieutenant colonel, Julian Alexander, confined to his tent with an armed guard for nine days without preferring any charges. The presence of an armed guard over an officer was highly unusual and considered deeply insulting.[1]

While Lieutenant Colonel Alexander languished in his canvas prison, Halstead called a meeting of the regiment, announced that Alexander was no longer an officer, and that he, Halstead, had appointed a replacement, something clearly not within his power. Brig. Gen. George Stoneman ordered Halstead to cease and desist, but Halstead ignored the general and threatened Alexander with fresh arrest if he did not resign. Halstead's method of communication with Alexander received particular emphasis in the court-martial records: "Colonel Halstead sent his Negro servant to Lieutenant Colonel Alexander with an order to 'stop in the street,' an oppressive and insulting act."

Other issues raised at the trial included Halstead's selling the sutler position of the regiment for four hundred dollars and half the profits, and appointing his own son as regimental quartermaster.

Halstead survived this proceeding and returned to duty, but in December 1861, in a trial presided over by Brig. Gen. Silas Casey, he was tried on new

*Col. William Halstead, author of a seven-volume law book, spent his army career quib-
bling over horsefeed and a hat, and was finally dismissed as unqualified to lead cavalry.*
BUREAU OF ARCHIVES AND HISTORY, NEW JERSEY STATE LIBRARY.

charges: violation of the 14th Article of War and conduct unbecoming an officer
and a gentleman. The charges surrounded his signing of a false certificate claiming that he had not drawn forage already for his five personal horses (other documents mention two horses), when he had already received such forage, at
government expense.[2]

A variety of clerks and accountants were called to court, and their testimony
fills thirty-five pages, all concerning "forage for two horses, from 6 September to
1 November, 1861, one month and 24 days, a total of $58.00, plus a hat for the
colonel's servant."

In addition, Colonel Halstead had a similar run-in regarding the date his pay began. Maj. John W. Newell, paymaster, U.S. Army, testified:

> Colonel Halstead came to my office at 17th and Pennsylvania on the 22nd of November, 1861, at noon. His account was not made out yet and I asked him to return in an hour. He returned at 2:00 p.m. and I paid him in a check upon the Treasury. He objected, claiming more time was due him, August 13 onward. My records showed September 3, 1861.
>
> Colonel Halstead said volunteers should be paid on the same basis as regulars, that is, from the date of the acceptance of their appointment to rank. He insisted upon it as his right. . . . He grew warm, rather energetic, in this brief discussion. The colonel said his point would be tested by legal authority and that he would not sign the receipt as it might signify a final settlement. I told him that upon proper authority from the Adjutant General's Office, I would pay him the balance, but until then I must go by the muster roll.

At the end of the testimony, Halstead submitted his final statement in writing, an impassioned and lengthy document commencing "On the honor of an officer, a gentleman and a Christian. . . ."

After considerable discussion, the court-martial board rendered its decision. On the charge of making a false certificate, he was found "guilty of neglect of duty." As to conduct unbecoming an officer and a gentleman (which results in automatic dismissal), he was found guilty of unofficerlike conduct, a lesser offense. He was sentenced to be admonished by the general commanding his division. The sentence was confirmed by Maj. Gen. George McClellan, without comment. Over $58 and a hat, the trial consumed the time of thirteen senior officers for three days.

December 1861 saw a further unraveling of his military career. A few days after his court-martial, Halstead was required to meet with a board of examination, consisting of five cavalry officers. Their unanimous decision was that "Colonel Halstead is unqualified to be a cavalry officer." He was discharged in February 1862, having served a total of six months.

It would seem that his long and prosperous career in the courthouse of Trenton, New Jersey, and in the halls of Congress had left him ill prepared for a life with different standards of accountability. His regiment went on to battles such as Cross Keys, Cedar Mountain, Fredericksburg, Gettysburg, Cold Harbor, and Malvern Hill.

After his death in 1878, his *New York Times* obituary noted, "Since his return from the war, he had lived in comparative retirement. The cause of death was old age and a general impairment of his vital forces."[3]

Chapter Five

An Extreme Case

COL. MORTON C. HUNTER

There are many types of courage—some are revealed in battle, some in painful social situations, and some in the eternal struggle with bureaucracy and protocol. Col. Morton C. Hunter exhibited the last type, and was court-martialed for conduct prejudicial to good order and military discipline.

He commanded the 82nd Indiana. His regiment had been in existence for only three months, but it had already fought in the Battle of Perryville and participated in the pursuit of Confederate General Braxton Bragg during his withdrawal into Tennessee. In November 1862, the 82nd Indiana was on duty at Camp Gallatin, near Nashville, when one of Hunter's officers, Lt. John McKinley, became sick with typhoid fever.[1]

For the vast majority of Americans today, typhoid is only a word, but in the world of 1862, it was a very different matter, a dreadful disease, caused then, as now, by the bacterium *salmonella typhosa*. The usual method of spread is by ingestion of human filth from sewage-contaminated drinking water, milk, or shellfish. The symptoms begin with a severe sore throat, grayish-green diarrhea, and a fever that rises daily over the course of a week to about one hundred five degrees Farenheit, and then subsides.

When the fever is high, the afflicted person is usually delirious, no longer in mental contact with the world. The lining of the intestine is highly inflamed, with areas of sloughing and ulceration, often accompanied by severe or fatal passage of blood through the rectum. Even when recovered, the patient will be weak for at least a month.

How did typhoid affect the Civil War soldier? In the Army of the Potomac, in 1861, there were 12,000 cases. In some units, more than half of those affected died. Seventeen percent of all deaths in the military during the Civil War were from this disease.

Colonel Hunter had adequate reason to be concerned about his lieutenant. The regimental surgeon gave his opinion that unless the patient was moved to a location that would afford better medical and nursing care, he would die. And soon.

Col. Morton C. Hunter risked his commission to save the life of a lieutenant with typhoid fever. Hunter's passionate defense is a classic of responsible morality. MASSACHUSETTS COMMANDERY MILITARY ORDER OF THE LOYAL LEGION, U.S. ARMY MILITARY HISTORY INSTITUTE.

Leaving the regiment required a pass. Colonel Hunter was more than willing to provide such, but it required the endorsement of a higher authority, in this case, Maj. Gen. William S. Rosecrans. Rosecrans was away for a week, however, and the authority of the brigade commander, Colonel Connell of the 17th Ohio, was not sufficient.

Colonel Hunter took the matter into his own hands and wrote the following document, which remains on record today: "Headquarters, 82nd Regiment Indiana Volunteers. November 17, 1862. Guards, pickets and all others concerned, pass Lieutenant John McKinley to the hospital in the city of New Albany, Indiana. He is a lieutenant in Company F of my regiment and is quite sick with an attack of typhoid fever. Morton C. Hunter, Colonel, Commanding."

Lieutenant McKinley used the pass, went to the hospital, survived, recuperated at home, and returned to his regiment five months later, but not before coming to the attention of the Department for Returning Deserters and Absentees, headquartered in Indianapolis.

On March 12, 1863, a bureaucrat, whose name is lost to the records, sent the following letter to the head of this department, Brig. Gen. Milo S. Hascall, a lawyer and West Point graduate:

> I enclose a copy of a paper given by Colonel Hunter of the 82nd Indiana to a lieutenant of his regiment, which will explain itself. By virtue of no other authority than this, the lieutenant has been absent at his home in Indiana ever since the date of that paper. I have ordered the lieutenant to proceed to the county where he lives, collect all the deserters and absentees therein, and proceed with them at once to his regiment. . . . I suggest that the whole matter be investigated.

General Hascall took immediate steps regarding this dangerous threat to army discipline: he referred the matter to Rosecrans, whose headquarters referred the matter to headquarters of the 14th Army Corps, with the order, "Have the officer who was guilty of this offense arrested and tried by court-martial."

On March 27, 1863, a court-martial board of two colonels, two lieutenant colonels, two majors, and seven captains convened. Colonel Hunter was clearly not in a litigious mood, as he declined challenging a trial board in which eleven of the thirteen members were his inferior in rank. The first prosecution witness was the typhoid patient himself, Lieutenant McKinley.

Q. What were the circumstances connected with your leaving the regiment on November 17th, 1862?

A. I had been sick for some two weeks with typhoid fever. The doctor saw fit to send me to the hospital in New Albany, Indiana, and the colonel got up a pass. The colonel said, "That is all I can do for you." I started on a train the next day and went to New Albany, Indiana.

Q. Did the colonel give you any advice as to whether the pass was or was not sufficient authority for your leaving?

A. He said that was all he could do.

Q. Did you ever state to Brigadier General Hascall that you had been privately advised by the colonel to go home, on the authority of that pass?

A. No.

Q. Had you any other authority than Colonel Hunter's pass for your absence from November 17, 1862, to March 22, 1863?

A. None.

Q. What was the condition of your health during the time of your absence?

A. I was not able to be out of bed more than half of the time, the latter part of the time I was able to take exercise.

Q. Did you procure the approval of any superior officer on Colonel Hunter's pass?

A. The approval of Colonel Connell, 17th Ohio, commanding brigade, was procured before starting.

Q. Did you go to Colonel Connell yourself to get this approval?

A. I did not, I was not able to go anywhere.

Q. Do you know how the approval of the colonel commanding the brigade was obtained, and whether the pass was or was not forwarded to any higher authority for approval?

A. I do not. I was too unwell to know anything at the time.

There was extended questioning along the same lines, clearly intending to elicit a statement that Colonel Hunter had given Lieutenant McKinley erroneous legal advice. The court obtained no satisfaction on this score. The next witness was Dr. William H. Lennon, surgeon with the 82nd Indiana Infantry.

Q. Will you state the condition of Lieutenant John McKinley's health about the 17th of November, 1862, and whether, in your opinion, he could have recovered by remaining in camp?

A. The lieutenant had been for some time previous debilitated from diarrhea and there then set in Typhoid Pneumonia, a very severe attack; from the precedent of such diseases in camp, I told the colonel that the lieutenant would have to be taken out of camp and that if he were not shortly moved to where he could get different treatment and diet, he would be unable to be moved within four or five days. We had endeavored to procure a house and put him in it, but had failed.

Q. In your judgment, if he had remained in camp, would he have lived or died?

A. I had expressed an opinion that he could not recover if he remained in camp.

Q. Did he return to his regiment as soon as his health would admit?
A. Yes, sooner than he should have returned. I was on leave myself and
   I examined him at home.

This concluded the testimony. At this point, Colonel Hunter introduced
the following verbal statement:

> I thought at the time this pass was gotten up, that in extreme cases, it
> was necessary for an officer to take some degree of responsibility on
> himself, when the life of one of his men or officers was at stake. When
> there was not sufficient time to go through with all the regular for-
> mula, that if the act of the officer was done in good faith, for the ben-
> efit of the service and not for its injury, that it was the duty of the
> officer to take the responsibility incident to the case presented to him.
> In this instance, General Rosecrans having been away from there, no
> pass could be procured from him, as I really thought, under seven or
> eight days, and before it could have been procured, the lieutenant
> would have been past removal. In order to save his life, I regarded it as
> my duty to send him to some convenient hospital; for that purpose,
> this pass was procured, in consequence of which, the lieutenant has
> again returned to the regiment, and without which, in my judgment,
> he would have died.

After deliberation, the court found Colonel Hunter not guilty, and acquitted him with the statement, "The Court is of the opinion that, while the conduct of the accused in the matter before the Court was irregular and
unauthorized by the rules of the service, his motives were good and that his acts
were intended for the good of the service and that, under the circumstances, he
was justifiable in assuming the responsibility that he did assume."

This opinion of the court is followed by another opinion, which in its
humanity and positive tone is a truly unusual document in the world of court-
martial records: "The General Court Martial (I am happy to say) has acquitted
you, honorably, and you will, by the hearty direction of Colonel W. and many
friends, return to duty forthwith."

Return to duty he did, with his happiness tarnished only two months later
as reflected in this request for home leave, "My child just died and my wife is ill
from protracted nursing. My presence home is indispensable to saving her life.
She is given up to grief." This request for leave was approved by Maj. Gen.
George H. Thomas.

The next entry in his records comes in March 1864, at which time he was
serving on court-martial duty. The commander who had authorized the court-
martial received an urgent telegram from Brig. Gen. John Turchin requesting
Colonel Hunter's return to the 82nd Indiana. "Lieutenant Colonel [Paul]

Slocum has been killed at Rocky Face Ridge. The regiment has no major. The 82nd Indiana is now commanded by a captain. Please send us Hunter." By November 1864, Hunter was commanding a brigade in Savannah, Georgia, and in early 1865, held the same post in North Carolina. The war drew to a close and he was mustered out in June 1865. Two years later, he was breveted as a brigadier general, "for gallant and meritorious service."

As with so many survivors of the Civil War, the experiences of field and camp seemed to have accelerated the aging process. In July 1890, he filed for a pension, based not on a military injury but on total disability. At age sixty-five, a stroke had left him almost speechless, with a paralyzed right arm and leg, and his "mouth drawn to the left." He was able to write only a few words. General Hunter was granted a pension of twelve dollars a month. His records do not indicate a date of death nor how he was employed in his years after the war.

Chapter Six

"Got for Dam!"

COL. CHARLES KNOBELSDORFF

The records of Col. Charles Knobelsdorff raise serious questions as to whether he ever did anything useful for his country. Although his pension papers list his prewar occupation as "land agent," in a newspaper recruiting notice he gave his rank as "Captain" and described himself as "an experienced soldier."

The newspaper clipping, found in his court-martial records, is dated "Chicago, June 6, 1861," and is captioned "Plan of Organization of a Volunteer Regiment of the North-West." It proposes a unit of

> Ten Companies having a minimum of 83 and maximum of 101 men, including commissioned and noncommissioned officers. Each company has to elect one captain, one first lieutenant, one second lieutenant, one orderly sergeant, four sergeants, eight corporals, one bugler, one drummer and one wagoner.

Knobelsdorff's plan is portrayed in noble terms:

> To express the harmony and fraternity of the Northwestern States, we the undersigned experienced soldiers, consider it as very practical to form an independent Regiment composed of companies of the Northwestern States, to wit: Illinois, Ohio, Wisconsin, Indiana, Michigan, Minnesota and Iowa, and to tender the services of such a regiment to the United States government, for three years service. There is not the least doubt that such a regiment would be accepted. The name of the regiment shall be the Northwestern Rifle Regiment. [It appears later as the 44th Illinois Infantry.][1]

The future colonel announced in the same notice that there would be "an indispensable uniform" to be furnished by each company which would consist of "a light grey coat with light green standing collar, the same caps and shoulder straps and United States buttons, a light grey lined pantaloons, a black felt hat with a wide brim, the right side of the same turned up and fastened with a

34

United States cockade, two grey woolen shirts and a blue woolen blanket." Further noted was a clothing allowance, a one hundred dollar cash bonus upon honorable discharge, and a land grant.

A final point, one upon which future events hinged, was the apparently benign statement, "As soon as ten companies have joined the regiment, Captain Charles Knobelsdorff will call a meeting of the ten officers of the various companies at Chicago for the purpose of organizing the regiment and effecting its acceptance by the United States government." The regiment was mustered in on September 13, 1861; Knobelsdorff was age thirty-three. Within two months, the complaints began. Records dated November 24th, 1861, from Sedalia, Missouri, described Colonel Knobelsdorff sending patrols throughout Pettis County, taking nearly all the horses, mules, cattle, wagons, and buggies; plundering the citizens' homes; and even stealing their blankets.

These complaints troubled Colonel Knobelsdorff not a bit. The following month, his mind was on other controversies. He had been appointed as commander of the Second Brigade, but was removed and replaced by Col. Peter Osterhaus. Knobelsdorff fired off several heated missives, claiming that he had senior date of rank. As he was busying himself with these issues, he apparently orchestrated the circulation of a petition urging his own appointment as a brigadier general.

Though Colonel Knobelsdorff may have thought rapid promotion was his due, some believed otherwise. The records of January 1862 have several complaints: one report notes that Knobelsdorff kept arresting his own officers, that General Fremont kept releasing them, and that Knobelsdorff kept re-arresting them.

One hundred men from the Buckeye State grew restive under Knobelsdorff's domination, and a letter from the Governor of Ohio removed Capt. Edwin Hayes's company from the 44h Illinois, to be re-assigned to "some other Ohio regiment." The War Department of the State of Illinois weighed in with their opinion: "The 44th Regiment of Illinois Volunteers, otherwise known as the Northwestern Rifles, is not in the Official Register."

Meanwhile, the colonel used administrative counterbattery fire, invoking the medical profession. In January 1862, he produced letters from two surgeons, both saying that he needed twenty days at home. The first diagnosis was "facial neuralgia," and the second spoke of "inflammation of the aveola," an organ not found in any current medical dictionary.

However, these maneuvers only delayed the seemingly inevitable: On April 24, 1862, at Camp Cross Timbers, Benton County, Arkansas, a court-martial was convened, under the presidency of Col. Jeff C. Davis of the 22nd Indiana, to hear the case of Colonel Knobelsdorff. There was a total of six charges.

On the first, fraud and conduct unbecoming an officer and a gentleman, it was stated that on August 14, 1861, at Camp Ellsworth near Chicago, Knobelsdorff held a "temporary election," which he said was necessary to draw supplies. There were as yet only 400 men and 13 officers in the regiment. The "permanent election" never happened, however, and the apparently rigged "temporary election" was the one that resulted in commissions from Gov. Richard Yates, all for Colonel Knobelsdorff's friends. The first charge also included the sale to Lt. William H. Gale the position of regimental quartermaster for the sum of one hundred dollars, and further, that Knobelsdorff, after receiving the commissions of Capts. Wallace Barrett and Edwin Hayes and of Lt. John B. Stoner, returned the papers to the governor, stating that these three men had been discharged from the service (which was not true). Knobelsdorff then took the swords from these three officers and gave them to other men. The final specification of the first charge was that at St. Louis, Sedalia, and Springfield, Colonel Knobelsdorff was so drunk and noisy "as to bring great reproach upon the service."

The second charge was "insubordination and using language unbecoming an officer and a gentleman." On September 22, 1861, it was alleged that Colonel Knobelsdorff demanded entry, without a pass, to the laboratory at the St. Louis Arsenal. When the sentry refused, the colonel shouted, "Got for dam, I shoot you like a dam dog, I run you through mit my sword." After this outburst, Knobelsdorff was in turn informed that "he and his command were put under arrest and would remain overnight at the Arsenal by order of Major General Fremont." Colonel Knobelsdorff's reply? "I do not give a damn for General Fremont's orders and I will march out my whole command." The final part of the second charge was that on November 3, 1861, at Springfield, Missouri, Knobelsdorff had made "an inflammatory and mutinous speech," denouncing Maj. Gen. David Hunter as a "Know-Nothing, an enemy of German-Americans, and a Bull Run coward."

The third charge, "oppression and usurpation in office," returned to the problems of Captains Barrett and Hayes and Lieutenant Stoner, noting that Major General Fremont repeatedly ordered them to report for duty at the 44th Illinois and that Knobelsdorff repeatedly arrested them.

The fourth charge, "disobedience," took note of Knobelsdorff's refusal to follow Fremont's orders in regard to the three officers, but also his neglect of Special Order No. 29, issued by Maj. Gen. Henry W. Halleck, which also ordered Knobelsdorff to restore Hayes, Barrett, and Stoner to duty, after which he arrested them once again.

There were yet more charges. On November 5, 1861, while field officer of the day, he was drunk; on March 7, 1862, at the battle of Leestown (Pea Ridge), Arkansas, he was so drunk "his regiment became very confused;" from December 15, 1861, to January 15, 1862, he was so drunk and noisy at night that he caused "great annoyance" to the entire regiment.

On March 8, 1862, at the battle of Pea Ridge, the colonel ordered his quartermaster to hitch up the wagons and retreat, without having received any orders to that effect. Three days later, he confiscated "from the privates of said regiment, swords, pistols, revolvers and other articles and appropriated them to his own use." While still at Pea Ridge, instead of chasing Maj. Gen. Earl Van Dorn's Confederates, Knobelsdorff busied himself circulating a petition calling for the resignation of his own major.

On the first day of the battle, he had sent one of his officers off on an errand; when night fell and the man had not yet returned, Knobelsdorff remarked, "It is no matter if he has been killed."

One might think that this would have exhausted the list of charges, but there was one more. On March 9, 1862, Knobelsdorff marched his regiment in the direction of Bentonville, Arkansas; entered three different Confederate hospitals; took nearly all the surgeons, stewards, and nurses prisoner; confiscated their ambulances and horses; and left the wounded to shift for themselves. One Confederate surgeon presented a pass signed by Gen. Samuel Curtis (Knobelsdorff's commander), which the colonel disregarded.

The trial opened on April 3, 1862, and wound to a halt fourteen days later. Thirteen colonels were occupied all day for two full weeks, which certainly could have impaired the efficiency of any army trying to pry gray-clad troops out of Missouri and Arkansas.

Capt. John Russell of Company G described the temporary election, its origin in the "need to procure supplies, and the failure to hold a permanent election." He described the colonel's drinking at his tent at Sedalia: "He seemed sufficiently drunk as to be unfit for duty." Capt. Edwin Hayes recalled:

> Colonel Knobelsdorff ordered me to give up my sword and my belt. I haven't seen them since, although I got another sword from Major [Thomas] Hobart. The colonel obtained commissions for the field grades, but we company officers were offered commissions from Governor Yates. We all refused to accept such. We said we would accept only commissions signed by Secretary of War [Simon] Cameron.

As to liquor, Hayes testified that on January 2, 1862, Knobelsdorff was so drunk "he couldn't talk plain," and made so much noise that the camp could not sleep. Lt. John Stevens of Company C stated:

> Yes, I have also seen Colonel Knobelsdorff intoxicated. It was hard to sleep with the noise and confusion around the colonel's tent. I have seen him so under the influence that he misused his men. Near Bentonville, I was on picket guard and was sick. I asked to be relieved. He said, "I know no sick men." But then he offered me a drink from his canteen and I felt better.

Stevens went on to say that he had bought his own sword in St. Louis for twenty-two dollars (almost two-months' pay for a private, then), that Colonel Knobelsdorff had taken it, and that he had not seen it since. "General Halleck issued an order restoring our swords, but Colonel Knobelsdorff re-arrested me and placed me under guard."

Captain Barrett of Company B described the colonel's visit to the laboratory of the St. Louis Arsenal.

There was a sentry at the door. The colonel tried to push his way through. The sentry stopped him. Colonel Knobelsdorff put his hand on his pistol and threatened to shoot the guard, then put his hand on his sword and threatened to run him through. The guard asked who he was. Colonel Knobelsdorff replied, "It is none of your business, but I'll run you through mit my sword."

Here, Colonel Knobelsdorff cross-examined the captain. "How did you know he was a guard?" Barrett replied: "He was wearing a United States uniform and the adjutant of the Arsenal said he was a guard."

Barrett then turned to the subject of arrests. "General Fremont ordered me to report to the camp of the 44th Illinois, to report for duty. Every time I did so, Colonel Knobelsdorff arrested me. Later, on the march to Bentonville, we arrived at a Rebel hospital and I saw Colonel Knobelsdorff arrest the doctors and nurses."

Lt. Charles J. Darke, aide to Brig. Gen. Peter Osterhaus, said, "I saw Colonel Knobelsdorff when he was acting as field officer of the day, and he was under the influence of liquor." Major Hobart was positive that Colonel Knobelsdorff was drunk at Pea Ridge.

He sent out skirmishers beyond sight of the regiment. I concluded he was drunk by his appearance and how he conducted the regiment. He spoke disparagingly of his superiors in the presence of other officers, referring to General Fremont as incompetent, General Halleck as no soldier, General Hunter as a Bull Run coward, and General [Franz] Sigel as unqualified to command. He said these things several times.

In his cross-examination, Knobelsdorff asked what might be seen as a leading question: "Did you not bring these charges against me from malicious motives, fearing that I would prefer charges against you for cowardice on the battlefield?" As might be expected, Hobart replied, "No."

A Lieutenant Halby, also of the 44th Illinois, testified on the subject of alcohol. "I saw the colonel ride at full speed into camp. He certainly looked drunk. He would come out of Captain Strauss' tent, staggering, in full view of the men."

As often happens, the clarity of this picture was soon muddied, in this case by Adjutant William A. Gordon, of the 1st Division of the Army of Southwest Missouri. "I never saw Colonel Knobelsdorff drunk and I know him well. At the door of the St. Louis Arsenal, there was no guard posted at all, and I certainly never heard him speak ill of any general."

After deliberation, the court acquitted him of four charges, found him guilty of two, and sentenced him to be "reprimanded in orders by the general commanding in the Southwest. The Court is thus lenient because the charges . . . are stale and prolix, and seems, as here reviewed in the light of the evidence, to be pervaded by a spirit which does not commend itself to impartial minds." The reviewing general added:

The testimony adduced fully justifies the finding of the Court. It was becoming [of] Colonel Knobelsdorff, who must expect obedience from so many, to set the example of obedience himself, when directed to restore Captain Barrett, Captain Hayes, and Lieutenant Stoner to the respective companies. By violating the orders of Major Generals Fremont, Hunter and Halleck successively, Colonel Knobelsdorff did a great wrong, not only to the officers under his command, but to the whole service to which he is connected and he has received a remarkably light sentence for his misconduct. He will be careful not to presume from the result of this trial that like lenity will be shown for similar acts in the future. He is released from arrest and will resume his sword.

In May, Knobelsdorff was placed in command of the Second Brigade, but in August 1862, some offense, not now in the record, caused a new court-martial to be assembled and, on August 15, 1862, he was dismissed from the service at Camp Irwin, Texas.

Having returned home, he set about clearing his name, and on December 3, 1863, his administrative "disability" was removed by the governor of Illinois and a few days later, he was promoted to brigadier general. Embarrassment seems to be an emotion beyond the ken of Colonel Knobelsdorff. In May 1864, he claimed $416 for provisions for 40 men, food consumed in the summer of 1861. The account books showed that he had been paid for this once before, and the government declined to pay for it a second time.

The records of the pension bureau shed light on his later years. In 1879, at the age of 52, he applied for a pension as an invalid, and submitted a statement that in September 1861, a "spirited horse" fell on him, and since then he had suffered from a spinal disease. He also certified that since he left the service, he had "lived by manual labor." This last statement is of interest, since A. T. Andrea's *History of Chicago* notes that Charles Knobelsdorff was president of the Germania Bank, which was chartered in 1869. In 1887, he filed a pension claim that he was unable to care for himself and needed constant nursing assistance.

In 1890, his personal physician, Dr. J. O. Day, certified that "the General had epileptic fits, was blind in the right eye, suffered from spinal neurosis, and was totally incapacitated." However, a government-appointed special examiner made a home visit and filed a very different report: "He is as healthy as any man his age [sixty-three years]. I was in his house more than two hours and I failed to see that he required any aid whatever. It is my opinion if he were examined by a Board not headed by his own physician, that he would never receive another pension."

In 1891, he applied to have his pension increased from thirty dollars a month to seventy-two dollars, certifying that he was "totally disabled from all work." Perhaps this time he was right—in 1892, he was dead. His widow, Luitgarde, drew a pension until 1925, when the books were closed on the family Knobelsdorff.

Chapter Seven

"And a Brandy for my Horse!"

COL. NEWTON B. LORD

Checkered is a word that barely describes the career of Newton B. Lord, the colonel of the 35th New York Volunteers. He began his military service in May 1861, at age twenty-nine, as a captain of Company K. In June he was a major, and by August he commanded the regiment. Within five months he was in trouble, and on January 22, 1862, at Upton Hill, Virginia, his first court-martial began. The principal charge was disobedience. The principal venue was Binn's Hill, near Falls Church.[1]

Colonel Lord was sent from brigade headquarters the following order: "As the section at Binn's Hill is particularly exposed, three sentinels will be established there, who will be relieved every two hours from the reserves. The presence of any other persons on the hill, except the occasional visit of an officer, is strictly prohibited." This written order was delivered by Lt. John A. Kress, aide-de-camp to Brig. Gen. James S. Wadsworth, who then repeated it verbally to Colonel Lord, along with instructions to keep the reserve near Patterson House.

Lord signed a receipt for the orders. Two days later he still had twenty men posted on Binn's Hill. Lieutenant Kress went to Lord again and repeated the general's orders. Lord again agreed to follow them, but another two days passed and the extra men were still on the hill.

Col. George Pratt of the 20th New York State Militia testified that Lord had received such orders. Maj. William Grigg recalled having seen twenty men on the prohibited hill. Lieutenant Kress testified again that he had seen Colonel Lord post a large number of men on the hill, even after he had received written and verbal orders not to do so.

The court asked Lieutenant Kress if he had been speaking for General Wadsworth. His reply: "In carrying out the General's orders, I was speaking for the General. I made three visits to Colonel Lord and each time there were many men on Binn's Hill." At the conclusion of the testimony, Colonel Lord submitted a 3,000-word defense, which began, "I do not desire to consume the time of the Court. . . ."

The principle thrust of his defense seemed to be that Lieutenant Kress had not prefaced his orders with a specific statement that he spoke for the general. Further, Lord seems to have seen malign intent in the lieutenant, some glimmer of personal animosity. Apparently convinced of this line of reasoning, the court acquitted Lord.

The commanding general, Irvin McDowell, wrote a finely reasoned rebuttal on the subject of delegated authority:

> That which is communicated by a staff officer in the name of, or by the direction of, his chief, is the act of the chief, and it is not necessary that every sentence used by the staff officer should be accompanied by a declaration of that fact. In cases of routine, it is to be inferred. It is enough to know that he is acting under the orders of his chief.
>
> The adjutant at evening parade orders the captains to forward march, but he is not required to say, "The colonel directs me to say forward march," or any equivalent.

After further illumination of the concept of the chain of command, McDowell concluded by noting that even if Colonel Lord felt a personal animosity toward the bearer of the general's orders, the colonel, through an exertion of *noblesse oblige,* should not dignify such conflict by taking notice of it.

Having escaped this difficulty with only a general's admonition, Colonel Lord seemed destined for further difficulties. His service record says little about the 35th Regiment's part in the battles of Cedar Mountain, Gainesville, and Bull Run, but something was amiss at South Mountain (Antietam) in September, 1862. Lord's records for that month contain letters from both the chaplain and the surgeon denying that the colonel was a coward at South Mountain. They both stated that Colonel Lord needed to spend the day of the battle lying in an ambulance because he was sick.

In January 1863 a letter by Brig. Gen. Marsena R. Patrick, the noted disciplinarian, contained some harsh words:

> Since Colonel Lord took command, there has been constant quarreling in this regiment, except when he was absent sick. The citizens of Jefferson County [the locale in New York where the regiment was raised] have requested of me that he be brought to trial. I may add that the major now in command is by far the best officer in the regiment, and the only one upon whom I could rely on as a commander.

The major was in command because Lord was under arrest again, this time for fraud in drawing forage, for drunkenness on duty, and for cowardice.

In February 1863 a third set of charges appeared in the record, illustrating Lord's talent for getting himself into trouble in multiple venues. At Alexandria,

Col. Newton B. Lord rode his horse into a saloon in his hometown, where they both had a brandy. He then shot holes into the ceiling with his army revolver. MASSACHUSETTS COMMANDERY MILITARY ORDER OF THE LOYAL LEGION, U.S. ARMY MILITARY HISTORY INSTITUTE.

Virginia, he was so drunk that he fell off his horse. He was drunk at brigade headquarters. At Cottage Landing, Virginia, he was so drunk that "he made an indecent exposure of his person in the presence of a lady," after which he rode his horse into a gully and fell headlong from the saddle.

Lord seems to have reserved his most dramatic acts for the home folks. At Brownsville, New York, in his native Jefferson County, "in full view of the citizens," he rode his horse into a bar, procured a drink of brandy for himself and a second brandy for his horse, then fired his revolver into the ceiling. After riding out into the street, where a large crowd of the curious had now gathered, he rode once again into the bar, and "repeated his performance."

In February 1863 the charges were dropped following his resignation. This would have ended the career of any ordinary man, but Lord was not ordinary. He returned to Jefferson County in June 1863, and by September had recruited enough men to form the 20th Regiment of New York Cavalry, with Newton Lord once again a colonel.

His new regiment, also known as the McClellan Cavalry, saw action in North Carolina and Virginia, and was present at the Appomattox surrender. Lord served eighteen months with the 20th New York Cavalry, resigning March 23, 1865. From the records available, he seems to have kept his horse out of the bars.

Chapter Eight

"A Miserable Reptile"

LT. COL. JOHN DUNN MACGREGOR

John Dunn MacGregor was born in New York State in 1827, served in the Mexican War, and joined the 4th New York in April 1861 as a captain. By the end of the month he was lieutenant colonel, a rank he held for the next thirteen months. He was listed sick in August 1861 and in May 1862, not unusual for those pest-ridden times.

After his superior, Alfred W. Taylor, returned to the regiment in April 1862, following lengthy litigation, an apparently smoldering feud erupted once again. Around June, MacGregor seems to have called Colonel Taylor "a liar, a thief, a coward and a low-down miserable reptile," and was soon under arrest.[1]

The trial commenced June 9, 1862, in Suffolk, Virginia. The charges were conduct prejudicial to good order and military discipline, and conduct unbecoming an officer and a gentleman. Apparently MacGregor had addressed these terms of disrespect toward Taylor in the presence of most of the regiment.

In a court-martial, the accused is entitled to challenge members of the court he believes to be prejudiced. In this case, MacGregor challenged the presence of Col. Samuel Alford, who "had sat on the trial of Colonel Taylor and disregarded all the testimony that went against Taylor. Colonel Alford is biased in favor of my accuser." The court rejected this challenge.

The first witness for the prosecution was Taylor himself. MacGregor cross-examined him: "Do you believe in the existence of a God and in a future state of rewards and punishments?" Taylor said that he did. Taylor then described the incident. "I heard an uproar and received a report from Lieutenant Henderson. I then sent a written report, placing Colonel MacGregor under arrest."

Capt. C. W. Kruger heard MacGregor say to a Lieutenant Walker, "You say Colonel Taylor is not fit to command, and here you are collecting money for a gift for the colonel. You are a hypocrite." Ens. Charles Anderson admitted that he had been promoted from sergeant by Colonel Taylor and had contributed ten dollars (three weeks pay for a private) toward a gift for the colonel.

Thomas Halligan, fife major, recalled: "I heard Colonel MacGregor call Colonel Taylor a liar, a thief and a coward. I was in my tent 20 feet away, but I

Lt. Col. John Dunn MacGregor, a dour and pious Scot, cross-examined his own commander, commencing with the question, "Do you believe in the existence of a God and in a future state of rewards and punishments?" MASSACHUSETTS COMMANDERY MILITARY ORDER OF THE LOYAL LEGION, U.S. ARMY MILITARY HISTORY INSTITUTE.

know his voice." Sgt. Samuel Willetts testified that "Colonel MacGregor said that Lieutenant Walker was circulating a petition to be published in New York, commending Colonel Taylor, and he said even the lieutenant knew more than Colonel Taylor." Six other witnesses seemed unable to recall anything of the incident, including Ens. Henry Chapman, who, himself, was under arrest for assaulting his captain.

MacGregor was acquitted of all charges, and a few weeks later was a full colonel, following Taylor's resignation.

To make the story even more complex, the month before his court martial, MacGregor had submitted his resignation, which was endorsed by Taylor in these words: "This officer is the main cause of the discord in this regiment. Harmony will not be restored while he remains. The discipline of the regiment will be greatly improved by his departure," but, as we have seen, it was Taylor who departed.

MacGregor seems to have served well. He was wounded in the left arm at Fredericksburg and wounded again at Chancellorsville, and was mustered out with his regiment in May 1863. In 1867, he was breveted brigadier general for "gallant and meritorious service in the field during the War." He died in New York City on April 23, 1878, and was buried in Brooklyn.

Chapter Nine

"I Will See You Damned!"

COL. JOHN H. McCUNN

The Irish Rifles, later designated as the 37th Regiment of New York Volunteers, was mustered in at New York City in June 1861, and served in the defense of Washington, D.C., until March of the following year. Defending the capital seemed to require a certain amount of time in Willard's Hotel. It was there that Col. John H. McCunn, commander of the 37th, encountered 1st Lt. Robert F. Hunter, then serving with the provost guard.[1]

In the court-martial, held in Washington, D.C., in August 1861, with Brig. Gen. Erasmus D. Keyes as president, McCunn was charged with conduct unbecoming an officer and a gentleman, and conduct prejudicial to good order and military discipline.

The specifics were as follows: In the afternoon of August 7, 1861, at Willard's Hotel, Lieutenant Hunter, who was then on duty, asked Colonel McCunn to show the pass authorizing him to be away from the camp of his regiment (during this dialogue, the enlisted men of the provost guard remained outside the hotel, awaiting the summons to subdue any miscreants).

Colonel McCunn, in reply to Lieutenant Hunter's request, retorted, "Go to hell. By God, sir, by what authority do you demand my pass?" Lieutenant Hunter replied that his authority was that of Col. Andrew Porter, the provost marshal. McCunn then replied, "By God, I do not recognize your authority." Lieutenant Hunter asked the colonel's name, which the colonel refused to divulge.

After several such exchanges, McCunn reached into his pocket and produced a piece of paper, which he flourished, exclaiming, "There, damn you, will that do?" It did not. Hunter clearly regarded the proffered paper as insufficient and improper, and explained to the colonel that he must give his name and regiment, and must go to his quarters under arrest. McCunn, undaunted, exclaimed, "I will see you damned before I obey your arrest, and besides, you and your men are all drunk."

This opinion was seconded by a defense witness, Edward Burke: "In my opinion, Lieutenant Hunter was acting under the influence of drink. I saw him several times during that day in the bar of Willard's Hotel, but only saw him drink a beverage twice."

Patrick McNamara, also a witness for the defense, observed: "I saw Lieutenant Hunter in the bar that day, drinking. His face was very red. He must have been in a state of intoxication or he would not have addressed the colonel as he did."

After much contradictory evidence was given, testimony came to a close. It was customary in that era to allow the accused to submit a written statement in his defense, before the trial board retired to deliberate. In his submission, McCunn's eloquence stands in contrast to the inarticulate and tongue-tied defenses offered by most accused today.

On the first note of alarm of danger to our capital, I volunteered in April as a private in the 69th Regiment of New York Volunteers. From then until now I think I have performed my duties as a soldier and as a gentleman.

I quit a quiet and happy home, and every endearment and comfort in life to help my struggling country. The charges made by Lieutenant Hunter are untrue in every particular. It is well known to all who know me that I do not drink, and that Lieutenant Hunter was an entire stranger to me. When he abruptly addressed me, I told him he was drunk and that I should report him. It is quite evident that Lieutenant Hunter preferred these charges lest I should report him. The first witness which Lieutenant Hunter called [Mr. Campbell] swears positively that he heard me use no profane language. His next witness, Dr. McMillan, swears that he heard me use no disrespectful or profane language, and says in addition that Lieutenant Hunter called me a fool. Colonel Murray of the regular army, who I offered as a witness, swears he saw the greater part of the difficulty and never heard me use a profane or harsh word.

The Court can see the trouble and heart-burning which this has brought to my door, can see the lasting disgrace which such men can bring upon the service, can see the deep humiliation that a man like myself must undergo by coming in contact with such a person.

I quit my high position and my happy home to assist my country and this is my reward. Notwithstanding, I will stand by the old flag that afforded me shelter when driven by the pelting winds of fortune, stand by the Constitution under which I have brought myself from poverty to plenty. Through this terrible ordeal we must and shall come triumphant.

After considering this statement and the testimony offered, the court found McCunn guilty of certain portions of the charges, including failure to display a pass upon request, failure to give his name, and accusing Lieutenant Hunter of being drunk. McCunn was sentenced to be "reprimanded in General Orders from the Headquarters of the General Commanding the Army of the Potomac," which at that time was Maj. Gen. George B. McClellan, a man who

By order of Maj. Gen. George B. McClellan, Col. John H. McCunn was barred forever from entering the lines of the Army of the Potomac. McCunn's obituary concluded, "even his closest associates mistrusted him." DIVISION OF MILITARY AND NAVAL AFFAIRS, NEW YORK STATE ADJUTANT GENERAL OFFICE, ALBANY, NEW YORK.

relished the admonitory and uplifting possibilities of court-martial reviews. Whether it was the wisest use of his time may be questioned, but he was more than equal to the task of writing a court-martial review that would stand any degree of literary scrutiny.

The General Commanding confirms the finding and sentence of the Court, but in doing so, he assumes that the sentence was made thus light in consideration of the inexperience of the accused. Colonel McCunn, it would appear from the record, is ignorant of the first great principle which should guide all soldiers of whatever rank, viz: implicit obedience to proper authority. The authority of Lieutenant Hunter, and his right to demand Colonel McCunn's pass, were most clear and unquestionable; it was the authority, directly delegated through the Provost Marshal, of the General Commanding this army, and should have been obeyed as respectfully and implicitly as if the demand had been made by the General in person. The manner of the officer making the demand should have had no influence, but the colonel should have obeyed the order respectfully and promptly. If the manner of Lieutenant Hunter was improper, and that it was so is by no means clear to the General Commanding, it was the duty of Colonel McCunn to have retained his self-possession and self-respect, and to have complied with the direction to show his pass, trusting to subsequent action for redress. Colonel McCunn showed by his demeanor, as it appears on the record, that he has yet to learn at least two things before he becomes competent to command a regiment: and these are—self-command, and respect for proper authority. The pass shown by Colonel McCunn was improper in form, and Lieutenant Hunter was perfectly right in declining to recognize its validity. The paper submitted during the trial by Colonel McCunn [a prior drunk conviction of Lieutenant Hunter] as his defense, is, in many respects, irrelevant, and in others, discreditable.

The court would have been entirely justified in refusing to receive it.

The General Commanding fully approves the finding of the Court, which characterizes the conduct of Colonel McCunn as prejudicial to good order and military discipline, and desires to express the hope that this instance will be a sufficient warning to him and all other officers who may feel disposed to place themselves in opposition to the constituted military authorities. The finding of the Court may be regarded as quite lenient, but the General is prevented from remanding the case to the Court, for reconsideration, partly because the time of many valuable officers would thereby be consumed, and partly because he is willing to attribute Colonel McCunn's misconduct mainly to the fact of his being an inexperienced soldier. Colonel McCunn will resume his sword and his duties."

As is so often true in life, there is a postscript to this story. In his defense McCunn had claimed that Lieutenant Hunter had a history of drunkenness. Review of the records shows that at Fort Ridgely, Minnesota, on October 30, 1858, Hunter, while drunk, beat and cursed Sgt. R. J. Reed and Pvts. James Gillan and William Lyon, and the following morning failed to appear at morning inspection. Hunter was sentenced to a one-year suspension from all rank and pay.

The reviewing officer in early 1859 offered the opinion that Lieutenant Hunter "may rest assured that a continuance of the vice which has brought humiliation upon him in this instance, will effectually unfit him for his profession." This was a sadly accurate prediction; two months after his encounter with Colonel McCunn at the Willard, Lieutenant Hunter was a civilian, having been dismissed from the army in disgrace for continual drunkenness.

However, the story of Colonel McCunn was not over. According to the *New York Times,* he "conducted himself with gallantry at Malvern Hill, and was breveted a brigadier general. Having made some disrespectful remarks about his commanding officer, he was ordered to be court-martialed, which he avoided by resigning. General McClellan then issued an order prohibiting him from ever entering the lines of the army."

The military service record of Colonel McCunn contains two remarkable letters, both written to General McClellan. Lt. Col. John Burke, the new commander of the 37th New York, noted: "Colonel McCunn resigned, as we officers found him to be wholly incompetent. Now that he is a private citizen, he has preferred charges against nearly every officer who signed the petition requesting his resignation." Two days later, Brig. Gen. I. B. Richardson warned that "McCunn has been trying to excite a commotion among the men of the 37th. If Lieutenant Colonel Burke cannot enforce discipline among his men, it shows he is incompetent for command. As far as I can see, the men are willing to obey, but the officers appear to be entirely incompetent in the discharge of their duties. I have more trouble with 37th New York than I have had with all of the others, even worse than the 12th New York. The officers of the 37th appear of low character and can never make anything of themselves."

Following his abrupt return to civilian life, McCunn obtained the Tammany Hall nomination for judge of the Superior Court, a post he held for nine years. In spite of his many political connections, he was then removed from office by the New York State Senate, because of "malconduct and malfeasance in office." This hearing, and its verdict, so enraged McCunn that he died a few days later. His obituary, which occupied the front page of the July 7, 1872, *New York Times,* described his leaving Ireland at age sixteen and coming, friendless and penniless, to America, where he worked four years as a cabinetmaker's apprentice. At age twenty, he expressed a strong interest in becoming a lawyer, and was hired as a messenger by the firm of Boardman & Benedict. "Having picked up a slight knowledge of the law in that firm, he was admitted to practice at the New York Bar at the age of twenty-one." The obituary concluded, "In person, Mr. McCunn was agreeable and popular with the rougher classes of society, being always anxious to keep them favorable to him. As a politician, he was mistrusted, even by those with whom he labored." With those words, McCunn passed into history.

Chapter Ten

"*A Mouthful of Tongue*"

COL. DIXON S. MILES

Col. Dixon S. Miles's tempestuous career traces its course from the dry deserts of New Mexico to the watery confluence of Harper's Ferry, where a Confederate shell put him beyond the reach of any "earthly tribunal," as a later investigation aptly put the matter.[1]

Four months after the Federal disaster at First Bull Run, a court of inquiry met to examine the allegations of drunkenness on the part of Colonel Miles in that conflict. The charge had been brought by Col. I. B. Richardson, who commanded the brigade, on the heights of Centreville, Virginia, on July 21, 1861.

The court of inquiry opened with a request by Colonel Richardson that he be allowed to appear as accuser in the case. Miles immediately objected, citing page 131 of the classic book on military jurisprudence, authored by De Hart. Miles asserted that only the judge advocate could appear as prosecutor. He went on to note that Colonel Richardson had an axe to grind in the matter and that if Richardson acted as prosecutor it would be mixing "private animosities with the stream of public justice."

Richardson then testified, not as accuser, but as witness. "I had made my disposition of the troops and had gone to some other part of the battlefield. On my return, I found this regiment deployed in line of battle and in another position." Richardson first met Col. Ambrose Stevens and asked him why the position had been altered. Stevens replied that Miles had ordered it. When pressed for details, Stevens added, "I don't know why Colonel Miles ordered the change, but I do know that I have no confidence in him. The man is drunk."

Colonel Miles testified next, denying that he was drunk and giving a detailed description of the troop movements at Centreville and his reasons for ordering the movements. Then he entered the argument *ad hominem*: "The testimony of General Richardson is manifestly actuated by malicious feelings engendered in former years in New Mexico, when he was a captain of the Third Infantry, of which I had the command."

Colonel Richardson took the stand again. "At the Battle of Manassas, July 22, 1861, I commanded the Fourth Brigade of Tyler's Division and had my brigade in position at Blackburn's Ford." After a long and technical description of terrain, troop dispositions, and multiple orders flying across the field through messengers and aides, he recalled that at about 6:00 P.M., he had noticed that Colonel Miles' voice was "guttural and his language incoherent, and I noticed he had difficulty to maintain his seat in his saddle."

Col. Daniel McConnell of the 3rd Michigan then spoke. "Colonel Miles was reeling in his saddle, very unsteady, his language, tones and utterances was thick, his general condition was like an intoxicated man."

The next witness was Dr. George B. Todd, assistant surgeon of the 12th New York. "It is my impression that he was intoxicated. It is not an easy matter to distinguish intoxication from eccentricity or peculiarity of manner. He was unsteady on his horse. His tone of voice was monotonous." Then the doctor arrived at specifics. "His command to the 12th New York Regiment was 'You are now where I want you. Lay there, damn you, and die there.' Also, I noticed that he was wearing two hats. I considered him entirely unfit at that time." Colonel Miles cross-examined the doctor: "Could extreme debility from diarrhea give unsteadiness in a horseman while riding?" Dr. Todd conceded that it might.

Capt. S. A. Judd of the 3rd Michigan then took the stand. "If I have ever seen an intoxicated person, I think he was one. He spoke with a mouth full of tongue. He rolled on his horse and could not keep his balance." Judd was followed by Capt. Frederick Shiver of the same regiment. "The colonel was well over on one side, well nigh off his horse."

Maj. W. F. Bragg spoke next, noting that Gen. Irvin McDowell had ordered him to position some artillery. "I was doing so when Colonel Miles rode up. He seemed very excited and asked in an angry and vexed manner by what right I was moving the guns. I replied, 'By General McDowell's orders.' Colonel Miles replied, 'I will not have my arrangements interfered with by any man.' I thought he had been drinking." Other witnesses described Miles' bowel troubles and the prescription of brandy for these symptoms.

These witnesses were followed by five men for the defense, who swore that Colonel Miles was cold sober on July 21 and that his behavior was steady and rational.

The court considered this conflicting testimony and agreed on a statement of facts: first, "Colonel I. B. Richardson was justified in applying the term drunkenness to Colonel D. S. Miles condition about 7:00 o'clock p.m. on the 21st July last."

Their second accepted fact related to medication: "Colonel Miles had been ill for several days before July 21 last—was ill on that day; that the Surgeon had prescribed medicines, and on the day of the battle had prescribed for him small quantities of brandy. The Court, however, considers his illness a very slight extenuation of the guilt attached to his condition July 21st last."

The court of inquiry then made its recommendations: There was not sufficient evidence for a court-martial to convict him of drunkenness, and the

Col. Dixon A. Miles's performance at Harper's Ferry was reviewed by a board of senior officers, who described "an incapacity amounting to almost imbecility" and criticized the general who had appointed Miles. MASSACHUSETTS COMMANDERY MILITARY ORDER OF THE LOYAL LEGION, U.S. ARMY MILITARY HISTORY INSTITUTE.

assembly of colonels and/or generals needed for a court-martial would be a great inconvenience to the army. They recommended no further proceedings.

The findings were approved by Maj. Gen. George B. McClellan, but this was not the end of the matter. Colonel Miles was relieved of his command and assigned to an out-of-the-way post—Harper's Ferry—where, presumably, he would be spared the pressure of combat. However, Confederate Maj. Gen. Thomas J. "Stonewall" Jackson had other plans.

Harper's Ferry lies at the bottom of a deep Y-shaped valley; the surrounding heights command the town itself. It is the opposite of a defensible place. On September 14, 1862, Jackson appeared on those heights and pointed his cannons down onto Colonel Miles's post. Behind the cannons were six divisions of Confederate troops. At Harper's Ferry, there were less than 15,000 Federals, looking almost straight up those Confederate gun barrels. Just at dusk, shells began to hurtle down upon the huddled Federals.

At dawn the next day, the barrage resumed. After an hour Colonel Miles recognized the hopelessness of the Union position. He ordered the Union colors lowered and a surrender offered. One of the last shells from Jackson's batteries killed the colonel. The Confederates took 11,500 prisoners, along with 13,000 rifles and tons of equipment badly needed by the Rebel forces.

A few weeks after the fall of Harper's Ferry and the closely related Battle of Antietam, a military commission investigated the surrender. The full proceedings occupy many hundreds of pages, but a few central points stand out.

The portion of the report concerning Colonel Miles opens with a touching and philosophical sentiment, rarely seen in bureaucratic communications:

> The Commission has approached a consideration of this officer's conduct . . . with extreme reluctance. An officer who cannot appear before any earthly tribunal to answer or explain charges gravely affecting his character, who has met his death at the hands of the enemy, even upon the spot he disgracefully surrenders, is entitled to the tenderest care and the most careful investigation.

The commission clearly felt that they had been both tender and careful. "These this Commission has accorded Colonel Miles, and in giving an opinion only repeats what runs through over 900 pages of evidence, strongly unanimous upon the facts, that Colonel Miles' incapacity, amounting to almost imbecility, led to the shameful surrender of this important post."

The commission went on to note that Maj. Gen. John Wool had ordered Colonel Miles to fortify Maryland Heights, a position of great natural strength directly above the town. The investigators were of the opinion that Miles's failure to order the building of strong points was "criminal neglect, to use the mildest term."

A review of the records shows that nine days before Stonewall Jackson's unwelcome appearance, Colonel Miles had ordered Col. Thomas Ford to build entrenchments upon the heights, but had failed to provide men, picks, or shovels in spite of Ford's frequent entreaties, both verbal and in writing.

Colonel Miles's state of mental capacity may be gauged to some extent by one witness from the engineering corps. He testified that Colonel Miles had ordered him to take up about a hundred feet of the pontoon bridge, and a few moments later countermanded the order—in person. The puzzled engineer sought the assistant adjutant general and asked him to obtain from the colonel "a distinct statement which of these conflicting orders were to be obeyed."

The engineer went on to explain: "I did this in my own defense, inasmuch as during my service under Colonel Miles I had frequently found his orders liable to be misunderstood, and I regarded the taking up of the bridge as a matter of the highest importance."

The conclusionary statement of the commission, in its investigation of Colonel Miles, offered the deceased commander one slight concession, just the barest hint of exoneration: "The officer who placed this incapable in command should share in the responsibility and, in the opinion of the Commission, Major General Wool is guilty to this extent, of a gross disaster and should be censured for his conduct."

Perhaps the dead-and-buried Dixon Miles was a handy scapegoat for the Union disaster, useful for deflecting attention from McClellan's penchant for snatching defeat from the jaws of victory, or perhaps Miles was indeed a drunken near imbecile. The men who knew him and judged him voted for the latter, a sad legacy for an old soldier.

Chapter Eleven

So Drunk He Fell Off His Horse

LT. COL. FRANCIS B. O'KEEFE

The troubles of the New World were often the troubles of the Old World, merely transplanted into fresh and more fertile soil. The relationship of Ireland and Great Britain is a mordant example. After a brief whiff of autonomy in the late 1700s, the Act of Union in 1800 extinguished Irish freedom, but not a sense of hope. The potato famine of 1845–46, which killed or drove overseas almost two million Irish people did not solve the problem but rather increased the bitter taste. Three years before Fort Sumter, the Fenian Movement was born, and its post–Civil–War invasion of Canada provided another moment of crisis in U.S.–British relationships.

This ancient quarrel formed part of the background of the 15th New York Engineers, mustered in New York City on June 17, 1861, as an infantry regiment and reorganized that October as an engineering unit. The 15th served until June 1865, and its regimental banner was entitled to note service at Richmond, Seven Pines, Malvern Hill, Fredericksburg, Gettysburg, and a dozen other fights.

The commander of the 15th Engineers was Col. John McLeod Murphy, whose second-in-command was Lt. Col. Francis B. O'Keefe, a twenty-nine-year-old New Yorker, mustered in on June 17, 1861, with the rest of the regiment.

Three months later, O'Keefe was court-martialed on charges of conduct unbecoming an officer and a gentleman, drunkenness on duty, disobedience of orders, absence without leave, and insubordination.[1]

The specifics noted included the following: On the march from Willett's Point to White Stone, Virginia, he took a horse belonging to a citizen named Gardiner and spirited the horse aboard the steamer *Atlas* for his own use; at Camp St. John, Virginia, he was drunk, noisy, and disorderly in the presence of his regiment; the following day at the same camp he was so drunk he fell off his horse at evening parade; in Washington, D.C., he was too drunk to march his regiment through the city; on one occasion, he left his camp overnight without permission, and, finally, had used "threatening and menacing language" toward Colonel Murphy.

The trial, which was held in Alexandria, Virginia, with Brig. Gen. Erasmus D. Keyes as president, produced a considerable amount of contradictory testimony, as well as a spirited defense by O'Keefe on the subject of falling off his horse: he explained that he had stood up in his right stirrup to untangle his left stirrup. Experienced riders at the trial scoffed at such an explanation.

The court finally concluded that O'Keefe was guilty of being noisy and disorderly at Camp St. John, of falling off his horse at parade, and of being absent without leave, but was innocent of the other charges and specifications. He was sentenced to be cashiered, and the sentence was confirmed by Maj. Gen. George B. McClellan, but this confirmation fell far short of closing the record.

O'Keefe immediately appealed his case to President Lincoln, in a 3,000-word statement. He began by pointing out that he had served in the Mexican War (he would have been fourteen years old at the time if the New York State records are correct), and based his initial argument upon the honor "of an old soldier who appeals to be saved from the ignominy unjustly heaped upon him."

O'Keefe then pointed out that only five of the thirteen officers of the board had voted to find him guilty, the others being absent or disqualified at various points of the proceedings. He also noted that a recommendation of mitigation (that the sentence be changed to one year of suspension from rank and pay) had been ignored. But O'Keefe failed to mention that McClellan, in his review, had been of the opinion that "noisy and disorderly conduct . . . under the influence of liquor" was sufficient to support the charge of conduct unbecoming an officer and a gentleman, and expressed no interest in mitigation.

Continuing his appeal, O'Keefe attributed Maj. Clinton Colgate's opinion that O'Keefe was drunk on August 8, 1861, to the "distortions of vision caused by the sight of a lieutenant colonel's epaulets, which, if torn from the prisoner, would most naturally fall into his possession."

Lt. Walter Cassin had testified that he had seen O'Keefe walking in a field with Judge James H. Welsh, and testified that O'Keefe had an unsteady gait and used "boisterous language." O'Keefe's rebuttal was that Lieutenant Cassin was too distant to hear the actual words.

During the trial, Judge Welsh was confined by sickness to Willard's Hotel. His sworn affidavit stating that on August 8 he was serving as regimental paymaster and that while walking in the aforementioned field, had seen no indication of drunkenness on the part of O'Keefe, was rejected by the court.

Capt. Thomas Bogan testified that on the parade ground, O'Keefe had been "excited," but attributed this behavior to Colonel Murphy's having publicly called O'Keefe a coward. Bogan hastened to add that on this occasion, O'Keefe was neither noisy nor disorderly and was in every respect "entirely sober."

Also testifying were Lt. David R. Smith, Capt. James McQueen, Lt. George Da Cunha, Capt. John Lalor, and Dr. James McNair, regimental surgeon. Each of these men swore that on August 7–8, O'Keefe was entirely sober, showing not the slightest indication of intoxication. O'Keefe went on to give his personal opinion that the testimony of Lieutenant Cassin was based on "personal enmity and the expectation of promotion."

As to the charge of being absent without leave, (specifically, "he did pass a night outside the limits of his camp"), O'Keefe defended himself even more vigorously. "I was an invalid, on furlough, sleeping in a house 60 yards from our camp, incapable of entering into my duties for some six weeks, as testified to by the Regimental Surgeon."

Coming closer to what might have been the heart of the matter—although O'Keefe's exact wording leaves some points unclear—he thundered, "A man who had nobly fought and won distinction in the Mexican War, having been called a coward by a mere tyro in military matters, although an apology was subsequently made, would necessarily desire to avoid, by the best possible means, all chance of collision with his superior officer." O'Keefe went on to say that the relationship between himself and Colonel Murphy "were such as to preclude the possibility of Colonel Murphy justly regarding, much less seeking to punish, the act as a violation of duty, or disobedience, especially while he permitted other officers to do likewise without censure."

O'Keefe went on to note that two of the most senior officers of the court had been called away briefly during the trial and were thus not allowed to participate in the final deliberations. "Had General Keyes and Colonel Berry been permitted to resume their seats, as they essayed to do, their experience and judgment doubtless would have prevented a great wrong."

In his summation, the appellant stated forcefully that there was "not a tittle of evidence" to support the charge of drunkenness, and that the charges against him were "a means of gratifying personal resentments," using "extreme means and stale and accumulated offenses." He concluded, "The accused, as a matter of simple justice, should be restored to rank and pay."

Attached to the appeal were two documents of considerable interest. The first was a petition signed by Capts. Bogan, Garrett, Lalor, Dodd, Perry and Hicks, and by Lts. Larkin, Wood, Luby, Da Cunha, Hogan, Brown, Horban, Green, Murphy, Sandfor, Place, Bronson, Bacon, Farrell, Lane and Smith. The text of the petition stated that O'Keefe was never drunk and that his "superior qualifications endeared him to both officers and men."

In a separate document, Brigadier General Keyes, who had been president of the court, expressed his personal opinion. "I heard a portion of the testimony. It struck me that the charges arose from a personal quarrel between Colonel Murphy and the accused, and that the latter may have suffered as much from personal hostility as from his own misconduct."

On October 19, 1861, in Washington, D.C., the judge advocate sent to the White House an analysis of the court-martial. "The case is now appealed to the President on the grounds that the verdict was contrary to the evidence. An appeal does not lie on that ground. The 65th Article of War defines cases wherein the approval of the President is needed . . . this is not one of them."

It was, instead, according to judge advocate of the army, John F. Lee, one where the sentence is to be confirmed by the officer appointing the court. A sentence of dismissal from the service can be remedied by the president only by a new appointment of that officer. "I submit, however, that this should not be done except in <u>obvious</u> case of wrong and injustice." Lee went on to point out that it would be a "great inconvenience to the President" to raise appeals where the law allows none, and further, it would seriously prejudice the authority of the commanding general, if cases could bypass him "in matters the law has carefully confided to him."

But Lee had found a valid error in the trial record. "The Order for the Court appoints 13 members and with no warrant for a lesser number. Yet only eight appeared at any time, and only five at the verdict and sentence." The judge advocate here cited the Supreme Court in *Martin v. Mott 12th Wheaton*, which ruled that when less than thirteen officers are to sit on the court, there must be expressed authority for such a decrease, stated in the original Order. Lee summed up his conclusions and recommendations as follows:

> The validity of [McClellan's] order discharging the officer from the service depends upon the validity of the proceedings of the court martial. The President only may discharge an officer of his own authority. If the proceedings of the Court are now referred back to General McClellan, with the appeal and the statements accompanying it, he may advise the President whether to order a new trial, setting aside the former as void in law, or to confirm his order in the case discharging Lieutenant Colonel O'Keefe. In the case of an officer of Volunteers who has had one fair trial by court martial, I am unwilling to recommend to the President to void the proceedings on purely technical grounds, and to put the service to the inconvenience of a new trial or to restore without trial. The appeal complains that General McClellan disregarded the recommendation of the Court to commute the sentence to one year's suspension. There are obvious reasons for it. The services of the officer are wanted now, if at all.

In the court-martial files, as they exist today, there is no record of the President's reply. The records of the State of New York show that Lt. Col. Francis B. O'Keefe was dismissed from the service as of September 2, 1861. In 1878, O'Keefe wrote a brief letter of inquiry to the War Department. The letter is attached to his court-martial file. No answer is recorded.

Chapter Twelve

"General Logan Can Kiss My Ass"

COL. FRANK L. RHODES

The southern tip of Illinois has been termed "Little Egypt," because of its proximity to Cairo, and in 1861, the "Egyptians" were strongly pro-Democrat and pro-secession. There were thousands of loyalists, however, and the 8th Illinois Volunteers were Union men, as was their commander, Col. Frank L. Rhodes (also spelled Rhoads). But Rhodes seemed more interested in fighting his own superiors than in fighting the Confederates.[1]

Rhodes was thirty-six when he was mustered in as lieutenant colonel in July 1861 at Cairo, Illinois; in August, he was under arrest, although the records do not say why. For the next six months, his life seems to have been uneventful, but by March 1862 he was not a well man. His doctor certified that he had "chronic diarrhea, followed by jaundice, also a refractory [persistent] erythematous [reddened] condition of the skin, and a stomatitis [inflammation of the mouth] of a diphtheric [making a thick membrane in the pharynx] type."

He seems to have recovered his strength enough to annoy a number of his colleagues and superiors and, in August 1862, he was court-martialed in Jackson, Tennessee. There were three charges. The first was violation of the Sixth Article of War, which prohibits military men from showing disrespect toward their superiors. It was charged that while his regiment was under the command of Maj. Robert H. Sturgess and exercising on the drill field as part of the Second Brigade, which itself was under the command of Col. Michael K. Lawler, Colonel Rhodes appeared in his fatigue uniform without his sword and ordered his regiment to halt. Rhodes shouted at the members of the 8th Illinois, "Do not obey any orders from those other colonels, only my orders." Colonel Lawler appeared on the scene and twice ordered Rhodes to move off the drill field, but Rhodes persisted in telling his regiment to obey only him, saying, "I have been ordered to report to a junior officer, Colonel Brayman, and I will not obey his order and my regiment shall also not do so."

61

The second charge was violation of the Seventh Article of War, which prohibits the commencement of mutinies and recommends death for those who do so. This difficulty occurred upon the same drill field, after Rhodes was placed under arrest by Colonel Lawler. Major Sturgess was still functioning as commanding officer of the 8th Illinois, and he was ordered to detail a group of men for guard duty. Rhodes felt strongly that any orders to his regiment ought to come through him, and he said that if a portion of his regiment was selected for guard duty, he would place himself at the head of such a unit and urge the men not to report for duty, "I had as lief to be shot for mutiny as anything else."

The third charge was based upon violation of the Seventy-seventh Article of War, which states that when an officer is under arrest he must be confined to certain limits and must be ordered to surrender his sword. After his arrest, rather than remain in camp, Rhodes went first to brigade headquarters, then to division headquarters and then to district headquarters "without permission and in defiance of his arrest."

The fourth and final charge, conduct unbecoming an officer and a gentleman, is a very serious one, because any officer found guilty of such charge must, by regulation, automatically be dismissed from the service. This charge stated that Colonel Rhodes, while under arrest, visited his superior officer and, in the presence of enlisted men, and within the hearing of ladies, used obscene language in the abuse of his superior officers:

> I have been shit on, and General Logan might kiss my ass. I will be
> Goddamned if I will obey any order coming from Colonel Brayman
> nor should any man in his regiment. If they expect any man in the
> Eighth Illinois to do guard duty, they had better bring twice their
> number along to make them turn out. I do not give a damn whether
> they call it mutiny or any thing else.

All these events occurred on August 16, 1862.

The trial began with Colonel Rhodes asserting that legally he was in command, not Colonel Lawler, that Col. M. Brayman had been illegally assigned to command the brigade and that he, Rhodes, was not bound to obey either one of them. He wanted the second charge "quashed," as "I have never been legally arrested," and he also wished the third charge dismissed, as no legal limits had been set for his arrest. As to the fourth charge, he wished that removed as well, claiming that the specifications were vague. The court considered all of his objections, denied them, and called as the first witness for the prosecution Maj. Robert Sturgess.

Sturgess described the situation on August 16, when the brigade was at drill under the command of Colonel Lawler. Sturgess was commanding the 8th Illinois and recalled that after they had been drilling for half an hour the trouble commenced. The men had just halted with "Order Arms," and Colonel Lawler had then given the next order, which was "Forward into Line." At that moment, Colonel Rhodes rode onto the drill field and shouted, "Eighth Regiment, halt." Then Rhodes brought his horse close to the 8th Illinois and ordered, "Stand fast! I am your colonel and you will obey my orders." Rhodes then rode over to Lawler and demanded an explanation. Lawler replied, "This is no time for explanations, I am busy drilling the brigade." This did not deflect Colonel Rhodes at all. He replied, "I don't care. I have been ordered to report to a junior officer, and, by God, I won't do it!" Rhodes then brought his horse back to the 8th Regiment and addressed them as follows: "Boys, I want you to stand by me. They can arrest me as they damn please, but I won't obey that order." At that point, Colonel Lawler rode up and said, "I do arrest you, instanter." Rhodes then left the drill ground and the men of his regiment "seemed mutinous and were making considerable noise." Major Sturgess quieted the men down and told them, "You may not like Colonel Lawler but he is your superior officer and you will obey him." When Colonel Lawler arrested Rhodes he did not demand his sword or set limits beyond which he could not go. This testimony was confirmed by the next witness, Capt. Hermann Lieb, commander of Company D.

Now, it was the turn of Corp. James White, also of Company D. He recalled that he was functioning as a clerk at headquarters and that Rhodes appeared demanding the original of the order appointing Colonel Brayman as commander of the Second Brigade. Corporal White declined to give out the original, noting that Rhodes had already been sent an official copy, but he eventually yielded to the demands and threats of Colonel Rhodes, who promised to return the original order in half an hour. White recalled that, "I next saw him at twilight at Mrs. Campbell's dwelling. I was in the tent at headquarters and I could hear Colonel Rhodes voice raised at Colonel Lawler. Colonel Rhodes was shouting, 'I have been shit on. The general can kiss my ass. I will be God-damned if I obey any orders from Colonel Brayman. I don't give a damn whether you call it mutiny or not.'"

Lt. John Hoover, of the 3rd Illinois, testified that he had been at division headquarters with General Logan. He remembered that it was after dark and that Rhodes had ridden up and expressed his unhappiness that Brayman had been given a superior post: "Colonel Brayman is junior to me by ten days and I will never take orders from a junior. If they want to confine me, they will find me at the head of my regiment. I have been shit on and the general can kiss my ass." Lieutenant Hoover remembered that there was one lady present at the headquarters.

After deliberation, the court found Colonel Rhodes guilty of the first charge only and ordered that he be suspended for thirty days. The case was then reviewed by Brig. Gen. John A. Logan, the object of Rhodes's scorn, who concluded, "This decision is not approved, upon the ground that the service suffers materially by such findings of courts martial, in cases of such gross violation of military discipline. I respectfully refer this decision on to District Headquarters." There, the case was reviewed by Maj. Gen. Ulysses S. Grant, who made the judgement: "Findings and sentence approved, except so much as suspends him from his command for 30 days. The suspension of an officer from his command without forfeiture of pay is no punishment adequate to the offence of which the accused is found guilty." Grant released Rhodes from arrest and ordered him back to duty.

In September 1862 Colonel Rhodes requested a leave to go home and visit his wife, who was "in a feeble condition." The following month he resigned his commission, stating, "The notoriety and disgrace of a general court-martial, coupled with a reprimand, have placed me in a false position in this command."

The rest of his records are a narrative of decline and disability. In 1872, one of his acquaintances described him as "never a well man, looked old and had to use a cane." In 1875, he was described as "mostly crippled." In 1879, at the age of fifty-four, Colonel Rhodes was dead. Two years later, his widow remarried, but in 1883, after only two years of marriage, her second husband died. The records resume in 1901, when Colonel Rhodes's widow applied for a pension. Over the next two years a thick but unrewarding correspondence grew, a dossier of despair and disappointment. On two occasions, her attorney wrote the Pension Bureau asking for an early decision, stating that, "The colonel's widow is blind and destitute," and urging an immediate decision. Based upon records of the War Department, the Pension Bureau finally replied that there was no proof that his military service had caused his death. The final entry in this thick pension file consists of a large purple rubber stamp mark: "Case abandoned." Rhodes' widow, although "in a feeble condition," had outlived him by twenty-four years.

Chapter Thirteen

"I'll Pull Your Nose on Dress Parade!"

COL. WILLIAM F. SMALL

Colonel William F. Small was a Philadelphia lawyer and, apparently, a man of violent opinions. He saw conspiracies everywhere, insulted both his regimental surgeons and left a contradictory record, in which he is both dishonorably discharged and promoted to brigadier general.[1]

In June 1861, at the age of forty-two, he was mustered in as colonel of the 26th Regiment of Pennsylvania Volunteers. After an initial baptism by fire by a surly mob in Baltimore, the first year of his service passed peacefully in Washington, D.C., and at Budd's Ferry, Maryland. The only recorded event for Colonel Small was a furlough at Christmas. In early 1862 a number of his chickens came home to roost; he was court-martialed on five charges, with seven specifications. The trial was held during McClellan's Peninsular Campaign at Camp Winfield Scott, near Yorktown, Virginia.

The first charge was the making of a false muster. It was asserted that he had made Donald Farquhar the commissary sergeant when Farquhar was not enlisted in the service. The second charge was conduct unbecoming an officer and a gentleman. In this, he had ordered Capt. Samuel Moffett to place Farquhar on the company rolls after Moffett had just arrested Farquhar, who did not belong to Moffett's company. On another occasion, the colonel quarreled with Lt. George Tomlinson and said to him, "You are a damned liar. I will pull your nose upon dress parade. I will waive my rank and fight you with my fists." The third specification of conduct unbecoming was that, when the regimental surgeon, Dr. John Mintzer, asked Colonel Small to examine the commission of the newly appointed assistant surgeon, Small not only refused to look at the document but pulled off his gloves, raised his fists in a threatening manner, and again offered to fight "any damned conspirator in the regiment, officer or private." When Dr. Mintzer said that it was his duty to report Small's refusal to examine the commission, Small replied, "If you or any man dare to write over my head, I will have him tied to a whipping post."

Under the heading of "conduct to the prejudice of good order and military discipline," there was yet another allegation regarding Donald Farquhar. The colonel did not require Farquhar to perform any military duties and allowed him to come and go as a peddler in the regiment. In addition, the colonel apparently created a sensation when he ordered the public whipping of Pvt. Caleb Weir of Company A, and then told Weir, "If you leave the regiment, I will not look for you." Understandably, Weir deserted. The third specification strongly suggests that Gen. Joseph Hooker had some doubts about the leadership of the 26th Pennsylvania. Hooker had appointed a board to examine all of the officers of the regiment. Colonel Small called a meeting of his officers, told them that the order was "an insult" and vehemently recommended that all of them refuse to be examined.

The fourth charge, that of "insubordination," reflected his refusal to follow General Hooker's order regarding the board of examination. The fifth charge, "disobedience," was connected with the appointment of assistant surgeon Joseph Alexander. General Hooker had ordered Alexander to report for duty with the 26th Pennsylvania and Colonel Small refused both the doctor and the written order.

The trial record contains ninety pages of testimony, almost all of it both heated and contradictory. A Captain Hill had run away from the regiment and resigned his commission. There was an argument about the events of Captain Hill's disappearance, and the venue of this encounter illustrates the amateur atmosphere that pervaded a volunteer army. The persons present at the meeting in the colonel's tent were Colonel Small, Mrs. Small, Lieutenant Small (the colonel's son) and Lieutenant Tomlinson. Tomlinson had asserted that there was some conflict between the colonel and Captain Hill. Small then called Tomlinson "a damned liar." Small was of the opinion that Tomlinson was a troublemaker, and he accused him of bullying a Captain Webb, saying, "If you don't improve your behavior, you will find me ready to fight and that would include either sword or pistol."

Apparently this internal dissention had come to public notice, and there was a rumor that in the marching order the 26th Pennsylvania was to be placed in the rear of the march as a sign of disgrace. Captain Moffett had gone to see Hooker himself to inquire into this rumor and Colonel Small was quite angry at Moffett.

The issue of the assistant surgeon, Dr. Alexander, occupies a considerable portion of the court record. Alexander testified that he had appeared at the camp during inspection, stood at his proper place during the formalities and was then approached by Colonel Small, who asked Dr. Alexander, "Are you a visitor?" Alexander replied that he was there by the authority of the governor of Pennsylvania and of the secretary of war and proffered his commission and the orders from General Hooker appointing him to the 26th Pennsylvania. The colonel replied that he still considered the surgeon to be only a visitor to the regiment and to have no official connection with it.

Col. William F. Small had one of his obstreperous privates flogged without a trial, and later threatened to have his regimental surgeon whipped for disagreeing with him. U.S. ARMY MILITARY HISTORY INSTITUTE.

The regimental surgeon, Dr. John Mintzer, stepped forward and told the colonel that he considered Dr. Alexander's credentials to be good. The colonel became very excited and replied, "I am the colonel and no one will go over my head. This is part of a conspiracy and I will fight any and all of you!" Dr. Alexander stated that he must report the colonel's refusal of his credentials. This further excited Small, who said, "Anyone who goes over my head will be whipped." Dr. Alexander returned to General Hooker and received a second order assigning him to the 26th Pennsylvania. He returned to the regiment and again presented credentials to Colonel Small, who said, "I will fight this to the Supreme Court! This is an independent regiment, organized by authority of the Secretary of War, not by the intervention of the Governor of Pennsylvania and I have no need to recognize the authority of the government or of the Surgeon General of the State of Pennsylvania." Alexander did add, in mitigation, that after he was finally taken into the regiment, the colonel had not interfered with his medical work or been uncivil to him.

The next issue was the flogging of Private Weir. The testimony on this point was from Dr. Mintzer. He recalled that a woman who was "about the regiment" had come to the colonel and complained that Private Weir had kicked her in the jaw. Dr. Mintzer examined her and noted that her jaw was "very swollen." Weir was brought to the colonel's tent, where he attempted to justify his kicking of the woman. Without any formal hearing, the colonel ordered that Weir receive thirty-nine lashes. Dr. Mintzer recalled: "The man was taken outside and stripped. The drum major administered four lashes, lightly, and then the colonel remitted the balance. Then the colonel told Weir that he was a disgrace to the regiment and bade him be gone. Even though there was no court-martial, I feel that the punishment was just."

Testimony on other subjects indicated a strong flavor of conspiracy and political infighting in the 26th Pennsylvania. Corp. Robert Tricker of Company G testified, "Lieutenant Tomlinson told me that he had been in the colonel's tent, trying to anger the colonel enough to provoke him to a duel. He thought the colonel would be dismissed for dueling and then Captain [Benjamin] Tilghman would be colonel. The lieutenant had bet money on it."

The final decision of the court was that Colonel Small was guilty of some of the charges, and it recommended his dismissal. The case was then reviewed by Maj. Gen. George B. McClellan, who noted that Captain Tilghman, who aspired to the colonel's place, had been judge advocate of the court.

> The documents show that a draft of the charge was made by Captain Tilghman before his official capacity as Judge Advocate, that he was the accusing officer, and that he had an interest in the successful prosecution of these charges. While DeHart states that the Judge Advocate is merely the ministerial official of the Court, it is clear that the influence which he may, and which in practice he does, exert upon the findings and the sentence, is sufficiently notorious to demonstrate that this dictum of DeHart is not supported by reason."

McClellan further noticed that the court refused to read the minutes of each day's proceedings prior to approval. "This is at variance with the practice of Courts of ordinary and civil jurisdiction." He went on to remark that evidence had been excluded without good reason, which pointed to a possible conspiracy. "The proceedings are disapproved and Colonel William F. Small is released from arrest and will resume his sword."

On May 5, 1862, at the Battle of Williamsburg, a musket ball passed through the calf of Colonel Small's right leg, injuring the posterior tibial nerve and chipping part of the bone. Two months later, a surgeon's certificate stated that the wound was healing and that Colonel Small was now able to get about using a crutch.

In June 1863, Colonel Small was discharged from the army for reasons not found in the record. In 1866, his April 1862 discharge was made honorable by "retroactive acceptance of his resignation by order of the President." Since his guilty sentence was overturned by the disapproval of General McClellan, it is unclear why this 1866 action was necessary. It is further confusing to find later records referring to him as General William Small, as no commission is found in his records, nor is he listed in the brevet section of Ezra Warner's *Generals in Blue*.[2]

In 1872 Colonel Small applied for a medical pension on the grounds of his leg wound, supported by the Surgeon's Certificate of Dr. Mintzer, who described a "partial loss of motion, worse in cold weather, with continuing inflammation of the tibial nerve." Small alleged "pain and lameness." From here, Colonel Small's life seems to have gone downhill. A letter from his doctor in early 1877 described "severe emaciation and prostration, with general wasting away secondary to sciatica." A few months later, in June 1877 his death certificate gave as the cause of death, "consumption of the lungs, superinduced by gunshot wound and sciatica." (Since the cause of tuberculosis was unknown at the time, almost any harm to the body was thought to contribute to the spread of this often-fatal illness.)

Colonel Small had married in 1837. In 1878, his widow, Mary Ann, was awarded thirty dollars a month, which continued until her death in 1884.

Chapter Fourteen

"Makes Us a Set of Niggers"

LT. COL. WILLIAM T. WILSON

In the early winter of 1861, the leaders of the 15th Regiment of Ohio Volunteers seemed to have expended more energy fighting each other than in fighting the Confederates. The unit had been organized at Mansfield in September, five months after the bombardment of Fort Sumter, and had served the last three months of 1861 in the occupation of Munfordville, Kentucky, ten miles north of today's Mammoth Cave National Park.

The regimental commander was Col. Moses R. Dickey; his immediate subordinate was Lt. Col. William T. Wilson. Maj. William Wallace was the third ranking officer. They were stationed at Camp Nevin, a post that has long since been forgotten. The day after Christmas 1861, a general court-martial, presided over by Brig. Gen. Thomas J. Wood, was convened, to hear charges against Lt. Col. Wilson.[1]

The first charge was "contempt and disrespect to commanding officer." Colonel Moses had apparently issued an order requiring officers to be included in roll call. On December 1, at regimental headquarters, Wilson encountered Major Wallace and exclaimed loudly, "That order is one of Dickey's damned tyrannical orders, and nobody else's, for no military man would issue such an order." Wilson then turned to the regimental adjutant, Lt. Calvin R. Taft, and continued his outburst: "It is a damned arbitrary thing and makes a set of niggers out of officers who are supposed to be honorable men—such a thing was never heard of in the military before."

Three days later, Colonel Dickey called Wilson to his tent and reprimanded him for language presented in such a public and inappropriate manner. Fully unchastened, Wilson replied "in an insolent, disrespectful and contemptuous manner."

"Col. Dickey, you shall not make such charges against me to my face." Wilson repeated this challenge several times, apparently urging matters toward a duel, which implication Colonel Dickey disregarded. (Offering or accepting a challenge to a duel is punished with dismissal by the army.) The first charge continues:

Lt. Col. Wilson, from the 12th day of October, A.D. 1861, until the
4th day of December, 1861, at Camp Nevin, Harden County, KY, had
continuously and habitually engaged, whenever opportunity offered,
in disrespectfully finding fault with the means of discipline used and
the orders issued by Col. Moses R. Dickey . . . in the presence and
hearing of the commissioned officers and privates belonging to said
regiment, thus attempting to bring the said colonel into disrepute and
destroy his influence with said regiment.

All these actions of Wilson were said to be "much to the prejudice of good
order and military discipline."

A second charge of "beginning to excite, cause and join in mutiny and
sedition," was based upon Wilson's undermining Dickey's order regarding sentries and guard lines. A member of the regimental band, claiming that a sentinel
had no right to challenge him, tried to force his way past the sentinel and was
arrested. Wilson arrived on the scene and told the assembled group that the
commander's order did not apply to musicians. This, of course, placed the sentinel, a private, in the position of having contradictory orders from a colonel and
from a lieutenant colonel.

The first witness for the prosecution was Major Wallace, who confirmed
the story that Wilson had denounced the colonel's orders for officer's roll call as
"tyrannical." The judge advocate then asked Wallace, "Has the accused been in
the habit of finding fault disrespectfully with the means of discipline used and
with the orders issued by Col. Dickey?" Wallace replied, "He has. In several
cases in the presence of other commissioned officers. It was frequent."

Colonel Wilson then questioned the witness: "State what order was ever
denounced by the accused, when and in whose presence?"

Wallace's memory was, perhaps, more complete than Wilson would have
wished. After a brief disclaimer, Wallace warmed to his subject:

I remember one order when we were about to move camp at Camp
Nevins. The colonel directed the men to be under arms at 7:00
o'clock in the morning and the accused remarked at the sutler's store,
in the presence of the men of the Regiment that it was an unnecessary
order, and his manner implied more than his words. The men were in
a state of uneasiness at the time, having been under arms from 7:00 to
nearly 2:00 o'clock. This was on the 21st of October.

A fresh thought overtook Wallace: "Another case has just come to my mind.
When the regiment was at Camp Anderson at Lexington, soon after coming into
the state of Kentucky, Col. Dickey was in the habit of giving his orders to the
companies himself, in person. About the 7th of October, Col. Wilson frequently

remarked in the presence of the officers and men that Col. Dickey had a damned queer way of giving orders, holding mass meetings over the regiment."

Wallace was cross-examined by Wilson: "Is it not true that the accused has proven himself a faithful, efficient and obedient officer?" The reply: "It is true that the accused has proven himself an efficient and obedient officer," a reply which clearly showed the absence of "faithful."

The next question took a wholly new course. "Is it not true that Col. Dickey and yourself joined in advising Governor [William] Dennison to appoint the accused colonel of a regiment now organizing in Ohio?" Wallace replied, "I did. I cannot answer for Col. Dickey."

The next witness for the prosecution was Lieutenant Taft. When asked if he had ever heard Colonel Wilson speak disrespectfully of his commander, Taft replied, "I never heard Col. Wilson use Col. Dickey's name. I did hear Col. Wilson speak of an order referring to roll call of officers, issued by Col. Dickey about three weeks ago. Col. Wilson remarked that it was making a set of slaves or negroes of a set of officers who were supposed to be gentlemen, and that such a thing was never heard of in the military."

The prosecution now summoned Colonel Dickey, who recalled a single instance of being addressed disrespectfully:

> That was at my headquarters, about the 4th of December. I accused him of having spoken disrespectfully of me to others, and he said, "Col. Dickey, you shall not make such charges against me," and repeated the same several times. This was after I had ordered him to his tent in arrest and he had gone and returned. He said he had expressed his opinion freely, and sometimes disapprovingly, of the orders issued by me, that he was not my slave, that he had the right to do so, and that he had spoken to camp officers in the same manner as he had to Major Wallace.

Wilson cross-examined: "Is it not true that the accused has shown himself to be a faithful, efficient and obedient officer?" Dickey's answer was qualified: "So far as assistance in drill and active labor is concerned, he has."

Wilson now returned to a subject that seemed crucial in his own mind: "Did you or did you not advise Governor Dennison about three weeks ago to appoint the accused as colonel of a regiment then organizing in Ohio?" Col. Dickey's answer contained a surprise: "I did not, but I wrote to friends to have it done, and at the request of the accused."

The final question by Colonel Wilson says much about his grasp of military protocol: "Is it not true that I claimed the right to criticize your orders, but expressly disclaimed any feeling of disrespect toward you personally or as an officer?" "I believe it is true," Dickey conceded.

The final witness for the prosecution was 1st Lt. Charles Carroll. He had observed Colonel Wilson telling the leader of the regimental band that he, like commissioned officers, had the right to cross the picket line. Colonel Wilson called no witnesses for his defense.

The court adjourned and after the "mature deliberation" required by the regulations, returned the verdicts: guilty of disrespect toward a commanding officer but not guilty of exciting mutiny. "The Court does therefore sentence him, Lt. Col. William T. Wilson of the 15th Ohio Volunteers, to be reprimanded in orders by the Commanding General of the Department."

Brig. Gen. Don Carlos Buell approved the sentence without comment. Eight months later, Colonel Wilson submitted his resignation.

PART TWO

Conduct Unbecoming an Officer and a Gentleman

Chapter Fifteen

"I'll Burst it to Thunder!"

COL. WILLIAM BISHOP

Missouri in the Civil War was a cauldron of passionate hatreds. Union and Confederate civilians lynched each other. The same group of night riders would be termed patriots by one faction, bushwhackers and marauders by another.

Martial law, assassination, horse theft, arson, and robbery were everyday events. It was no time for the fainthearted, and William Bishop was a man for the time. In June 1861, Brig. Gen. Nathaniel Lyon authorized Bishop to raise three regiments of northeast Missouri Home Guards, and added, "all those who enlist and are sworn in and render service will have a claim against the government." Bishop later wrote that in June 1861, "few in northeast Missouri were bold enough to stand by the government, when to talk and act treason was popular." Bishop reported that he recruited and swore in more than 2,500 men, who later formed the principal portion of the 21st Missouri Infantry.[1]

On the last day of July 1861, he was appointed by Maj. Gen. John C. Fremont to raise a battalion of cavalry, a number that was raised later to a full regiment, known variously as the Blackhawk Cavalry and Bishop's Battalion.

In January 1862, while serving as colonel, he was put under arrest and cited on four different charges. It was claimed that Bishop intended to defraud the government by entering John D. Park on the muster roll of the regiment "knowing full well that said John D. Park was not then nor ever had been Lieutenant Colonel of said regiment." The first charge further asserted that Park had never been appointed by any competent authority.

The second charge alleged that when, in September 1861, Brig. Gen. Benjamin Prentiss ordered Bishop to report his force to the district headquarters, Bishop refused to go.

The third charge, "neglect of duty," stated that Bishop had not instructed his regiment or inspected its quarters since August, nor had he established proper sentries or outposts, even when near the enemy.

The fourth and final charge was "conduct unbecoming an officer and a gentleman," and centered mainly around a December 1861 incident in which the colonel said, within earshot of two other officers, "I will rule this regiment or burst it to thunder!"

Sadly, the actual transcript of the trial has disappeared somewhere in the intervening decades, but it went on for several weeks, strongly suggesting many witnesses and much testimony. The court's final decision was to acquit him on each and every charge, and after review by General Halleck, Colonel Bishop was ordered "to resume his sword."

However, in the period between his arrest on February 19, 1862, and his acquittal in late April, events had marched forward. Bishop's Blackhawk Cavalry had disappeared.

Because the Blackhawks were understrength, the governor of Missouri combined the five companies of Blackhawks with Louis's Independent Cavalry Battalion, and a few days later, with two companies of the 22nd Missouri Infantry. This new combination of units was named the 7th Missouri Cavalry.

In a letter to the adjutant general of the army, Bishop noted that he had "earnestly protested these changes," and noted that it was done "without authority from me." The Blackhawks had been a militia organization, while the new 7th Cavalry Volunteers were state troops. The colonel of the newly formed 7th Cavalry was Daniel Huston, Jr., a West Point graduate.

One of the letters submitted by Bishop in defense of his claim was by an R. E. Hill, who declared, "Colonel Bishop is a gentleman of strict integrity and well qualified for this post."

However, matters seemed to go from bad to worse. In late March 1862, Bishop submitted a surgeon's certificate describing "acute hepatitis and nervous derangement for five weeks." On the strength of this document, Bishop applied to General Halleck, who, by now, had succeeded Fremont as the local commander, for a leave of absence, which was disapproved.

A few days later, the new regimental commander, Colonel Huston, reported that "Lieutenant Colonel Bishop broke his arrest by leaving this post on the 3rd of April, 1862, and has not been heard from since. His present whereabouts are entirely unknown to me." Was Bishop physically sick, perhaps with malaria that had indeed affected his liver, was it more the apprehension and anger felt by someone on trial, or was it more a fit of pique? On these points, the record is silent, but his pension files give a longer view of his life.

Bishop died May 2, 1879, in Clark City, Missouri. His doctor's diagnosis was "paralysis resulting from apoplexy," in other words, a stroke. A later affidavit by his wife described the cause of death as "congestion of the liver and paralysis."

The appraisal of his estate, a matter of public record, is a poignant reflection of a man cast down from a higher plane. The total value of his personal holdings was $515.00. A few of the dozens of items listed have a sadly inglorious and homely ring: a hat rack, worth $1.50; 275 books for $68.75; a bathtub valued at $1.00; a watch worth 25 cents; and seven sheep at $1.00 each. At the estate sale, a Mr. Ware bought a sausage grinder for $1.15, and a Mr. Stuby purchased a mouse trap for 5 cents. Other familiar items of everyday life were purchased at similar prices.

Twenty years later, his widow, Mary, filed for a pension, but her application was rejected on the grounds that Bishop's death was not service connected. She refiled the next year, citing economic distress. A claims examiner noted that she owned a forty-acre orange grove near Eustis, Florida, but a home visit by an appraiser found that the Freeze of 1894 had killed every tree.

Mrs. Bishop was awarded a small pension, which in 1904, by means of a private bill passed in Congress, was increased to thirty dollars a month (and inadvertently gave her husband a posthumous promotion: he is described as "late Colonel of the Seventh Regiment Missouri Volunteer Cavalry.")

Mary Bishop died on March 8, 1920, seventy-one years after her marriage to William Bishop.

Chapter Sixteen

A Wild Night at the Old Spanish Fort

LT. COL. JOHN CREIGHTON

The case of Lt. Col. John Creighton of the 6th New York has at least two unusual features: he encouraged his men to fire at a Federal boat, and his case was terminated by a closely reasoned legal opinion, written by a surgeon. The time was the summer of 1861; the site was Camp Brown, near Fort Pickens, on Santa Rosa Island, Florida.

The 6th New York had been a colorful unit since its inception. It was organized as Wilson's Zouaves, by Col. Billy Wilson, a New York City alderman, described by some biographers as both brave and bombastic. The officers were from families with new money and political connections, and the enlisted men were mainly Irish and German immigrants, ready for a brawl or a celebration. But even in this group, Creighton stood out.[1]

The charges against him included the following: "The said Lieutenant Colonel John Creighton, under the influence of intoxicating liquor, and therefore unfit for duty, at about 2:00 o'clock in the morning, on July 15, 1861, did lie on the beach opposite the Warrington Navy Yard, still under the influence of liquor, and could not be awakened. . . ." 1st Lt. F. Silloway of Company H made a valiant attempt to rouse his passed-out-drunk colonel, but without success. Further efforts were made by Lt. B. Barker, of Company F, with equally unsuccessful results. The colonel snored on, oblivious to the attempts of his subordinates to rescue him from shame and disgrace. This evening, on the warm Florida sands, formed the basis for the first charge against the colonel: "Conduct prejudicial to good order and military discipline."

Sadly, this had not been Colonel Creighton's first escapade. His behavior forty-eight hours earlier had been even more outrageous. At about 1:00 A.M., July 13, Creighton, who was not on duty, and who had no business visiting the posted sentinels, appeared before the astonished eyes of Pvt. James Degan, of

Company J—who was posted as Sentinel No. 9 near the Old Spanish Fort—and seized the young soldier's musket.

Breathing whiskey fumes into the night air, and lurching left and right in an attempt to keep his balance, Creighton raised the musket to his shoulder and took a shot at the Federal guard boat that was visible just offshore, on its way to Fort Pickens.

Creighton then called to all the other sentinels within hailing distance and ordered them to also open fire on the same boat. To their credit, they did not obey him, but Creighton himself rammed home and fired two more shots at the boat before it disappeared into the mists of the night.

On July 15, at 9:00 A.M., an hour when it might have been hoped that sobriety and lucidity would have come to Creighton, he had the following to say about his feat of arms: "What I did was perfectly justifiable and I am only sorry that the sentries did not shoot someone in the boat." He was then informed that the commander of the detachment, Col. Harvey Brown, was quite indignant about the incident, and that Brown had reprimanded Col. William "Billy" Wilson, commander of the 6th New York, for not maintaining discipline. Creighton was more than nonchalant: "I am only sorry that Colonel Brown was not in the boat, where I might have shot him. If Brown sends for me, I will give him my opinion about him and his orders. It's time to show Brown that we have been kept down long enough."

On August 17, around 11:00 P.M., the officer of the day, Capt. Robert Hazeltine, was in his tent, about to make his rounds. Colonel Creighton suddenly appeared in his habitual condition of drunkenness and picked a quarrel with the captain. Soon the colonel's voice rose in "reproachful and provoking language." Hazeltine advised the colonel to go to bed and sleep it off. Creighton was not at all satisfied with this response and challenged Hazeltine to a duel. The captain advised Creighton not to be a fool. The colonel, making up in promptness what he lacked in wit, punched Hazeltine in the face with his closed fist, thus violating in one incident the 9th, 24th, and 25th Articles of War.

The court-martial of Colonel Creighton began on August 26, 1861, and the following persons were called as witnesses: Lts. James Heary, A. D'Orsille, J. Silloway, A. Entwhistle, B. Barker and J. M. Hieldt, Pvts. Patrick Daley and James Degan, and the chaplain, Rev. Michael Nash. The president of the court was Col. William Wilson, Creighton's immediate superior. The judge advocate was a surgeon, Dr. D. Pease.

In the weeks preceding the trial, Creighton seems to have desisted from his previous activity of marinating his brain, and applied himself with some degree of alertness to his own defense. When asked if he had objection to any member of the court-martial board, he replied in the affirmative. He objected to Colonel Wilson on the grounds that not only had Wilson preferred the charges against him, but that Wilson would appear as a principal witness for the prosecution.

Creighton argued that one person could not fairly serve as judge, prosecutor, and prosecution witness. Creighton then objected to all the rest of the other members of the board, on the grounds that they were officers of his own regiment, as well as junior to him.

Confronted with this challenge, the court then turned to Dr. Pease, who was acting as judge advocate, for a legal opinion. Pease noted that he was no lawyer, but promised an opinion the following morning. He was as good as his word.

When the court convened the following day, the doctor submitted a carefully reasoned, twelve-page written opinion, citing a wide variety of military jurisprudence authorities and precedents. It was his conclusion that the board was not legally constituted. At this point, the court voted to dissolve itself and to refer the matter to Washington, D.C.

On October 19 of the same year, the assistant adjutant general, writing from Washington, stated, "This case is to be submitted to the Secretary of War. The General-in-Chief [Winfield Scott] recommends that authority be given to Brigader General [Harvey] Brown, Commanding, Department of Florida, to discharge Colonel Creighton if he [Brown] is satisfied the charges against him are correct."

The final document in this record is dated October 26, 1861: "The Secretary of War has authorized General Brown to act as suggested."

Colonel Creighton was not only expunged from the army, but also from the collective memory of the regiment. A regimental history, published in 1891, by J. E. Taylor, makes no mention of Creighton. Reverend Nash had written a series of very perceptive letters during the war, which were later collected and published. In Father Nash's missives, too, Colonel Creighton is conspicuous in his absence. He was not in the postwar New York Militia, nor does he appear in any of the numerous postwar biographical cyclopediae. Colonel Creighton was a man who dissolved himself in alcohol and disappeared without a trace.

Chapter Seventeen

"Damned Hungarian Humbug!"

COL. HENRY C. DE AHNA

The clash of titanic egos is marked by sparks and thunder. In a setting such as wartime Missouri, a border state where partisan strife, neighbor against neighbor, murderous violence, and even more murderous reprisal, the possibility, even the need, for the exercise of strong-willed egos was everpresent. St. Louis, Missouri, in the summer of 1861, was nominally under Union control, but Confederate recruiting went on openly and Union soldiers were not safe in the streets. Armed bands of secessionist marauders roamed the countryside, and units of Rebel regulars menaced the key river town of Cairo, Illinois, where the Ohio flows into the Mississippi.

Into this melee stepped John C. Fremont, a man of action and a soldier remarkably free of self doubt. His sobriquet—the Pathfinder—was well earned. His exploration and mapping of the Rocky Mountain passes was instrumental in the great western migration, and he played a key role in tearing California loose from Mexico and joining the Golden State to the federal union. He was one of California's first two senators, became a selfmade millionaire, and was the Republican party's first Presidential nominee. In the early months of the war, Abraham Lincoln was far too preoccupied with eastern affairs to devote much attention to the west. He put that into the hands of Fremont, giving the Pathfinder a major general's commission and a parting benediction: "I have given you carte blanche. You must use your own judgment and do the best you can."

Fremont—millionaire, former senator, and freshly returned from a triumphal visit to France—was just the man to appreciate the opportunities latent in carte blanche. He established his residence and his headquarters in the opulent Brant Mansion, one of the finest homes in St. Louis. On the larger scale, he relieved the plight of Cairo with a hastily gathered force of 4,000 troops and three gunboats, and he caused St. Louis to be surrounded with a ring of fortifications.

Closer to home, he established a personal entourage, a bodyguard in the Imperial style, the Fremont Huzzars, an elite unit of 300 cavalrymen, who surrounded him with galloping hooves and flashing sabres whenever he sallied forth from his regal headquarters.

The Fremont staff was a colorful mixture of emigré European revolution-aries, rabid abolitionists, California business cronies, and regular officers. The European officers, in particular the Italians and the Hungarians, resplendent in feathers and loops of gold braid and bearing such titles as Adlatus to the Chief, were a particular vexation to the egalitarian American regulars.

Ulysses S. Grant, then an obscure brigadier, described an audience with Fremont. "He sat in a room in full uniform with his maps before him. When you went in, he would point out one line or another in a mysterious manner, never asking you to take a seat. You left without the least idea of what he meant or what he wanted you to do."

Requests for a meeting with Fremont were channeled through his chief of staff, who determined which visitors were deserving of attention. Worthy sup-plicants were placed on Fremont's appointment calendar. Entrance to the man-sion was through a series of numbered sentry posts. Into this gauntlet, at 10:00 P.M. August 24, 1861, strode Col. Henry Charles de Ahna, a native of Bavaria, commander of the Indiana Legion, a thirty-day regiment that included Capt. Hezekiah Brown's Independent Company, Capt. Edward G. Keashey's Inde-pendent Company, Capt. Thomas Bassett's Independent Company, and Capt. Daniel P. Monroe's Independent Company. In this mansion the frontier spirit of democracy was about to clash with the imperial household of Major General Fremont, and that clash resulted in de Ahna's court-martial for "conduct unbe-coming an officer and a gentleman."[1]

The trial took place in St. Louis. The opening session was held on August 12, 1862; the president of the court was Brig. Gen. John Pope. After the usual swearing in, the charges and specifications were read and testimony began. Sgt. T. Huehlen testified, "About a quarter past 9:00 on Saturday evening, Guard No. 1 called me. I saw the accused entering the hall and I told him politely that he was not on the list of those permitted to enter. He went in anyway." Huehlen then called Capt. Charles Zagonyi to report the intrusion. The sergeant recalled that the sentinel did not order the colonel to halt. Regarding the list of approved persons, Huehlen recalled, "My orders were not to let anyone in who was not on the list, except ladies, who could go up the steps."

Pvt. Henry Griff spoke next. He had been sentinel at Post No. 2, and had told Colonel de Ahna that his name was not on the list. De Ahna pushed his way past Griff, saying, "I am a colonel of Fremont's Guard and can go in or out at any time."

Captain Zagonyi recalled that he had been "astonished" to see de Ahna appearing in the hall. The colonel sat down at a desk and began to compose a letter to Fremont, while loudly demanding to know who was responsible for these new orders about coming in and out. Zagonyi claimed that he had previ-ously been on good terms with de Ahna, that he had explained five or six times that the orders came from Fremont himself, but that de Ahna would not hear of it. As the discussion became more heated, de Ahna exclaimed, "You make yourself big with your damned bodyguard. Damned Hungarian humbug!" Zagonyi did not take kindly to this talk about Hungarians, and stepped outside to cool off. When he returned, the colonel was making a noise that could be heard on the third floor, where Fremont and his wife lived.

The next witness was Theodore Heide, who testified through an interpreter, Julius Busch. Heide was a first lieutenant in the Fremont Huzzars, and had come by rail with de Ahna (who seems to have spoken some German) in order to meet a Mr. Woods, a political associate of Fremont's. Heide recalled, "The guard, who had issued no challenge, took the colonel by the sleeve." De Ahna turned on the guard and shouted, "What manner is this to pluck at the sleeve of a colonel in full uniform? I am to see Mr. Woods every day in order to report on the progress of my regiment, and have no need to deal with you."

At this point, Captain Zagonyi arrived and de Ahna upbraided him for having sleeve pluckers as guards. The conversation was half in German and half in English, and Heide confessed that he only understood part of it. (Here, de Ahna became dissatisfied with the services of Mr. Busch as interpreter, and replaced him with a Mr. G. A. Rutter.)

Heide continued: "Captain Zagonyi began to shout at the colonel, who shouted back and then threatened to have Zagonyi arrested." The captain then said, in an aside to the sentry, "Why did you not shoot this man?"

After several more witnesses gave similar descriptions of the noisy encounter, both prosecution and defense rested. After deliberation, the court found de Ahna guilty and sentenced him to "be dismissed [from] the service of the United States." The sentence was approved by Fremont, but the story does not end there.

Three weeks after the trial, de Ahna's case was reviewed in Washington, D.C., by John F. Lee, the judge advocate of the army, who wrote: "I do not find in this record sufficient cause to prevent the President's pardoning or restoring, or reappointing Colonel de Ahna, if he is a good officer capable of useful service." Lee, in his analysis of the case, was of the opinion that the serious charge of conduct unbecoming an officer and a gentleman was excessive, and that the lesser charge of conduct to the prejudice of good order and military discipline would have been more appropriate. "This record presents a case of insubordination and temper and not of disreputable conduct."

The case was then reviewed by Lt. Gen. Winfield Scott, still the commander of the Union army, who noted, "Pope is brigadier general of volunteers and not of the 'Army,' as set out in the Order. If he were of the 'Regular Army,' he could not be on this Court [Pope had been a regular army captain in January 1861], and the trial would be void. I concur with the Judge Advocate." The case then went to the White House, where de Ahna was pardoned, and his rank and commission restored. Orders sent from the headquarters of the army January 2, 1862, directed de Ahna to return to St. Louis, where he was to resume command of his regiment. That unit, however, was mustered out of service by order of General Halleck on January 8, 1862, leaving de Ahna in command of nothing. Undaunted, he arranged to be nominated by Lincoln as a brigadier of volunteers. While this nomination was under consideration by the Senate Committee on Military Affairs, Senator Latham received a most unusual telegram from General Halleck:

> A man who calls himself Henry C. de Ahna, and who was a so-called colonel under Fremont , by whom he was court-martialled and dismissed from the service, has succeeded, as I have learned, by worming himself into the confidence of Secretary Seward and Francis P. Blair, to get himself nominated to the Senate for a brigadier general. I would rather trust my dinner to a hungry dog than give such a responsible position to a foreign adventurer of this stamp. I have not the least doubt he would take pay on either side and fight on none.

This ended de Ahna's military career. He entered government employ as a civilian, holding posts all over the country from 1863 to 1883; in 1877, he was collector of customs at Sitka, Alaska. In 1891, at the age of 68, he died of bronchopneumonia and heart failure. In the intervening years he had a considerable struggle in supporting his nine children.

In 1911, his widow filed for a pension. She soon found herself in the Byzantine maze of the pension office, and the file is thick with papers. Among other requests, she was asked to prove that her husband had not been previously married in Germany. The records do show that de Ahna's dismissal had been wiped out in 1866 by administrative action and that he was "honorably mustered out." Mrs. de Ahna's last plea, in 1915, that she was destitute, was met by a final letter of denial, fifty-four years after de Ahna's fateful outburst against the "Hungarian Humbug."

Chapter Eighteen

"Perjured Felons"

COL. CARTER GAZLEY

James A. Garfield, a future president of the United States, and president of a court-martial board in August 1862, puzzled over the merits of the case of Col. Carter Gazley. One hundred and thirty years later, the question of whether justice was done still presents a challenge to those who seek historical truth.[1]

Gazley was age thirty-three when he was mustered into the 37th Indiana Volunteers on September 15, 1861. In April of the following year, he became the commander of that regiment. The regiment had spent March in Murfreesboro, Shelbyville, and Tullahoma in Tennessee, and was present at the capture of Huntsville, Alabama, on April 11, 1862.

In May, he was at Athens, Limestone County, Alabama, and there it was charged that Colonel Gazley "did sell to one Henry Eastman, a pair of horses that had been stolen, the property of Mary Ann Walton, he then well knowing that the said pair of horses were stolen at the time he made such sale." It was further charged that Gazley had sold to the same Henry Eastman twenty-two bales of cotton, stolen from John M. Malone.

Witness George Anderson testified that at about the time Col. John Turchin's forces left Athens, Mr. Eastman came to him, wanting to swap a horse for a buggy. They went together to a stable, where Anderson saw a pair of horses that he recognized as belonging to Miss Walton. "I know those horses. I certainly do. I was satisfied that they had been stolen or taken from her. I asked Eastman about the horses and he said he had bought them from Colonel Gazley, who claimed he had got them from Nashville." Later, Eastman left town with the horses, and came back without them.

The other two witnesses also gave evidence against Gazley; the court convicted him on all charges, and sentenced the colonel to be dismissed from the service. Gazley disagreed violently with the decision of the court, and launched a series of appeals. First, he wrote a long letter to Abraham Lincoln.

> I was sick at the time of my trial, and could not prepare. I had gone to
> Huntsville, where I was counsel for Turchin, during his trial. Then I

waited in Huntsville for eight days for my trial. I needed to return to my regiment to secure witnesses for my own defense, but was refused permission to travel. I was not permitted to prepare a defense.

Gazley went on to say that Anderson, the witness against him, was a "convicted felon," who wished to extort money from him. Gazley further complained that his request for a copy of the trial record and for a retrial had been refused.

In September, Turchin, now a brigadier general, wrote from Chicago on behalf of Gazley. "He is a very efficient and brave officer, and a highly intelligent and honest gentleman." The charges against him are "infamous." Further, stated Turchin, "Colonel Gazley would have been acquitted had it not been for his bold and manly defense in my case, as my counsel." Turchin ended by stating he would write to Gov. O. P. Morton on Gazley's behalf. Apparently Turchin's letter spurred the governor.

A few days later, Morton wrote to the secretary of war, urging him to grant an appeal. This request was passed on to the judge advocate general, who replied in late October.

The sentence of the court martial, confirmed by the commanding general, is final. Colonel Gazley can be restored to the service only by a re-appointment. A careful reading of the testimony has satisfied me such re-appointment would not be sanctioned by the government. The colonel did not apply for a postponement. He personally conducted his own defense. It is well known that such offenses bring discredit upon the service.

This opinion reached the secretary of war the same day that it was written, and he recommended that "this officer not be permitted to enter the service."

Col. L. R. Stanley was another officer who came to Gazley's defense, and he wrote to Governor Morton as follows: "I have 20 years experience in court. This court martial board had three officers from Kentucky, three from Ohio, (one a decided pro-slavery man), and only one from Indiana. Colonel Gazley was anti-slavery. The only witnesses against Colonel Gazley were a convicted felon and two secessionists. I urge a new trial."

In October, Gazley wrote to the chief of staff of the army. "I was dismissed based on the perjured testimony of Henry Eastman, who has since been convicted of fraud and swindling. I have new evidence, and I request a new trial." No reply appears in the record.

Was Gazley rightly convicted of selling stolen goods, had he been framed by a Confederate cabal, or was he being punished for his vigorous defense of Colonel Turchin, a man who generated impassioned enemies? Any answer must lie in the realm of the unknown.

What is known is that in 1908, Gazley applied for a pension. He was then eighty years old, "five feet eight inches in height, with grey eyes." He defended his eligibility for a pension by citing his combat service after his conviction. "After my dismissal, I was acting under General [Don Carlos] Buell's orders in holding Stevenson, Alabama, about August 30, 1862. I had a horse shot from under me and was shot in the right leg while commanding the troops under Colonel [Michael] Shoemaker. I was not treated in the hospital, as I went to my home as soon as General Buell's army passed Stevenson."

A year later, the pension board replied to Colonel Gazley. "Your application has been rejected, as you did not receive an honorable discharge."

Chapter Nineteen

"Inexpressible Regrets"

COL. WILLIAM H. IRWIN

Colonel William H. Irwin, commander of the 49th Pennsylvania Infantry, seems to have had more than the average share of conflict and trouble. In 1847, during the Mexican War, he was "totally disabled by a musket ball wound of the left hand" at the Battle of Molino del Rey. He seems to have been age fourteen at the time.

Disabled or not, he was mustered into service in July 1861, and elected colonel of the 7th Pennsylvania Infantry, but he soon took over the 49th when it was organized at Harrisburg. By November 1861, he was under arrest on charges that are no longer in the record. He objected to being confined to camp and wrote to the commanding general asking that "the limits of my arrest be extended to Washington, D.C., as I have business there." The general's reply included a note that "Colonel Irwin is a man of pride."

In January 1862, three relevant events are recorded: the colonel asked that his leave of absence be extended for "important business," charges were preferred against him by 2nd Lt. James W. Miller, and on the twenty-eighth of that month, his second court-martial began, headed by Brig. Gen. Winfield Hancock.[1]

The first charge was neglect of duty, it being specified that the colonel had held no school of tactics and when officers "respectfully" asked that he do so, he replied, "Go to hell!" Secondly, he was charged with being "so intoxicated as to be unable to perform the duties of a commander at the Grand Review at Munson's Hill, Virginia, on 21 November 1861 and at Camp Griffin, Virginia, on 22 January, 1862."

The third charge, "conduct prejudicial to good order and military discipline," related to his highly unusual behavior of forming the entire regiment under arms, between the hours of retreat and tattoo, and publicly asking their permission to absent himself from the regiment. The final charge was based upon having Lieutenant Miller confined to his own tent under an armed guard.

The first testimony concerned the incident of November 20, 1861, at the grand review of the Army of the Potomac.

Capt. George Smith testified that Colonel Irwin was very much under the influence of liquor. "He did not seem to know what he was doing." Lieutenant Parker agreed: "At the Grand Review, I believe the colonel was intoxicated. His face was red and he had a wild appearance. He rode around a good deal."

However, there were contrary opinions. Lt. William Mitchell recalled, "I was with the colonel all day and he had one glass of ale. His horsemanship and his orders were normal in every respect. After considerable questioning on the subject of the colonel's behavior, the final question addressed to the witness was, "Are you the stepson of Colonel Irwin?" The answer: "I am."

Maj. Thomas Hulings stated flatly, "He was sober at the review. I am from the same town and have known him for years. He is a sober person."

The court may have given additional weight to the testimony of the final witness, General Hancock himself. "I saw him frequently at the Grand Review. I did not think him drunk. He was excited, but I attributed that to the soreness he felt at my language to him, in an altercation we had on a point of duty. The colonel thought himself aggrieved. I knew him briefly on the field of Molino del Rey. He was wounded there and breveted a major for good conduct."

The evidence on the other charges fills ninety-two pages of testimony, again much of it contradictory. The long statement submitted to the court by Irwin is a remarkable essay on some of the finer points of drinking.

I was perfectly sober at the Munson's Hill review and am proved to have been so by cumulative and irresistible testimony. There remains under this charge only the specification relating to the evening of payday, the 22nd of January, 1862. I do not deny that on that evening I drank with some gentlemen who called at my quarters, but I deny, and repel with disdain, the allegation that I had thus become unfit for my military duties. I had perfect command of myself. It is proved that I drank and was exhilarated, and if before this Court it was proved that I drank every day and was exhilarated every day, yet entirely fit for duty, it would be impossible to find me guilty of this charge. Before I can be convicted of the crime of drunkenness on duty, it must be conclusively proved by legal testimony that I was in such a state of intoxication as to be unfit for my duty.

No order has ever been issued to this army forbidding the temperate use of wine or ardent spirits by the Officers; therefore, no violation of orders and certainly no breach of discipline in a temperate use of wine or ardent spirits . . . nor in inviting officers who might be present to use them. The right of an officer to do this in the absence of an order to the contrary is as clear as his right to invite a brother Officer to dinner, to offer him a cigar, or a glass of water.

In his court-martial, Col. William H. Irwin eloquently defended the right of an officer to offer a guest a drink and a cigar. MASSACHUSETTS COMMANDERY MILITARY ORDER OF THE LOYAL LEGION, U.S. ARMY MILITARY HISTORY INSTITUTE.

But there is no evidence of drunkenness . . . no unusual noises . . . no incoherence in my conversation . . . no violence of word or gesture . . . no riotous or disorderly conduct.

After many days of hearings, the court reached its decision: not guilty of neglect of duty and not guilty of drunkenness, but guilty of conduct prejudicial to good order. Irwin was sentenced to be suspended from command for thirty days and to be reprimanded. In an addendum, the court recommended remission of the suspension from command.

The regiment remained in the defense of Washington, D.C., until March 1862. After a brief advance on Manassas, it returned to Alexandria and embarked for the Peninsular Campaign, arriving in time for the siege of Yorktown and the long march west to the outskirts of Richmond.

Irwin's records show him requesting a leave of absence in January, after his trial, to attend to "important business." In July he asked to have his leave of absence extended. He was apparently present at Antietam in September 1862, but was absent with bronchitis in November and December.

In January 1863, he was made supernumerary and sent on recruiting service. On April 29, 1863, he was wounded near Fredericksburg by a musket ball that lodged itself at the base of the first and second toes of his right foot. He was absent, listed as wounded, May through August, and in September 1863 he was ordered to hospital by a board of examiners. In October Surgeon C. H. Wilson described Irwin as "so utterly prostrated physically and mentally, by reason of wounds and long service . . . he is entirely unfit for field service." Another doctor the same week certified Irwin as "mentally deranged." A few days later, he submitted his resignation "due to continued ill health," and concluded, "I withdraw from this noble army with inexpressible regret."

A few years after the war, he was breveted brigadier general for "gallantry at Antietam," the rank to date from March 13, 1865. In May 1865 he was rated as "one-fourth incapacitated" and issued a pension of four dollars a month. In 1884 he wrote to the Pension Bureau on his Indiana Coal Railroad Company letterhead, requesting additional benefits. A year later, having received no satisfaction, he wrote to his congressman, asking for "instant action."

The following year, the bureau received a letter from Dr. H. K. Pusey, superintendent of the Central Kentucky Lunatic Asylum. "General William H. Irwin died 17 January 1886 from exhaustion resulting from mental derangement from . . . pain, loss of sleep and nervous irritation of wounds he had received in the U.S. Army." Later that year, his widow's claim was rejected on the grounds that the cause of death was not service connected.

Chapter Twenty

"Their Pants Unbuttoned"

COL. JAMES E. KERRIGAN

In August 1861 Confederate pickets on Munson's Hill, just eight miles west of Washington, D.C., could look down on the Federal drill fields and, beyond them, to the unfinished dome of the capitol. Their occasional long-distance sniping, and the impudence of being so close to the center of Federal power, resulted in a skirmish in late August. The Rebels were not dislodged, but some Yankee honor was satisfied.

One of the least active in upholding such honor was Col. James E. Kerrigan of the 25th New York Volunteers, also known as the Union Rangers and Kerrigan's Rangers. In his February 1862 trial, Kerrigan was charged with "shameful abandonment of his post, in this: That he, the said James E. Kerrigan, Colonel as aforesaid, did, on the 27th of August, 1861, shamefully abandon his post which he had been commanded to hold, at Munson's Hill, Fairfax County, Virginia."[1]

Serious as this charge was, it was only one of the nine charges made against Kerrigan at his trial, held in Washington, D.C., which was presided over by Brig. Gen. Silas Casey. The other charges were as follows:

> Habitual neglect of duty, in that the said James E. Kerrigan, in command of the 25th Regiment of New York Volunteers from June 28 to October 18, 1861, . . . wherever said regiment has been, habitually failed and neglected to give his officers and men . . . practical or theoretical instruction in the tactics of the School of the Battalion and Company, or either of them.
>
> Conduct to the prejudice of good order and military discipline, in that, the said James E. Kerrigan did, at Hall's Hill, in Virginia, at the camp of said regiment, on the 14th and 15th days of October, 1861, suffer and permit the privates of said regiment, and the noncommissioned officers thereof, to engage in loud and unseemly dispute and brawls, to use disorderly language, and to make noisy disturbances, without any attempt on the part of said Kerrigan to repress same.

The said James E. Kerrigan . . . at the encampment . . . at Hall's Hill, upon an inspection and review then and there held of said regiment, permitted many private men of said regiment to appear on parade in a state of unseemly disarray and filth—their pants unbuttoned and their underclothes and persons exposed.

The list went on and on. Pvt. Patrick Goffery, who deserted from Company I and was gone two months, was restored to duty without a trial and received his full pay, even for the time he was a deserter. On September 27, 1861, on the march from Morton's Farm to Upton's Hill, Kerrigan was drunk. On the night of October 14th, Kerrigan was absent from his regiment until the following morning, without permission.

On October 16, 1861, Brig. Gen. John Martindale, a West Point graduate, visited Kerrigan's regiment "for the purpose of examination and instruction." Kerrigan, apparently bored by the proceedings, walked away and, even after direct orders to return and participate, "did wilfully and positively refuse to obey said command and order."

On August 27, 1861, when the Confederates were advancing upon his position, Kerrigan, against orders, withdrew his pickets. The final charge against him was that on several occasions, between July 25 and October 1, 1861, Kerrigan "did leave the camp of his regiment in Fairfax County, Virginia and visit and communicate with the enemy in said county."

From October 1861 until February 1862, Kerrigan engaged in some fancy legal footwork, attempting to delay his trial or have the charges dropped. October found him under arrest, and on the last day of that month, Fernando Wood, mayor of New York City, wrote to Lincoln on Kerrigan's behalf.

Wood opened his appeal by hoping that it would "not be considered improper . . . to address Your Excellency," and went on to say, "I have been requested on behalf of his family and friends, who are very numerous in this city," to help obtain an early hearing date. Mayor Wood's appeal for speed was somewhat blunted by Kerrigan's own maneuvers: he filed three separate requests for postponement, citing the need for his counsel "to visit the Supreme Court."

The mayor's letter continued: "Though I have not the most remote idea of the nature of the accusations made against Colonel Kerrigan, I can assure you that neither those friends, nor myself, would feel any sympathy, were we not convinced that he was guiltless of any offense involving disloyalty to the government, and to the cause in defense of which he was engaged in arms."

Wood went on to point out that Kerrigan was a member of Congress and that his district included the city hall of New York, "a constituency containing thousands of the most ardent supporters of the government. It is natural that they should take a deep interest in the result of the charges . . . the favor of a speedy investigation would excite among them the liveliest feelings of gratitude and enthusiasm, while delay may suggest uncertainty and doubt. Permit me then, as a personal friend of Colonel Kerrigan, and in view of the deep distress of his family, to appeal to your clemency that the opportunity to vindicate his character will not be long delayed."

While it is not difficult to imagine the conflicting forces impinging upon Lincoln, faced with the necessity of pacifying both New York City's tumultuous politicians and the army's need for discipline, one would be wrong to suppose that the President was much influenced by this appeal for clemency. The authorities, perhaps provoked by some fresh—but unrecorded—outburst on Kerrigan's part, confined him to Old Capitol Prison to await trial, a most unusual step in the case of an officer. Enlisted men were usually jailed awaiting trial, but officers, considered to be bound by honor, were given certain geographic limits, within which they were "under arrest" until told otherwise.

At last, the trial began. Maj. Henry Savage had this to say about his thirty-three-year-old colonel and Congressman: "He never instructed us in drill or tactics. I was elected major, but have yet to receive an appointment to that rank."

Capt. Archibald Ferguson, also of the 25th New York, agreed that there had been no military instruction, and elaborated upon the discipline in the camp:

> There was loud, drunken singing in the officer's tent, and much quarreling in the camp. A sergeant and a lieutenant had a conflict and the lieutenant hit the other man on the head with a pistol. The colonel took no action. Our regiment lagged behind in discipline and knowledge. There was much drunkenness, and gambling on dog fights. At the Grand Review, in October 1861, our regiment was in rags and very much in want of pantaloons. About five men in every company had no shoes.

General Martindale testified:

> When they came under my command, I visited their camp. There seemed to be no means of preserving order. Officers and men were quarreling in a boisterous manner. They were not soldierly. Many men had their pants unbuttoned or wore drawers instead of pants. Many were without shoes. Their persons were dirty and their weapons foul, very foul. Their drill and marching was irregular. When I assembled the officers of the regiment for instruction, Colonel Kerrigan walked off without permission and refused to return. I had him arrested.

The trial went on and on, generating 240 pages of testimony. Colonel Kerrigan's written defense, submitted the last day of the trial, ran to 56 pages, but it was in vain. Of the 42 charges and specifications, he was found guilty of 12 and sentenced "to be dismissed [from] the service of the United States."

Having pronounced this sentence, the court unanimously requested clemency, in a gesture more insulting than beneficent. "In consideration of the fact that Colonel Kerrigan has but recently entered the military service, and his

manifest inexperience and want of knowledge of military affairs, and his unfit-
ness to command a body of men . . . we recommend that he be allowed to
resign rather than be dismissed." Whether resigned or dismissed, he was a civilian again on March 7, 1862.

The court-martial board was more generous than it knew, since Kerrigan
had extensive military service, although some of it a bit offhanded. He had
served in Company D of the 1st Regiment of New York Volunteers in the
Mexican War, and afterward had joined the Walker filibustering invasion of
Nicaragua, serving briefly as *alcalde* of that nation's capital.

Having given the Nicaraguans the benefit of his administrative expertise, he
returned to New York City, where he was elected alderman from the sixth
ward, and served as clerk of the Tombs police court. He was elected to Congress in March 1861 and served one term.

Being removed from the army was hardly the end of Kerrigan's involvement
in public life. Though he continued in Congress for another twelve months after
his dismissal, his major efforts were devoted to Irish independence. He was
active in the Fenian Brotherhood, both during and after the War.[2]

The Fenians, a secret Irish brotherhood organized in the 1850s, sought to free
the mother country by involving the United States and Great Britain in war. To
this end, they launched several invasions of Canada between 1866 and 1870. Kerrigan led one company in the 1866 attack. His only military success was at the
Battle of Limestone Ridge, and the chief result of the invasions was to extinguish
the movement in Canada that had favored annexation by the United States. One
Fenian marching song may illustrate this unpleasant footnote in American history:

> We are the Fenian brotherhood,
> Skilled in the art of war,
> And we're going to fight for Ireland,
> The land that we adore.
> Many battles we have won,
> Along with the boys in blue,
> And we'll go and capture Canada,
> For we've nothing else to do!

During the unrest along the U.S.-Canadian border—a Fenian handbill
promised volunteers 200 acres in Canada—Kerrigan commanded the steamer
Erin's Hope, which landed weapons and gunpowder on the Irish coast. When
the authorities intercepted the vessel, Kerrigan managed to escape arrest.

He last appears in the court-martial records in 1896, when his attorney,
Thomas W. Pittman, wrote to the judge advocate general requesting a copy of the
1862 trial proceedings. By now, Kerrigan was sixty-eight years of age. What use
he made of the trial record is unknown. Three years later, he died in Brooklyn.

Chapter Twenty-One

Fling Wide the Banner

COL. JOHN MCCLUSKEY

Col. Joshua Lawrence Chamberlain and the 20th Maine were heroic figures in the 1860s, who lapsed into historical obscurity with the passing of the generations. A recent novel, *The Killer Angels*, and the cinematic version of that book, have granted a well-deserved resurrection to the memory of the 20th Maine and to its gallant commander. Chamberlain, who combined the brightest aspects of scholarship, personal courage, and political responsibility, now glows as America's Bayard, *le chevalier sans peur et sans reproche.*

A far more enigmatic figure was Col. John McCluskey of the 15th Maine. His court-martial in 1862 raised many questions. Was he negligent in preparing his troops for combat or was he so dedicated as to pay a drillmaster out of his own pocket?[1]

Was he a Victorian-era saint, washing the ailing soldiers of the 15th Maine with his own hands, or was he an example of moral evil, as he sat in the officer's cabin, gambling away the long nights at sea?

Was he a temperate and sober leader, who took a political risk to avoid ethnic strife in his regiment, or was he an excitable drunk, raving in his cabin with a brace of loaded pistols, and, finally, in an agitated fury, flinging into the sea the very symbol of community support, a regimental banner presented by the governor of Maine himself?

The 15th Maine was mustered in on January 23, 1862, and was ordered to the Department of the Gulf, commanded by Maj. Gen. Benjamin F. Butler, soon thereafter.

On March 6, 1862, the ship *Great Republic* passed the breakwater of Portland, Maine, and sailed south, its destination a tiny dot of land off the delta of the Mississippi River. Ship Island, until 1861 a sleepy spot of marshy sand and weeds, home to fishermen and other seafaring folk, had been transformed by the war into a major Federal stronghold, a base of operations for the eventual recapture of the Mississippi.

There, the *Great Republic* landed, on April 5, 1862, after a thirty-six-day passage. Ten days later, a court-martial board, under the presidency of Col. Henry W. Birge, commander of the 13th Connecticut Volunteers, was convened.

Colonel McCluskey faced three charges: conduct unbecoming an officer and a gentleman; violation of the 24th Article of War; and neglect of duty.

The specifications of the first charge were that McCluskey, when spoken to by two of his junior officers about allowing gambling among the men, had remarked, "If any brat of a boy attempts to teach me morals, I will slap his face." Further, on the night of April 2, the colonel was "drunk or intoxicated," and in such a state that he had thrown the regimental flag overboard into the sea.

The second charge was that McCluskey had used threatening language and gestures to his immediate subordinate, Lt. Col. Isaac Dyer, and toward his adjutant, J. Nowland. The third charge was that McCluskey had "wholly failed to perform the duties appertaining to his office, during the whole period of his connection with the regiment." The charges were preferred by Capt. J. B. Wilson.

Seventeen witnesses were called for the trial, all men of the 15th Maine. They included Lt. Col. Isaac Dyer; Maj. Benjamin Haws; Capts. William R. Swan, B. B. Murray, S. W. Leonard, Charles E. Smith, Lawrence Joyce, F. M. Drew, and J. B. Wilson; and Lts. W. S. Locke, D. M. Prescott, J. E. Cobb, A. Mowry, John B. Nickels, and Ransom E. Pierce. Other witnesses were Adjutant J. Nowland and regimental chaplain, the Rev. J. J. Brown.

The trial lasted from April 15 to May 3, 1862, and produced a forty-one-page record. The first three days of the trial were consumed in procedural matters, and included consideration of McCluskey's legal objections to the trial itself. Even today, to the layman's eye at least, the colonel's protests appear as monuments to legal obfuscation:

> I respectfully protest against the authority of this Court to proceed to the investigation of the charges now before them against me, and to pronounce sentence in the case for the reason that the Court is not properly and legally organized in accordance with Article 882 of Revised Army Regulations. Section 884 provides that "in the detail, the members will be named, and they will take place in the court, in the order of their rank." This does not provide that the members shall be <u>named</u> in the order of their rank; so that the order in which the members are named is no decision in regards to rank. In this case, no decision of the proper authority in regard to the rank of the members has been made. If the detail of the members were the decisives in regard to their rank, then the President would be appointed by the form of the order appointing a general court martial, and Section 882 would be rendered negatory; and moreover, if this were the interpretation the second sentence of Section 884 should read <u>the decision</u> instead of "a decision."

In the second part of his protest, Colonel McCluskey addressed himself to the issues of whether a delay in beginning proceedings was legal, and a consideration of what *might* happen if a court member were called away.

I respectfully protest against a delay of my trial until next Tuesday on the motion of the Judge Advocate by a vote of the court without application being made to the authority convening the Court. Section 886 of Revised Army Regulations provides for "delay or postponement of trial" in general terms and is applicable to either the prosecution or defendant. In the case on trial it was made by the prosecutor to the Court and it should have been "referred to the authority convening the Court." The reasons for this are plain: the public exigencies, known only to the commanding officer, might require the immediate services, in the field or elsewhere, of the members of the Court, in which case he would order the Court "dissolved and the charges reserved for another Court."

The court considered McCluskey's protests, ruled against him, and the trial began.

The charges that involved gambling produced the first spate of contradictory testimony. One witness said that the colonel spent long hours playing cards with the other officers, and that the cabin door was left ajar so that the enlisted men could see gambling in progress. Another witness stated, however, that Colonel McCluskey never played for money, and if he did, he returned the money. Yet another witness stated that on the quarterdeck, Capt. John B. Wilson and Lt. H. A. Shorey had encouraged the colonel to prohibit gambling aboard the ship, and the colonel's reply had been, "If any brat of a boy attempts to teach me morals, I will slap his face," but a fourth witness swore that he had heard no such statement.

To further confuse matters, Lt. Nowland clearly recalled the colonel saying, "If any brat of a boy should presume to teach me about conduct or about playing cards, I will slap his face for him. No brat of a boy will set himself to teach morals to me or anyone else."

Passing on to the matter of military training, or lack thereof, Captain Wilson stated that Colonel McCluskey, while in Maine, had issued a written order prohibiting battalion drill, which had been taking place already under the guidance of Lieutenant Colonel Dyer. Wilson further recalled that the colonel had issued only one written order between the time of the formation of the regiment and its arrival at Ship Island, had given the officers of the regiment no instruction in military tactics, and had never appeared at dress parade.

Colonel Dyer testified that in January and February, the regiment drilled by companies from 10:00 A.M. until noon and by battalion from 2:00 to 4:00 P.M., weather permitting, and that after muskets were available, Colonel McCluskey ordered that the companies should be drilled in the manual of arms. Dyer stated further that McCluskey arranged a subscription among his officers to hire a professional drillmaster to teach the men the manual of arms, and that McCluskey himself was the first to contribute to this fund.

The court then turned its attention to the matter of health and sanitation among the men of the regiment. In Maine, McCluskey was disturbed that the men did not wash sufficiently; he insisted that the officers should moniter the men's hygiene more carefully and expressed surprise that well-brought-up Maine men should revert to being "brutes" upon joining the army. One witness described the colonel as "not only a servant, but a slave" to the regiment, caring for the sick men and horses, washing the invalids with his own hands, and supervising the preparation of gruel and boiled rice for the sick.

The portrayal of McCluskey as an angel of mercy was contradicted by Dyer, who recalled no such maternal behavior other than the issuance of a single verbal order by McCluskey encouraging the men to wash themselves.

The question of the regimental banner occupied the majority of the Court transcript, and is in sufficient detail to permit a recreation of those long-ago events.

The regiment, when formed, contained "both Americans and Irish." The state of Maine had a suggested format for regimental banners, but certain elements proposed "an Irish banner" instead. The non-Irish grumbled that they would not fight under any Hibernian emblems.

On February 22, two weeks before the regiment departed for the Gulf of Mexico, a crowd gathered in front of the state house in Augusta. Notables present included the governor and the heads of the various branches of the state government. Following a flowery, patriotic, and prolonged oration by Mr. W. H. McCrillis of Bangor, a purple silk banner, a gift of the ladies of Aroostook, was unfurled. On one side it bore the coat of arms of the state of Maine and on the other side a harp and a shamrock. This attempt to please both sides of the controversy appears to have pleased no one.

Colonel McCluskey, in his speech accepting the flag, pledged that the banner would be carried proudly over the regiment and that it would never trail in the dust. But the feeling was far from universal. Lieutenant Colonel Dyer grumbled that he would never fight under an Irish flag, and an anonymous writer published an article in the *Kennebec Journal* denouncing the whole affair. Thus, the *Great Republic* set sail carrying with it a full cargo of ill will and dissension, along with the men of the 15th Maine.

The long passage along the Atlantic coast did little to abate the tensions. There were mutterings among the "Americans" about serving under an "Irish flag," while the Irish spoke of shooting any man who would speak ill of the regimental banner.

In the officer's main cabin, the aft bulkhead was decorated with ornamental woodwork, the intricate carving that lends grace to the functional ribs, blocks, knees, and spars of a working vessel. To this woodwork was tied the flag that so excited the men of the 15th Maine.

It would seem that this undercurrent of tension was working on Colonel McCluskey himself, generating a subterranean head of steam that was to burst forth on the night of April 2. Ordinarily, the display of behavior recorded in the court transcripts would be attributed to whiskey, but several witnesses stated that they had never seen the colonel touch a drop.

On the fateful night, McCluskey, the ship's doctor, Lt. A. Leavitt and a Mr. C. S. Crosby, the ship's captain, played cards in the officer's cabin until 10:00 P.M., at which time the colonel retired to his own small stateroom. About an hour later, the colonel's voice could be heard, gradually increasing in volume, until it was sufficient to awaken several of the other officers.

The colonel spoke to himself, apparently pacing about the cramped space by his bunk: "No, by God, I'll not disgrace that flag. No, by God, that son of a bitch Dyer will never have his way in this matter. I swore an oath, a sacred oath, that this flag will never trail in the dust. It was entrusted into my hands by the governor himself. It bears with it the sentiments of the ladies of Aroostook, and now, by God, those scoundrels make it a subject of unrest and rebellion. That son of a bitch Dyer thinks he will have his way with it."

These sentiments, repeated in louder and louder tones, alarmed the ship's captain, who called Lieutenant Leavitt and asked him to intervene. Leavitt, clad only in his underwear, persuaded McCluskey to open his cabin door. To Leavitt's horror, the colonel was brandishing a pair of loaded pistols, to which he had just fitted percussion caps. He shouted, "By God, I'm going to Dyer's room and we're going to settle this matter here and now. An oath is an oath; our flag will never trail in the dust." Leavitt, who seems to have had some personal influence over McCluskey, gradually calmed the colonel enough so that he could return briefly to his own cabin to put on his trousers.

In those few minutes, McCluskey seems to have worked himself into a fresh frenzy, and his shouted and repetitious thoughts on the subjects of flags deeply concerned Leavitt, who briefly quieted the colonel by pointing out that further such inflammatory outbursts would incite a mutiny or a riot, which would be a considerable hazard at one o'clock in the morning, three days from land.

In time McCluskey was persuaded to put away his pistols, but then he asserted that he wished to go forward in the ship, wake up all the enlisted men, and "explain the matter to the men." Leavitt persuaded the excited colonel that this, too, was not as splendid idea as it might appear. McCluskey's voice roared on into the night, in counterpoint to Leavitt's pleas for calm and discretion.

Suddenly, McCluskey burst from his room and into the cabin. He seized the regimental banner, which resisted his efforts to tear it down. He threw all his weight onto one corner, pulling loose part of the woodwork and bringing down that corner of the flag; an equally violent tug on the opposite corner freed the flag entirely. The colonel bundled up the silk in his arms, the shattered wood filigree dangling from the corners, and he climbed up to the darkened deck near the wheelhouse and on out of sight. A few minutes later, he returned empty handed.

"Well, by God, I have committed it to the sea itself. I have fulfilled my oath: never will it trail in the dust. Now that flag will never be dishonored, nor will it be a subject for dissension or dispute. The matter is finished." With this, he returned to his cabin and, at around 4:00 A.M., peace settled over the *Great Republic*.

On Saturday, May 3, 1862, "the prisoner having no further testimony to offer," the court meeting at Ship Island adjourned and deliberated. Their verdict was not guilty on all charges and all specifications.

In a clarification, the court issued an additional statement that agreed that McCluskey did, indeed, destroy the flag in question, but that since it was not an *official* regimental flag, "as defined by the Army Regulations and that since the accused acted under the impression that its possession by the regiment was productive of discord," such actions may have been "injudicious," but no criminality could be attributed to the act itself.

The decision of the court was reviewed and approved by General Butler: "Colonel John McCluskey, 15th Regiment Maine Volunteers, will resume his sword." There the matter rested. However, McCluskey seems to have lost further interest in his command. In August, four months later, he submitted his resignation.

Chapter Twenty-Two

Drunk at Cloud's Mill?

COL. ROBERT P. MCDOWELL

The 5th Regiment of Pennsylvania Infantry and its commander served only three months, but that was sufficient time for its colonel to get himself court-martialed. The 5th Pennsylvania was organized at Camp Curtin, near Harrisburg, on April 20, 1861, and served the next four weeks at Washington, D.C. It then crossed over the river and stayed at Alexandria until mustered out at the end of July.

Col. Robert P. McDowell, a Pittsburgh native, came to trial on July 3, 1861, charged with the 45th Article of War, with the specification that "while on duty as Officer of the Day, did get so drunk as to be unable to perform his duty properly on June 27, 1861, at Alexandria."[1]

The first prosecution witness was Lt. Col. John A. Creiger of the 11th New Jersey.

> On the 27th, the Confederates captured two of our officers near Cloud's Mill [near the old Springfield train station], and an attack on our pickets stationed there was anticipated. Colonel [Noah] Farnham told me to return to camp as quickly as possible, take a company and go to the mills. While at the mills, I saw Colonel McDowell, who was Officer of the Day. He appeared under the influence of intoxicating liquor and unfit for duty. I did not see him direct a force. He seemed sleepy, with his hat pulled over his eyes. He sat on his horse with his head hanging and his body settled down.

Maj. Charles M. Leaser of the 11th New York recalled Colonel McDowell that day:

> I had arrived with two companies and learned that the alarm was false. I asked Colonel McDowell how he would like to dispose these troops. He seemed unable to decide. While waiting for my troops to come up, I went into the mill with Colonel McDowell, and other officers, to take a drink of whisky. The colonel seemed confused, under the

influence of intoxicating liquor, and not fit to take command. His general appearance and indecision was that of an intoxicated person. He looked intoxicated even before we had a drink together."

Lt. J. J. Sweet of the 2nd New York Cavalry was called next: "I was ordered to take men from Alexandria to Cloud's Mill, as one of our pickets had been attacked. I met Colonel McDowell. He asked me what he should do with my troops. I thought he was drunk, so much so he could not perform his duties. I was with him about six hours. He drank while I was with him—three or four times. His face was flushed."

Here the Court adjourned, and the next day, took up witnesses for the defense. They told a different story. Surgeon William Brodie of the 1st Michigan Infantry recalled seeing McDowell at 10:00 A.M. on the 27th: "He looked sober to me." Colonel O. B. Willcox of the 1st Michigan described reconnoitering roads with Colonel McDowell from 5:00 P.M. to 11:00 P.M. on the 27th—but made no comment on McDowell's appearance that evening. Capt. Charles M. Lynn, also of the 1st Michigan, said, "I saw Colonel McDowell twice at Cloud's Mill. He was perfectly sober. I was with him an hour and he did not take a single drink."

Now, the colonel spoke in his own defense. "I had been in the saddle 20 out of 24 hours for three days running, when the alarm occurred at Cloud's Mill. Yes, it is true that I had a drink, as I needed a stimulant to keep going. However, I was never drunk."

The court deliberated on this testimony and acquitted him. The reviewing general agreed and that was that. Colonel McDowell's military service record contains a single piece of paper. Not even his age is given. The longest documentation of his military career is the transcript of his court-martial.

Chapter Twenty-Three

Death at Buzzard's Roost

COL. GEZA MIHALOTZY

An Austrian major and a future President came face to face at a court-martial held in Athens, Alabama, on August 13, 1862. The defendant was thirty-five-year-old Geza Mihalotzy, commander of the 24th Illinois Regiment of Infantry; the president of the court was Brig. Gen. James A. Garfield. For both men, the future held a rendezvous with a bullet.

The regiment was formed in Chicago in July 1861, and passed the remainder of that year in Missouri and Kentucky. With the coming spring, it moved south and spent most of May 1861 in Athens, Alabama, twenty miles south of the Tennessee border. At his court-martial, Colonel Mihalotzy was charged with disobedience of orders.[1]

The first specification was that Mihalotzy, "in contravention of General Order No. 13-A, from the Headquarters of the Department of the Ohio, in the following terms, to wit: 'peaceable citizens are not to be molested in their persons or property,' did, on or about the 2nd day of May 1862 quarter two companies [almost 200 men] of infantry in the house of J. H. Jones, in the town of Athens, Alabama, to the molestation of the inmates, and the destruction of their property." The second specification was that Mihalotzy had also quartered himself in the same house. The transcript of the trial has disappeared over the years, and only the charges and outcome remain. He was found guilty of the first specification, but not the second, and was sentenced to be suspended from rank and command for one month, and to be reprimanded in General Orders. Maj. Gen. Don Carlos Buell, the reviewing officer, disagreed with the Court:

> It appears from the evidence, that the demonstration of some persons in Mr. Jones' house, on the occasion of the [Confederate] attack on the troops in Athens, on the first of May, made his claim to protection as a peaceable citizen very questionable, though he seems really to have been so himself. The worst feature connected with the occupancy of the house was the bad conduct of the troops while in it. That cannot be excused under any circumstances, but it does not enter into the

charges against Colonel Mihalotzy, and it is due to him that he exhibited a commendable zeal and determination to suppress it when brought to his notice.

Buell restored the colonel to his command.

The 24th Illinois, after its brief sojourn at Athens, went on to more active combat, and fought at Perryville and Stone's River, Tennessee. In June 1863, Mihalotzy requested appointment to a commission as brigadier general, to command a Colored Troops unit. In the credentials he submitted, he listed his Austrian army services: cadet, from 1838 to 1841, and lieutenant, from 1841 to 1847. The following year he was a captain in the Hungarian Army, and from 1848 to 1851, he served as a brevet major. He came to the United States in 1851. Nothing in the record indicates why his request to command Colored Troops was rejected.

On September 20, 1863, he was wounded at the Battle of Chickamauga, and was on leave for two months recuperating. Four months after returning to duty, he was wounded again, this time at Buzzard's Roost Gap in Georgia. The wound was severe, and he was moved to a hospital at Chattanooga, Tennessee, where he died March 11, 1864, after two weeks of suffering. He is buried in the Chattanooga National Cemetery. To honor his memory, Fort Putnam, in the defenses of Chattanooga was renamed Fort Mihalotzy. Urbanization has covered the location, and what once held four siege guns and four field pieces is now 221 Boyntown Terrace.

The colonel's widow, Hannah, applied for a pension. In her application, she described her 1856 Chicago wedding when she was twenty-three years old. The month after her husband's death, she began to receive a monthly check for thirty dollars. There the record ends.

Chapter Twenty-Four

A Sharp Tongue

LT. COL. JAMES PECKHAM

If there were any shy, retiring colonels in the service of Missouri during the Civil War, they are not apparent in the records. The turmoil and bitter feeling in the border states, where neighbor against neighbor was an everyday tragedy, are strongly reflected in the records of such men as James Peckham.[1]

On July 4, 1861, at the St. Louis Arsenal, he was mustered in as the lieutenant colonel of the 8th Regiment of Missouri Union Volunteers. Within days he was fighting Confederate guerrillas, bushwhackers, and bridge burners along the route of the Northern Missouri Railroad. In August the 8th Missouri joined armed expeditions to Price's Landing and St. Genevieve, Missouri, and then spent the next five months at Paducah, Kentucky. There a Confederate musket ball found him: a November 1861 surgeon's letter notes that Peckham's "gunshot wound is healing." In January 1862, he submitted a letter of resignation, citing "urgent private business." The next month, the 8th Missouri took part in the successful attack upon Fort Donelson, apparently without Peckham being present.

Two months later, he was recommissioned in the same regiment at the same rank. Perhaps his potential successor, Maj. John McDonald, was annoyed by the return of Peckham and the abrupt evaporation of McDonald's vision of silver oak leaves on his own shoulders. Whatever the reasons, the two men's antagonism boiled over in late March 1862, in a shouting match held in front of the entire regiment. McDonald accused Peckham of political maneuvering. Peckham replied that he was entirely within his rights to have been recommissioned. McDonald retorted, "You are no gentleman and no white man; you are a son of a bitch."

Peckham responded by telling McDonald that he was under arrest and that he must hand over his sword. The major would have no part of it. "Kiss my ass. You can't have my sword, you or any other son of a bitch!" Peckham repeated his arrest order. McDonald suggested that they each take off their marks of rank and said, "I'll whip you with my fists."

This offer of pugilism was refused by Peckham, and the two men fell to cursing, calling each other "cock-sucker" and "son of a bitch" until the major finally yielded to his arrest.

The battle of Shiloh briefly distracted the two Missourians from their feud, but it came to a legal head near Corinth, when McDonald was court-martialed on charges of conduct unbecoming an officer and a gentleman, based upon their shouting and cursing match. McDonald was found guilty, but his punishment was remitted by Maj. Gen. Henry W. Halleck. Peckham himself was not court-martialed for this public display of bad temper, but the following month resigned his commission for a second time and never returned to the Eighth Missouri.

During his brief sojourn as a civilian, Peckham married. His bride was Catherine "Kate" Bohannon; they were joined at the Methodist Episcopal Church in Jefferson City, Missouri, by Rev. A. C. McDonald.

In September 1862, he enlisted again, this time in the 29th Missouri and, again, as a lieutenant colonel. He was immediately in trouble, once more, brought up on charges filed by Surgeon E. Kramer of the 1st Wisconsin Cavalry. The first charge was unusual: "illegitimate orders," and the second was the customary "conduct unbecoming an officer and a gentleman."

The two men were at the Federal camp near Cape Girardeau, Missouri. Peckham ordered Kramer to treat a man whom Peckham considered to be sick. The doctor replied that he was the doctor and that he would decide who was sick and who was not. Peckham then ordered Kramer to treat a particular civilian who was associated with the army. Kramer again objected, saying that he was an army doctor and did not treat civilians. The quarrel, held on a public street, escalated. The record quotes Peckham as shouting, "With the good pay you get, you ought to attend to that man, and if you don't take care of him, I will take your commission away."

At the trial, Surgeon Kramer stated that he had been placed under arrest, and was not allowed to treat the many sick and wounded patients in the hospital, which was insulting to him and deprived the patients of needed care. Not much came of this trial and Peckham continued with the 29th Missouri, appointed full colonel in March 1863.

The 29th saw much active service. They fought on November 24, 1863, at Lookout Mountain, Tennessee, where Peckham was severely wounded in the right arm. The surgeon's reports describe a musket ball entering the front of the deltoid muscle and exiting the back, leaving his arm largely paralyzed. Gangrene and sloughing followed, leaving a deep, contracted scar.

Peckham's service came to an end at Vicksburg, where he was again severely wounded. Some records describe the wound as in the left arm, though others describe the left groin. He never recovered fully, and was mustered out in March 1864, disabled by his wounds. It seems unlikely that his sharp tongue and ready temper were made any milder by the chronic pain of his injuries. Dr. G. W. Lawrence, resident physician at Hot Springs, Arkansas, described the "wound in the left inguinal region, with severe pain in the left thigh and great distress in portions of the abdominal viscera. The irritative action of old wounds, the adhesions and contractions, tend to exhaust the vital forces." Dr. F. G. Porter, examing surgeon for the Pension Office noted, "Upon any undue excitement or over exertion, in the ordinary affairs of life, undue nervous excitement, with prostration, supervenes."

In spite of these difficulties, Peckham went to work. In a notarized statement he described his brief employment. "I was in the civil service of the United States as an Inspector of Tobacco for the First District of Missouri for the entire period from March 3, 1865 to June 6, 1866. This is not a salaried office, but simply dependent on fees received from merchants, no salary being paid or compensation received from the government."

The difficulties caused by his wounds compounded, however, and at 5:15 A.M., June 1, 1869, Colonel Peckham died at Hot Springs, Arkansas, at the age of thirty-nine. His widow was awarded a pension of thirty dollars a month, plus an extra two dollars a month for her infant daughter.

Chapter Twenty-Five

"I Felt of Her Bosoms"

COL. J. LAFAYETTE RIKER

The case of Colonel J. Lafayette Riker (of the 62nd New York Regiment, also known as the Anderson Zouaves) has all the elements of Shakespearean comedy: an aristocratic name, mistaken identity, changes of gender, misrule in high places, archaic costumes, a bit of Shylock, and a surprise ending. There are darker elements as well: blood-stained sheets, the self-deluded rescue of fallen women, undue familiarity on short acquaintance, children where they should not be, and the opinion of four different officers regarding one pair of breasts.[1]

On March 3, 1862, a court-martial, presided over by Brig. Gen. Darius N. Couch, was convened. The members included five colonels, two lieutenant colonels, and a major. The accused, Colonel Riker, was charged with neglect of duty, creating a false muster, attempt to sell a commission, receiving illegal profits and rebates from a vendor, and keeping a woman in his quarters.

The court first considered neglect of duty. Several officers testified that they had provided regimental drills themselves, but that Riker was "too busy" to bother with such activities, or to instruct his officers in military matters. One captain, who had previous military experience, volunteered to train his fellow officers in "field movements," but he, too, was ignored by Colonel Riker. Another officer testified, "This regiment is unable to do the drills prescribed in Volume 2 of the Drill Book." (Riker's regiment was mustered in at New York City in June 1861 and was part of the defenses of Washington, D.C., from August 1861 through March 1862.)

On the subject of financial kickbacks, the lieutenant colonel of the regiment testified that Colonel Riker had "entered into an agreement with one T. E. Isaacs and others, to share the profits of the sutlership of the 62nd Regiment, New York State Volunteers, in the months of June and July 1861 or thereabouts." The witness also testified that Colonel Riker "became very distant with me since I raised questions about the regimental sutler."

Lt. Samuel C. Thwait then testified that before he had received his commission through the usual channels, Colonel Riker had offered to sell him a commission for $500 in cash; the colonel then added that he had been able to accummulate more than $6,000 in the five months since he joined the regiment, presumably through illegal transactions.

Serious as these charges were, the 140 pages of testimony centered chiefly around the subject of Pvt. Walter Harold, who was assigned to the company of Capt. Albert Meeks. The captain testified that Colonel Riker had asked him to put Private Harold on Meeks's muster roll, though Harold was never active in the company and lived at the colonel's quarters. Meeks noted that Harold was five-feet-two-inches tall and wanted to be a drummer boy, since a musket was too heavy for him.

All witnesses agreed that Private Harold was on the regimental payroll and drew a soldier's pay. As to the more crucial question—what was the role of Private Harold in Colonel Riker's personal life—opinion was more divided.

Capt. A. Johnston, testifying for the prosecution, recalled meeting Harold for the first time on Riker's Island (a bit of government land between the Bronx and Queens). The young soldier was dressed as a Zouave, a uniform with baggy pants, which tended to conceal the wide hips noted by other witnesses. Johnston then described another encounter, one which tells as much about the captain as it does about the private. Johnston had taken his laundry to Washington, D.C., to be washed at a house near the intersection of 14th Street and Pennsylvania Avenue, at that time the very center of "Hooker's Division," a neighborhood of saloons and brothels. There he met a woman who saluted him by name. On this point, the court queried Johnston in greater detail.

Q. What did you say?
A. I replied, "I do not know you."
Q. Her answer?
A. She said, "You know Walter Harold!"
Q. Are you confident that Walter Harold is female?
A. I am positive.
Q. For what reasons?
A. General appearance, mannerisms. I think I can tell a female.
Q. Do you have any evidence beyond that of sight?
A. Yes, I do.
Q. What is that?
A. I felt of her bosoms.
Q. Anything further?
A. No, I was only there a few minutes.
Q. What were Private Harold's duties at the colonel's quarters?
A. Nothing in particular—just looking out the window.

The next witness was Capt. Edwin Dans. At drill, he had noticed Private Harold's inability to shoulder a musket, as well as the large hips, small hands, and small feet. "I suspected something. I took her to Maj. Oscar Dayton's tent and we examined her there, just the two of us. I opened her shirt; I examined a breast, took hold of it, exposed it to the major."

After this impromptu bit of gender determination, Dans then went to Colonel Riker with his findings. Dans recalled the colonel's reply: "Let her stay here. I will examine into the case."

The impact of the captain's narrative was diminished by the next witness, Major Dayton, who recalled no such examination, denied having had Harold's breast exposed to his gaze, and, in essence, called Captain Dans a liar.

Captain Meeks, who had previously addressed the issue of muster rolls, added his recollection of the controversial soldier: "She had coarse features. We have a hundred boys in the regiment who would be taken for a girl as soon as he. He wanted to be a drummer, since he could not shoulder a musket."

The court then heard from Joseph Yates, quartermaster. "I know that Walter Harold is a woman and has been living at the house of Eliza Johnson in Washington City. Eliza is better known as 'Black Liz,' and her occupation is that of conducting a house of prostitution. The woman called Walter Harold is a common prostitute, and her presence in the regiment is part of a conspiracy of officers to discredit Col. Riker."

Puzzling in light of today's military family arrangements was the testimony of Colonel Riker's fourteen-year-old daughter, who had been living at the regimental headquarters. (According to her New York City death certificate, Mrs. Riker had died in 1851 at the age of twenty-five of "hysteria.") The daughter told the court that she and her father were the only persons occupying his room. She then described a scene, when the colonel was absent, in which Private Harold confessed to her that he/she was a woman. "She said she enlisted in order to keep an eye on a man that she loved; she feared that he might become engaged to another woman. My father knew nothing of Harold's gender."

Lieutenant Thwait returned to the stand and added yet another dimension to an already complex story.

Q. Have you ever been in bed with Walter Harold?
A. Yes.
Q. Narrate the occurrence.
A. While I was on recruiting service in New York, she came there, and I found her laying on the boards among the rest of the men. I told her I did not like to see her there and would give her a bed to sleep in. She told me she didn't like to go home with me.
Q. Then what happened?
A. I had told her I would take her to my own house, and afterwards she consented, provided I would promise not to injure her or take advantage of her in any way. I told her I knew her secret. I gave her my word as a gentleman that I would not take advantage of her, that she should sleep perfectly safe.

Q. And then what transpired?

A. She took me at my word and went with me. I went to bed first. She blew out the light, undressed herself and went to bed. In the night, I woke up, put my hand out and felt her breast. I had known she was a woman from heresay before, but now I was certain. We both got up in the morning and both went back to the tent in Union Square.

Q. Did you sleep with her again?

A. Not exactly. When I came back to my dinner, I went upstairs to my bed and turned the sheet down. There was clean sheets put on the bed after I left. I found blood on the tick of the bed. I told her of it when I saw her again and she said she had her curses.

Q. Please continue your narrative.

A. I told her notwithstanding that she could come and sleep there again, that the people in the house would have no suspicions of her being a female. She went back with me, but instead of going to bed, she sat up on a chair. She slept on the chair all night and in the morning went back to Riker's Island.

Q. Did you have any other evidence of her being a woman than feeling her bosom and [seeing] the blood?

A. No, except from her general appearance and the formation of her body. Her breasts were very prominent and her skin was very white and clear.

Q. Do you mean that you saw enough of the general formation of her body, apart from her bosom, to satisfy you that she was a woman?

A. Yes, sir.

Q. Was her whole body or what part exposed?

A. Nothing but her breast exposed. I formed my opinion of her general appearance by her appearance with her clothes on: small shoulders, broad hips, small feet, ankles and hands, and tapering fingers. Her voice was also an indication.

Q. You then had no better observation of her body in bed than when she was up?

A. No, sir.

Q. Did you have carnal connection with her?

A. No, sir.

Q. Did you see Walter Harold at Riker's Island?

A. Yes, sir.

Q. What was she employed as there?

A. In the colonel's quarters, when I first saw her.

Q. Was she there often?

A. Most all the time, whenever I went there.

The final witness was Walter Harold himself. He began by explaining that he was indeed female and that before the war was known as Helen Lambert.

Q. Did Colonel Riker know you were a woman?
A. Yes.
Q. Did he examine you?
A. Yes. He said he'd make it public and have the surgeon do it if I didn't let him examine me, so I gave him permission.
Q. Who was in your room at Riker's Island?
A. Colonel Riker and his aide, George Elder, but usually just the colonel.
Q. Where have you resided since you left the regiment?
A. At first with a Negro woman at 10th and "V" Streets, then in York, Pennsylvania.
Q. Did Lieut. Thwait take you to York?
A. Yes.
Q. Has he supported you since that time?
A. Yes.
Q. Did Colonel Riker have carnal connection with you?
A. No.

Having heard this—and much more—testimony, the court deliberated and turned in the final surprise of this convoluted bit of Americana: It found Colonel Riker not guilty on every charge. Riker had little time for future domestic experiments; he died May 31, 1862, of a gunshot wound received at Fair Oaks near Richmond, Virginia. Later, his daughter's guardian petitioned for a pension until she came of age. She was awarded $30 a month, from May 1862 to July 1867, at which time she would turn sixteen and be responsible for her own welfare.

Chapter Twenty-Six

He Drank Himself Sober

COL. CHARLES L. SUMMALT

In April 1861, Washington, D.C., was a city surrounded and besieged: across the Potomac lay hostile Virginia; to the north Maryland was filled with southern sympathizers, eager to interrupt the rail lines to the capital. On May 6, 1861, newly minted Maj. Gen. Benjamin F. Butler seized the initiative and secured the vital Baltimore & Ohio Railroad junction at Relay House, Maryland.

In a less heroic mode, the same location was the site of the self-marination of Col. Charles L. Summalt, commander of the 138th Regiment of Pennsylvania Volunteers. This regiment was organized in Harrisburg on August 16, 1862, and two weeks later was sent to guard the rail link at Relay Station, a duty performed until the regiment moved to Harper's Ferry in June 1863.[1]

During his seven months in command, Colonel Summalt had generated such a record of malfeasance, that his court-martial opened with a total of three charges and fifteen specifications.

The first charge was drunkenness on duty. The offenses specified were as follows: he was so drunk on November 4, 1862, that the lieutenant colonel had to take command; on December 6, his drunkenness produced "grossly improper conduct"; on December 20, he was so drunk at Camp Relay House that he was "totally unfit for duty"; on January 2, 1863, he was so drunk that "he behaved in an unseemly and disgusting manner"; and he was described as "very drunk" on December 4, December 13, and December 25, 1862.

The second charge was conduct prejudicial to good order and military discipline. On December 2, 1862, while very drunk, he entered the officers' mess tent and vomited on the floor next to the supper table, "rendering the scene so nauseating as to oblige them to eat elsewhere." Two days later the regiment held dress parade. After the men had been dismissed, Colonel Summalt, who had been drinking, called a second dress parade and, after having the men assembled for the second time that day, delivered a long and rambling harangue. On January 13, 1863, he used "very profane language," and on several occasions he called the guards from their guard posts and obliged them to drink with him.

116

On September 20, 1862, only a few days after assuming his new duties, he fired his gun at night, for no good reason, creating a false alarm.

The final charge was conduct unbecoming an officer and a gentleman. The first specification was that he had visited the home of a well-known secessionist, got drunk, and announced his sympathy for the South and his support of John C. Breckinridge, the presidential candidate against Lincoln in 1860, who ran on the breakaway Southern Democrat ticket. (At the time of the trial, Breckinridge was a major general in the Confederate Army.) The second specification under "conduct unbecoming," was that on December 18, 1862, in the tent of the regimental surgeon, Summalt tore up charges against him and threw them into the stove, while calling Maj. Gen. John Wool names "too indecent to be spread out upon this record."

The first witness was Pvt. Amos Bennett of Company H: "While we were at dress parade, the colonel said that he felt sick and entered my tent and threw up. I held his head because he seemed very sick. He smelled like liquor." Capt. R. L. Stewart of Company K was also a recipient of the colonel's emetic proclivities. "I saw him throw up in my quarters, but he did not seem intoxicated. On a different occasion, though, he definitely seemed drunk and excited, especially when he was trying to get off his horse."

The hospital steward, James Wells, stated: "The colonel was in Captain Stewart's quarters. Colonel Summalt said that he felt sick and then he vomited profusely on the floor. It smelled of liquor. I needed the colonel to sign some important papers, but he did not."

Steward Wells was also with Colonel Summalt during the visit to the home of Mr. William Dorsey, the alleged "well-known secessionist":

> At Mr. Dorsey's home, Colonel Summalt had several drinks and amazed the family with quotations from Shakespeare. Then he did his classic representation of Ajax defying the lightning. After that, Colonel Summalt passed out drunk on the settee and I could not awaken him when dinner was called. We carried him into a different room and put him on the sofa. At 9:00 P.M., he woke up and asked for coffee, and then he asked for whisky to put in his coffee. After he was a little more wide awake, he repeated his quotations from Shakespeare. Then the colonel requested that Mr. Dorsey's daughter sing "Maryland, My Maryland," and then he and I returned to camp.

Steward Wells also recalled Summalt's speech, defending his voting for Breckinridge in the 1860 election.

Wells's final contribution to the testimony was in describing a visit to the tent of Regimental Surgeon Custis P. Harvey: " The colonel came into the doctor's tent and pulled a paper from his pocket. He said it was from General Wool and then added 'that damned old secessionist may kiss my ass.' Then the colonel threw the order into the fire."

Dr. Harvey now contributed his narrative to the proceedings. "Colonel Summalt came into my office, staggering from the influence of liquor. He showed me a paper said to be from General Wool and then he cursed the general and put the paper in the fire. On December 25th, I was called to see the colonel about 3:00 o'clock in the morning. He was lying on his back and was insensible. I considered him to be dead drunk and returned to my own quarters."

Lt. E. Epick, of Company A, described an uncomfortable supper shared with the colonel: "I was invited by the colonel to dine at his public table at the hotel. The colonel had been drinking. That was very clear. He raised a great fuss and cursed at the proprietor about the service at his table. It was not a very pleasant meal."

Lt. Edward Moon, quartermaster of the 138th Pennsylvania, had his own unpleasant recollections of being invited to join the colonel.

> I met Colonel Summalt near my quarters. He invited me to go to the Relay House. I replied that I had regimental business I needed to tend to, ordering and receiving supplies, et cetera. He ordered me to go with him. I replied, "Of course, Colonel, I would obey an order to join you." The colonel was already staggering drunk. At the Relay House, he insisted on playing billiards. He was so drunk he only made seven or eight points. When it was time to go, he went outside and fell off the platform into the ditch water. I helped him up. He then said he wanted to fire off his pistol. I begged him not to, as there had been an alarm and the men were in the rifle pits with loaded guns. The colonel fired four shots into the air. I called the Sergeant of the Guard. The colonel did not know the password, but the sergeant recognized him and let him pass by. I took Colonel Summalt to his quarters and left him there.

As in most of these trials, there were contrary witnesses, for the defense. Several men of the regiment testified that they had seen no intoxication and recalled Colonel Summalt as a sober and steady commander.

At the close of testimony, Summalt introduced an eighteen-page statement, rebutting the witnesses against him. He first took up the Breckinridge issue:

> I concede all that Wells testified, that prior to the last Presidential election, I was a Breckinridge man and that I voted for him. If thus to have voted and thus to acknowledge a military offense, so must it be. Another section should be added to the Articles of War, and a permanent court-martial established in every battalion of the army. Even Steward Wells would not testify to the utterly groundless residue of this charge, that I said my sympathies were with the south in the present rebellion.

The Relay House, a tavern at an important railway junction, was the site of Col. Charles L. Summalt's drunken plunge off the porch and into the ditch. MASSACHUSETTS COM-MANDERY MILITARY ORDER OF THE LOYAL LEGION, U.S. ARMY MILITARY HISTORY INSTITUTE.

Now, Colonel Summalt turned to the most dominant theme of the trial, the overuse of alcohol. A Mr. Luckett, a guest of the Dorseys, had testified that Colonel Summalt was sober and his behavior entirely proper during the after-noon and evening at the Dorsey home. The colonel's defense follows:

> As to intoxication on that occasion, Wells is more full and explicit and would appear plausible and entitled to some degree of credit, were not his own statement contradictory and had he not been contradicted in every material statement by James H. Luckett, who is more than his equal in intelligence and character. According to Mr. Wells, Mr. Luckett started drunk, and after large potations, drank himself sober (as a little

drink intoxicates the brain, and drinking largely sobers us again) while I
started sober and drank myself drunk, and he alone, a sick man convalescent, in just the condition to be most easily affected by liquor, started
sober, drank and kept sober, a sort of a male Vestal virgin among bac-
chanals. He says I was in the dining room before tea. Mr. Luckett says I
was not. Wells says I lay down in the dining room; Mr. Luckett says I did
not. Wells says I was carried from where I first lay down into the parlor,
and lay down there. Mr. Luckett says that I lay down at the instance and
constrained by the urgency of himself and Mr. Dorsey's family and continued to lie where I first laid down.

He says I was drunk. Mr. Luckett says I was not. He says that he
drove up to camp on our return. Mr. Luckett says he did not. But both
agree that more than once when there, and both before tea and after, I
did what I could to entertain the company there, and did so at the
request of the Ladies there, and this circumstance I submit is conclusive,
that Mr. Luckett is right and Wells is wrong on the points where they
differ. Intelligent and accomplished ladies do not treat with that courtesy
the man who, almost a stranger, forgets or disregards in their presence
the politeness and decency of civilized life. It is true I was at the time off
duty and ten miles from my camp, which in itself would be a sufficient
defense, but I rest my defense rather on the ground that I did not do the
acts alleged. I say that Mr. Luckett is a credible witness throughout, and
if he be believed, not one allegation of the charges can stand.

Regarding the specification of drunken vomiting on November 4, 1862,
Summalt offered the following rebuttal. "The specification is sustained by the
evidence of Moses Bennett and Andrew Bothel and no other. And all that they
testify is so perfectly consistent with perfect sobriety on the occasion that I
called no witness to speak in reply. It only appears that I complained of being
sick (as I was) and vomited in consequence, as thousands of other sick men have
done before and have done since."

There were sixteen more pages of defense, following the general trends just
expressed. Apparently the court was not impressed, because Colonel Summalt
was found guilty of most of the charges and was dismissed from the service of
the United States on March 30, 1863. He had been in the army a total of seven
months. He made no application for a pension.

Chapter Twenty-Seven

Bad Blood in the 4th New York

COL. ALFRED W. TAYLOR

It is not hard to imagine the atmosphere in a regiment where the commander and his immediate junior cannot stand each other, where the commander is so drunk his hat falls off, and where the commander's brother-in-law threatens to shoot him.

The 4th Regiment of New York Infantry (also called the 1st Scott Life Guards) was mustered in at New York City in May 1861. The colonel was Alfred W. Taylor; the lieutenant colonel was John Dunn MacGregor. After brief training, they spent four weeks at Newport News, then for almost a year served at Havre-de-Grace, Maryland, thirty-five miles northeast of Baltimore.

After only five months of service, Colonel Taylor was tried for drunkenness on duty, conduct unbecoming an officer and a gentleman, and conduct prejudicial to good order and military discipline. The specifics occupy several pages. At Baltimore, at a review in early August, he was so drunk he was "unable to communicate in a proper manner with his superior officer" (this was Maj. Gen. John Dix). Taylor was also noted to be drunk in public in New York City on September 6, 7, 8, 9, 10, 11, and 12. The final dereliction is one couched in the phrases of a bygone era.[1]

"Colonel Alfred W. Taylor . . . did publicly receive and submit to gross indignities and personal chastisement in the presence of officers and soldiers of his regiment, at the hands of Captain Joseph Henriquez, of Company A of the same regiment, without resenting the same in a proper manner or taking any measures to punish the offense."

The 156 pages of testimony ranged far and wide over Taylor's life. He began his defense by entering into evidence his 1853 brevet major commission, in the 1st Regiment of New York Volunteers, which honored his service in the Mexican War, although it was never clear how this related to his drunken antics nine years later.

The court then turned to witnesses who spoke of events during General Dix's August 3, 1861, review of the regiment. Maj. J. Belger recalled, "Colonel Taylor seemed as if he had been taking a drink, but did not appear to be much under the influence." Capt. G. H. Camp said, "Colonel Taylor was not in a condition to command, because of intoxication. He failed in nearly every command that he gave at parade. He mixed the battalion up." Capt. Andrew Constantine tried to soften the blow, saying, "He talked rather fuddled, but was not so intoxicated as to stagger," but then added, "he was intoxicated when General Dix visited. He was not in a condition to communicate with a superior officer, nor did he stand very straight."

The parade of witnesses continued. Capt. Charles Kruger stated, "He was intoxicated. He attempted to drill the battalion, but could not get through with it; he was so drunk he could hardly draw his sword. The privates called out, 'There is the colonel, blind drunk. When we get drunk, we get bucked and gagged.'" Capt. John Downs agreed. "His action was loose and unsteady. He got the regiment in a circle. The men were laughing. He was drunk."

Lt. Joseph Thornton told the court, "Colonel Taylor was too much under the influence of liquor to give a command intelligibly," and Lt. Charles Rodman added, "He staggered and could not stand steady. He was so intoxicated he could not give a proper command. General Dix turned away from him."

General Dix himself, by now a veteran of forty-five years of military, political, and legal strife, was called to the stand. His views were clear. "Colonel Taylor was very much under the influence of liquor. I thought it useless to hold very much conversation with him. I afterwards gave him a friendly admonition." (A "friendly admonition" from Dix—senator, lawyer, general, and railroad tycoon—would have terrified most men into a lifetime of sobriety.) Witness Lt. James McDonald was somewhat indecisive: "Colonel Taylor was not sober, but he was not what I would call drunk."

Dr. George Lovejoy, assistant regimental surgeon, was not ambivalent. "Colonel Taylor was not in a condition to command. In attempting to draw his sword, he staggered." Quartermaster James Bayles stated, "He drank so much August 3 that he could not attend to his duties. I had seen him drink since, at Barnum's Hotel and at Havre-de-Grace." The witnesses, however, were not all in agreement. Adjutant W. H. Henriques told the Court:

> I saw Colonel Taylor August 3—his orders were judicious and intelligent. I did not think him drunk. I do not know how to define the word "drunk." He gave one wrong order, but he is not perfect as a drill officer. I saw no confusion and no problem drawing his sword. I never saw Colonel Taylor drink a glass of liquor, in fact, he ordered the liquor tent broken up when he returned to camp.

Three other witnesses gave Colonel Taylor support. Sgt. Maj. Charles A. Anderson said, "The colonel did not look intoxicated." Capt. Joseph Henriques recalled, "On August 3, he may have been drinking, but I don't think he was drunk. I knew him in Mexico and never saw him drunk." Capt. James Mooney added his somewhat qualified help to Taylor's case, saying, "He was under the influence of liquor, but not what I call drunk. He gave one incomplete order and then corrected it. His other orders were in a proper and intelligent manner."

The court now addressed the events in September in New York City. Corp. W. Fogarty said, "I saw Colonel Taylor in the liquor department of Russel and Company. He came in intoxicated and when he left he was drunk. He staggered considerably and used language usually heard on the street. His hat fell off and was placed back on his head by a helpful onlooker." John Vreeland, a citizen, recalled: "About 9:00 P.M., I saw him at Russel and Company. He got so tight he held onto the counter. He was in full uniform. His hat fell off and someone had to pick it up for him. I saw him two days later in Thompson Street. He was so drunk then he did not know where he was going."

Now, the court took up the matter of the unseemly scuffle with Captain Henriquez at Havre-de-Grace. Sergeant Major Anderson gave his evidence:

> Colonel Taylor was arriving on the boat. He came down the gangway with a lady on his arm. Captain Henriquez hurried up, very excited, followed by Dr. Wainwright, and shouted to the colonel, "You son of a bitch, you stole my sister. Oh, that I had my pistols here!" The lady got behind Colonel Taylor, her husband. The colonel held the captain by the jacket, kept him at arm's length, and said, "Arrest that man." No one did anything. Dr. Wainwright grasped the captain's arms, then the captain kicked the colonel several times. Colonel Taylor reached inside his jacket, I thought for a pistol, and I jumped in between the two men. Then Mrs. Taylor fainted, pulling her husband's arm away from his jacket, and the doctor dragged the captain away.
>
> I don't think the affair caused the colonel to lose favor in the eyes of the enlisted men. The men raised a pole in front of the colonel's tent and when they saw him coming, they gave him nine cheers.

The court convicted Colonel Taylor and sentenced him to be reprimanded by General Dix. The rather lenient sentence was because "the intoxication of Colonel Taylor was accidental . . . and a recurrence is not likely."

Maj. Gen. George B. McClellan reviewed the case and wrote a long critique. The high point was as follows:

> You found him not guilty of Drunkenness on Duty, but guilty of "being under the influence of intoxicating liquors while on duty." This is only a circuitous way of saying he was <u>drunk on duty</u>. Why should there be any difficulty in coming to the Saxon word "drunk," the major general finds it hard to conjecture. It is not intended by the 45th Article of War to punish only the officer who is <u>dead drunk</u>.

The court reconsidered its conclusion and recommended that Taylor be cashiered. The finding was approved by McClellan. But that hardly ended the matter. Over the next several months, there was a lively correspondence involving Taylor's lawyer (a man who can afford to raise his own regiment can afford a lawyer), the judge advocate general, the adjutant general of the army, and even the President.

Taylor's attorney, J. Morrison Harril, wrote to "His Excellency, the President," and argued several points. First, Harril suggested that McClellan had not written the review himself, but only "'some staff officer who acts for him." Then Harril made light of the August 3 drunken escapade in front of General Dix, suggesting that since it was only a parade, "not an occasion of serious service," the offense should be mitigated. Harril's closing request, using the finest legal logic, was that the entire affair should be remitted, since the colonel's drunkenness was "accidental."

On March 7, 1862, the judge advocate wrote to the adjutant general of the army, "The records arrived in this office without any statement by the reviewing authority [McClellan]. I note that some order was made on March 5, but I cannot tell what." From the loss of records, or from Mr. Harril's pleading, or perhaps from some invisible string-pulling, the adjutant general admitted defeat and recommended to the White House that Taylor be pardoned. This was done, and on April 15, 1862, General Dix received a memorandum from the adjutant general, restoring Taylor to command.

On April 16, Harril wrote to Maj. John F. Lee, the judge advocate, "I was with Colonel Taylor when he was restored to his regiment. His men cheered him as he entered camp. When he left for New York on business, the whole 800 men ranged along the road and gave him three cheers. The Republic will probably take no harm by his restoration."

Something must have gone awry after Taylor's triumphal return. Within three months, he resigned, and his archenemy, Lt. Col. John Dunn MacGregor was a full colonel, in command of the 4th New York.

PART THREE

Failure to Provide Proper Leadership

Chapter Twenty-Eight

Malaria and Hemorrhoids

COL. JOSEPH W. BELL

The career of Col. Joseph W. Bell left few traces in the record of his country, though he was entitled to call himself general at the end of his military career. He was the commander of the 13th Regiment of Illinois Cavalry, which was organized at Camp Douglas, Illinois, in the winter of 1861–62. Bell himself was mustered in December 1861, at the age of forty-seven. The regiment's first six months of service was in the District of Southeast Missouri, and in April 1862, Bell was commanding the Federal post at Pilot Knob.

There he received a letter of criticism from Maj. Gen. Henry Halleck, then in charge of the District of Missouri. The letter raised issues concerning contraband slaves, the protection of trains of supply wagons, and the protection of the countryside from marauders. Colonel Bell replied to General Halleck:

> General [Frederick] Steele ordered me to send escorts with the trains going south. It requires nearly all my forces to do so. My telegram to you was based upon evidence from soldiers in the camp. I may be in error, but my judgment is that the post needs heavier forces, if it needs any. I have made no arrests for secessionist proclivities, but I have sent in statements regarding each case, along with the names of the witnesses. In Colonel Welton's letter, he refers to Order No. 3, in regards to slaves coming within the lines. I find no such order on file at this post. I feel pained at your severe rebuke, but I wish to do my duty and await your orders.[1]

The next document in Bell's records is a Surgeon's Certificate, dated August 1862, written at Helena, Arkansas. The doctor certified that the colonel suffered from "malarious influence, intermittent fever, abdominal venous congestion, constant migrating pains, and hemorrhoids," and needed thirty days in a better climate to recuperate. The request for a leave of absence was rejected by General Steele, who noted that a Surgeon's Certificate valid for such leave must state that the leave is "necessary to save life."

Col. Joseph W. Bell wrote to Maj. Gen. Henry Halleck, "I feel pained at your severe rebuke." Bell was later found unqualified for cavalry service because of severe hemorrhoids. MASSACHUSETTS COMMANDERY MILITARY ORDER OF THE LOYAL LEGION, U.S. ARMY MILITARY HISTORY INSTITUTE.

Apparently, Bell went home anyway, as in September 1862 he wrote a long (and mostly illegible) letter absolving himself of blame for being away without leave, citing the pressure of "personal business."

The next month, the governor of Illinois received the following letter from Bell's superior. "Colonel Bell left this command August 10, 1862, without authority. He ceases to be an officer. Lieutenant Colonel [Theobald] Hartmann is a competent officer, but the disaffection long existent in the regiment would be best quieted, and its efficiency and usefulness restored, by the appointment of some other suitable person. I suggest combining several of the independent companies into the 13th Illinois Cavalry."

In November 1862, after he was dismissed, Bell traveled to Washington, D.C., where he must have exercised a talent for persuasion, as he arranged to be reinstated. Six months later, however, his military star was once again eclipsed. In April 1863, the 13th Illinois Cavalry was consolidated with several other units and Colonel Bell was designated as "supernumerary," in brief, having no job. This action may reflect the opinion of one of his superiors, who wrote, "The 13th Illinois Cavalry needs an efficient and permanent commander."

In May 1863, Bell again applied for a leave of absence, this time for twenty days, based upon a new Surgeon's Certificate, citing further trouble with hemorrhoids. This request was also disapproved: "If the Colonel is suffering severely from hemorrhoids he is unfit for cavalry service and should resign." Bell replied in a brief letter that "I am too sick for service and tender my resignation."

Brig. Gen. John Davidson, who reviewed the request on May 19, 1863, noted, "The resignation is approved, although I have charges against this officer for encouraging marauding—but it is so difficult to get court martials to do their duty that I recommend immediate acceptance of his resignation." After Bell's departure, the regiment continued to serve, mainly in Arkansas, until it was mustered out on August 31, 1865. Its combat experience may be estimated by the mortality among enlisted men: 21 soldiers died of wounds and 360 died of disease.

One final document appears in Colonel Bell's military service records. In October 1867, he was given the rank of brevet brigadier general for "gallant service in the war." It would appear that his maladies did not continue into civilian life, as there is no record of an application for pension.

Chapter Twenty-Nine

"The Blood Spurted"

COL. HENRY B. CARRINGTON

The first battle fought by the 18th Regiment of U.S. Infantry was against its own men, and its commander's first conflict was with the families of his own recruits. The 18th Infantry Regiment (U.S. Regular Army) was formed in July 1861 and organized at Columbus, Ohio. It did not leave the state until Christmas of 1861, when it moved into Kentucky.

The commander was Col. Henry B. Carrington, a Yale graduate, classical scholar, ardent abolitionist, and influential lawyer. His law partner was William Dennison, Ohio's Civil War governor. In 1857, Salmon P. Chase, Dennison's predecessor in the governor's house, asked Carrington to organize the State Militia. His success in this led to his appointment as state adjutant general. In 1861, with this background, Carrington was able to swiftly arm nine regiments of Ohio militia and send them to aid George McClellan in western Virginia. Carrington's reward was a commission as a colonel in the regular army and assignment as commander of the yet-to-be-organized 18th Infantry Regiment.[1]

With his well-known name, political connections and recruiting experience, he soon filled the approximately 900 spaces open in his new unit. In his speeches and public pronouncements, Carrington emphasized several points: service as a regular was somehow superior to service as a volunteer; as colonel, he would be a father to his men; because of his wise guidance, the 18th would be a model regiment; his soldiers' lives would be the best in the army; and under his leadership, only the highest moral tone would be allowed. The passage of nine months clarified Carrington's degree of success as a father to his regiment.

On April 7, 1862, the *Cincinnati Daily Commercial* devoted almost 3,000 words to the subject of the 18th Infantry. The editor began with the observation: "We frequently receive letters from soldiers making most bitter complaint about their officers. We do not question that these are often just, but they can seldom be published with probable advantage, and we generally put them aside as belonging to a department of the history of the war, the time for the publicity of which has not arrived." The editor concluded, however, that the hour was at hand to shine the light of day on some of these issues. The remainder of the feature story was devoted to letters by many men of the 18th Regiment, written in March and April of 1862.[2]

One man described how his lieutenant, at Lebanon, Tennessee, would get into a drunken fit and lash about with his sword. He cut off the tip of the elbow of Pvt. Michael Coon and laid open the elbow joint. A few days later the wounded arm had to be amputated.

A captain of the same company regularly got drunk, knocked his men down, and stamped on their heads. At other times, he took them by the throat, choked them, and called them "damned sons of bitches." One night, two sick soldiers had been allowed the privilege, by another officer, of standing near the fire. Captain "X" approached with a club and knocked the two men down, believing them not to be entitled to the comfort of warmth.

The letter writer noted that Colonel Carrington was rarely at the regiment and that Lieutenant Colonel Shepherd could not be approached or appealed to, except by the permission of the same captain who beat them. "Many of the men who were induced to join this regiment with falsehood and flattery now find themselves, not soldiers in the regular army, but regularly enslaved. A general discontent reigns through the camp, every man feels his yoke of bondage. Every man hates Captain "X" and no one will rescue us." The correspondent noted the daily prayers of loved ones at home, whose anxiety was that the sword of the Rebels would cut down the boys in blue, but opined that it would be more useful if the prayers were directed toward protecting the Union soldiers from their own "heartless and drunken commanders." The editors noted, "We would not publish the above unless we believed it to be substantially correct." A soldier of the 18th Regiment wrote from Nashville on March 12, 1862:

> I am not sick of saving my country or doing what I can to end this nefarious war, but I am heartily sick of the tyranics which I see inflicted on these injured and deceived men. Non-commissioned officers are reduced on the merest pretense, at the whim of an officer; men are tied up by the wrist and thumbs for the least offense, and all kinds of brutality are exercised by those having a little brief authority.

The same writer went on to describe a white-haired seventy-year-old recruit whose pitiful cries could be heard all over the camp, after he was tied up by Captain Wood.

The same writer continued, "An enlisted man is nothing but a dog to be kicked and cuffed about at the mercy of his master. If it should come to my turn . . . I think I should desert or commit suicide. The spirit is being so utterly crushed out of our men that they will be utterly unfit for battle."

Another private in the 18th Regiment wrote from Spring Hill, Tennessee, on March 27, 1862, "We had a great excitement here yesterday. A man was tied up by his wrist to a tree in front of the guard house. Some of the boys of the 9th

Col. Henry B. Carrington was a lawyer, politician, and scholar who turned a blind eye to the "barbarous system of punishment" administered by his subordinates. MASSACHUSETTS COMMANDERY MILITARY ORDER OF THE LOYAL LEGION, U.S. ARMY MILITARY HISTORY INSTITUTE.

Ohio and 2nd Minnesota saw it and came down in force and cut him down. He was again tied up and again cut down. Lieutenant Colonel Shepherd and other officers then went down to see what the trouble was and were greeted with sticks and stones." The officers of the 18th finally called out a company, whose bayonet charge drove back the Minnesota and Ohio boys.

A soldier wrote on March 30th from Columbia, Tennessee: "The other night, Captain Wood tied a man up by the heels so that he swung clear of the ground for 25 minutes. Then, when the poor fellow was half dead, his limbs numb and powerless, he tried to make him get up and walk. The man nearly died from the effects of this punishment. The men are almost in a state of mutiny, but the affair has been hushed up."

An outsider's view of Colonel Carrington's unit was presented in a long letter from a G. Tafel of the 1st German Regiment, originally printed in the
Cincinnati Volksblatt. After a panegyric upon the beauties of the spring landscape
at Camp Somerset, Tennessee, the writer then struck a more ominous note.

"The monotony of camp life was yesterday and the day before yesterday
broken in a very unpleasant manner. Occurrences of the most exciting character took place and it required but little to cause bloodshed. When I relate to you
the reasons for it, you will hardly believe that such barbarities can be practiced in
the 19th Century, and in the freest land on earth." Tafel related that he had heard
in Nashville of the "inhuman punishments" used by officers of the 18th Infantry,
but that it was an entirely different matter to see them with his own eyes.[3]

The 1st German Regiment was camped immediately beside the 18th Regiment. One morning the cry ran through the German camp that the officers of the
18th had again hung up several men. The day before a man had been punished
the same way, and Col. Robert McCook had ordered the man released, but on
this fresh occasion, McCook was absent and the torture proceeded undisturbed.

Upon a tree that marked the boundary between the two regiments, a man
was hung up by his wrists, so that he could barely touch the ground with his
toes. The soldier had recently served as a guard over men sentenced to hard
labor; his crime was that of having not been severe enough with his charges.
Near this unfortunate victim was another man staked out flat on the ground for
having visited the neighboring village without permission.

Men of the 9th Ohio and some Minnesota boys put a block of wood under
the toes of the suspended soldier, which relieved the pressure on his wrists.
Another more daring soldier took his knife and cut the rope that attached the man
to the overhanging limb. This deliverance brought such a cry of joy that the officers of the 18th came running, and ordered him strung up again. His order
brought "numerous expressions of disgust and sundry cries of disapprobation." The
lieutenant colonel of the 18th called the volunteers "sons of bitches" and knocked
the cap off of one volunteer's head and received "a shower of missiles" in reply.

The lieutenant colonel then ordered the guard of the 18th to load their
rifles and shoot any man who crossed the camp boundary. The adjutant of the
18th came to the headquarters of the German regiment to enter a protest, but
withdrew under a hail of stones.

At this point, Herr Tafel was summoned to Regimental Drill, but when he
returned later, he found that the Minnesota boys had cut the man down several
more times, whereupon the officers of the 18th ordered a bayonet charge into
the camp of his rescuers. The privates of the 18th, who had little heart for this
business, allowed their officers to get ahead of them, where, among the German
supply wagons, they received a variety of bruises and goose eggs.

The following day, the officers of the 18th hung five more of their men, this
time in the center of their camp, out of the reach of the other regiments. One man
was hung upside down by the heels off the ground "until the blood spurted from
his mouth and nose." Soldiers of the 18th demanded that the now-unconscious

man be cut down, but the lieutenant colonel posted a full company of men with loaded guns to surround the limp figure, who was not brought down until the regimental surgeon arrived and ordered it. "Today, the report becomes current that the abused man has died. I leave your readers to their own reflections."

Attached to Tafel's correspondence was a note by the editors of the *Volksblatt,* urging the German and English press to reprint his letter, in order that "the public may be reminded of the barbarous system of punishment which, to the reproach of mankind, is still perpetrated in the Army of the Great Republic, by officers who are even lower in the scale of creation than beasts."

Other letter writers bitterly observed that while they were in Tennessee, suffering repression and abuse, Colonel Carrington was safe at home with his wife and children in Columbus, Ohio.

The *Ohio State Journal* reprinted the following message from Colonel Carrington, which was sent from "Headquarters, 18th US Infantry, Columbus, Ohio." "To those in Ohio who have entrusted to my command their sons, I owe a debt of personal gratitude and for their satisfaction I will notice recent criticisms upon myself and my regiment."[4]

The colonel went on to explain that he was still in Ohio recruiting more men, as required by "Act of Congress, increasing the Regular Army," but that he expected to join his regiment in the very near future, where he would "unite the entire command and share its fortunes."

As to the reported torture of enlisted men, which he refered to as "alleged abuses," he loftily replied, "Army Regulations amply provide for the protection of all, whether soldiers or officers, and no one need doubt that the Regulations can, and will, be practically and effectively enforced."

These bland reassurances apparently satisfied the editor of the *Ohio State Journal.* Whether he was more impressed with the promises, or with Carrington's powerful political connections, the editor immediately rose to Carrington's defense: "The above card, concise and to the point, speaks for itself. There is not a man in Ohio who knows Colonel Carrington, who will doubt that he will deal to the extent of the law with officers, however high, who maltreat a soldier or violate Regulations."

The *State Journal* editors confidently concluded that Carrington's joining his regiment would "gladden hearts" and that "there will be court martials one of these days."[5] (The records of the National Archives, covering the years 1861 and 1862 indicate no courts-martial, of any type, for Colonel Carrington, Lieutenant Colonel Shepherd or Captain Wood. The statements of Carrington and of the newspaper editors appear, upon factual review, to be nothing but empty promises and political blather.)

More than newspapers and agonized mothers took an interest in the young men of the 18th Infantry. On April 14, 1862, the powerful Congressional Committee on the Conduct of the War asked for an inquiry into charges of "brutality," and a few days later Congressman Cyrus Aldrich wrote to Lorenzo Thomas, adjutant general of the army, asking for an end to mistreatment in this new regiment. A formal court of inquiry was convened and thousands of words recorded. One medical witness, Dr. Webster Lindsley, assistant surgeon, stated that hanging a man by his heels was "very harsh treatment" and that he had ordered such a man cut down. However, the line officers testified that the instances of privates being shot to death and slashed with swords were necessary treatments for recalcitrant recruits. The court concluded that there were no grounds for any charges against Colonel Carrington, and the matter was closed.[6]

Soon, larger and even more desperate issues occupied the minds of the men of the 18th Regiment. The same day that these letters appeared in the *Cincinnati Daily Commercial,* the 18th Infantry was engaged in the bloody near disaster at Shiloh, Tennessee.

Certainly, in the winter of 1861–62, Carrington had other things on his mind besides his officers' brutal treatment of his own soldiers. Confederate sympathizers in Ohio were active in an organization called the Sons of Liberty, and the colonel was equally vigorous in suppressing them, through heavy punishments meted out by military tribunals, conducted by the army. The sentences imposed upon the Sons of Liberty were later invalidated by the U. S. Supreme Court, since Ohio technically was not "in rebellion" and Carrington's tribunals had no legal standing. The legal shortcomings of the army tribunals were probably no secret to Carrington, an experienced lawyer and politician, but their lack of merit did not seem to have deterred him.

In November 1862, Carrington was made brigadier general of volunteers and was instrumental in raising 120,000 Indiana volunteers. In 1865 he was too sick to travel because of coughing up blood, but he recovered. The year after the war, he commanded the expedition that built the first road through the Bighorn country of Wyoming, and constructed Fort Kearny as part of the subjugation of the Sioux. In 1867 an accidental gunshot of the thigh, while on the march from Fort Casper, left him with a contracted scar that compressed the femoral artery and caused unpredictable collapse of the knee.

While this wound slowly healed, he served as professor of military science at Wabash College and began a productive writing career, which produced more than twenty books and dozens of articles, including one based on newly opened British archives detailing military operations in the American Revolution. Carrington returned to Indian affairs, and was soon embroiled in controversy with the headstrong Capt. William Fetterman, who denounced Carrington as "an incompetent commanding officer." (This insult was considerably blunted when Fetterman, who had announced that "a single company of Regulars could whip a thousand Indians," led his eighty-one man scouting party into an ambush, where he and every one of his troopers were killed.)[7]

In 1891 he headed an expedition that forced the Flathead Indians onto their new reservation in western Montana. Later he was official historian of the Legion of Veterans of Indian Wars. He died in Boston in 1912 of "senility," at the age of eighty-eight.

Chapter Thirty

"Shit in Your Breeches"

COL. CHARLES A. DE VILLIERS

Col. Charles A. de Villiers, despite the aristocratic ring of his name, established a minor record by having no less than thirteen specifications attached to the charge of conduct unbecoming an officer and a gentleman against him. He was the commander of the 11th Regiment of Ohio Volunteers, a unit mustered in at Camp Dennison, Ohio, in June 1861.[1]

A sixty-mile line drawn southeast from Columbus, Ohio, will reach the Ohio River, the border between Ohio and today's West Virginia. Here the Kanawha River, flowing northwest, enters the mighty Ohio, bringing the waters from the Kanawha Valley, a region roughly forty by eighty miles. About halfway up the valley is Gauley Bridge and, a little past that, Hawk's Nest, now the site of a state park. The 11th Ohio was ordered to the Kanawha Valley July 7; ten days later de Villiers was captured by Confederate forces.

This challenging period of captivity brought forth de Viller's better attributes. At Richmond's Harwood Prison, he buoyed the spirits of his comrades through astonishing feats of soldiers' drill and pantomimes of musket and broad-sword exercises. Soon, he bettered these accomplishments by escaping from prison, making his way through night marches to Norfolk, and, once there, assuming the guise of an elderly, nearblind Frenchman. So convincing was de Villiers that he was granted passage north, where he resumed command of the 11th Ohio.[2]

While he was away, his regiment saw action at Hawk's Nest, but was otherwise mostly confined to garrison duty. After his return, there were skirmishes on November 10 at Gauley Bridge and the following day at Cotton Mountain.

From then until the following April, the 11th Ohio was based at Point Pleasant, where the Kanawha and the Ohio join their waters. This relatively quiet period of garrison duty seems to suggest that there is truth in the adage, "The devil finds work for idle hands." It was certainly true for Colonel de Villiers, whose court-martial was convened February 26, 1862, at Charleston, which sits astride the confluence of the Elk and Kanawha Rivers. Colonel Hugh Ewing of the 30th Ohio presided.

It seems that Colonel de Villiers was impartial; he had conflict not only with his own men, but also with the secessionist civilians. On November 17, 1861, de Villiers took possession of seven head of cattle near Gauley Bridge. It was usual in seizing Confederate property to have it first declared contraband of war by a court of judicature. De Villiers simply seized the cattle (whose ownership is unrecorded, except that they were found in a nearby field), had them driven into town, sold them to Quartermaster E. H. Rice for $100, and put the money in his own pocket.

Right after Christmas, the colonel had arrested one James A. Lewis, a resident of the Kanawha Valley, and refused to release Lewis until he paid the colonel the sum of $11.50. At the same time, he seized two slaves, one belonging to a James H. Lewis and the other to William P. Hawkins, and refused to release them until he received $20. The total sum from these transactions, $31.50, also went into de Villiers's pocket.

On November 15, 1861, while still stationed at Gauley Bridge, de Villiers drew an order on John W. King, sutler of the 11th Ohio, for the sum of $410, claiming that the draft had been approved by the council of administration, which was not true. The sutler seems to have been stuck with this piece of worthless paper. Another angry voice was that of Lt. Col. N. W. Finzell of the 11th, who wrote to Brig. Gen. Jacob Cox, complaining that he had "received an ungentle-manly and dastardly insult from Colonel deVilliers when on dress parade."

Perhaps it was a matter of whose ox was being gored, but a contrary view was expressed on December 17, 1861, when a number of Point Pleasant citizens signed a petition praising Colonel deVilliers, citing his efforts to maintain order and enforce the law.

The most serious charge involving civilians was de Villiers's treatment of the property of a Point Pleasant lawyer, Mr. Henry J. Fisher. The witness for this charge was Mr. John W. English, another Point Pleasant attorney. "Colonel de Villiers summoned me and said he was supposed to arrest me, but would not just now. He demanded my political sentiments. I told him I had voted for secession. He then told me we must go to Mr. Fisher's house and open the safe. He knew that Fisher was away and that I had the key to the safe."

English then described the visit to the Fisher house, in which de Villiers opened the safe and took out about $300 in currency, as well as a considerable quantity of bonds, notes, and mortgages. De Villiers left the silverware in the safe, but kept the key. (Later, the silverware was gone, including a $130 silver coffeepot.)

English and de Villiers then visited the Fisher library, a room sixteen-by-eighteen-feet, with books from floor to ceiling. When de Villiers announced his intention of quartering his officers in the library, English volunteered to move the books to Fisher's office. The colonel forbade such a move. (During the stay of the 11th Ohio, all of the books disappeared.) Later, de Villier returned to the Fisher home and took all the sheets, towels, blankets, tablecloths, and napkins.

The colonel defended himself against these charges by blaming "Negroes," and in a passionate oration, concluded, "Can anyone guarantee the honesty of these Negroes?," a rather deft bit of blame-shifting and *non sequitur*. His case was not helped by an affidavit from Barbara Weiss, his former cook, who swore that de Villiers had told her that he had the key to Fisher's safe.

De Villiers's relationship with his own men seems to have been no better than his dealings with the citizens of Virginia.

Lt. N. S. McAbee of Company F testified that he had been acting adjutant during the combat of November 10–11, 1861, and had been carrying messages all night to the 1st Kentucky Infantry, which was protecting the right flank of the 11th Ohio.

> I had returned to our headquarters about 4:00 in the morning and sat down to rest when Colonel de Villiers came up to me and told me to carry a message to the 2nd Kentucky. I started to obey and he shouted, "Come, fly around, quick, spring." I told him that the springs were just about played out in me. The colonel replied in the presence of many officers, "Lieutenant, you are a coward. You have more shit in your breeches than you have in your guts. You had better resign and go home."

Colonel de Villiers then cross-examined the witness.

> Q. Was this not in a time of great excitement and in the heat of action?
> A. No, sir, I don't think it was. There had been considerable excitement earlier, but at that exact moment there was nothing worth mentioning.
> Q. Was this not at the time of the fight at Cotton Hill?
> A. It was afterward, sometime after any shots were fired.
> Q. Did not my order dispatch you on a dangerous service and did you not express an unwillingness to go?
> A. It was not dangerous, and I expressed no unwillingness.
> Q. Is Colonel de Villiers [referring to himself in the third person] a man when under excitement is in the habit of making use of violent and vehement language?
> A. He is.

On the same night as the hot words with the lieutenant, the colonel addressed the following words to Capt. Philander P. Lane of Company K: "Captain Lane, you are not fit to command a company. You are a coward and every man in your company is a coward. I ought to tear the captain's shoulder straps off your uniform." This little speech was made in the presence of a gathering of officers and enlisted men of the regiment.

The following month, Captain Lane called the colonel a scoundrel and circulated a petition asking that de Villiers resign. Lane was acquitted of these two charges, but convicted of failing to promote two sergeants recommended by the colonel.[3]

The colonel continued with his morale-building efforts, by giving a speech, in German, to some men of the 2nd Kentucky, in which he said, "Welcome, gentlemen, I am glad you have come. The officers and men of my own regiment are all cowards." The men of the 11th included many German-speaking soldiers, and they were not happy with their colonel's remarks.

This era of bad feeling continued. On December 5, Lt. J. E. Alexander, who was officer of the day, was taking his dinner at the Virginia House in Point Pleasant. Colonel de Villiers stomped in and demanded to know why the lieutenant was not with his company. Alexander tried to explain that he was officer of the day and therefore was not at his usual post. The colonel shouted, "I will take off your shoulder straps. I will have you court-martialed. You are not fit to be an officer." In the words of the court record, "The said Colonel de Villiers refused to hear any explanation, but continued his abusive, provoking and ungentlemanly language, all in the presence of numerous citizens, also officers and privates of the regiment aforesaid."

In early January, a Surgeon's Certificate described DeVilliers as having "a cold of the lungs, coughing up blood," but this was not enough to suppress the colonel's taste for administrative combat. On January 10, 1862, de Villiers, apparently getting wind of Captain Lane's petition and preferring of charges, called several members of Company K into his headquarters, forced the administration of an oath upon them, and questioned them closely for information which might enable de Villiers, in turn, to prefer charges against Lane. He was too late. The records still contain a telegram, classic in its brevity: "Arrest Col DeVilliers on charges preferred by Capt Lane. By order of Genl Rosecrans."

By mid-February 1862, de Villiers was under arrest and the 11th Ohio was commanded by Lt. Col. A. H. Coleman. Colonel de Villiers, although under arrest, advised a Corporal Elliott of Company K not to obey the orders of Coleman, orders which were issued at dress parade on February 15.

The final de Villiers action cited in the court charges occurred at a familiar location—the Virginia House. Earlier, de Villier had arranged for Pvts. William Wehe of Company B and Robert Frank of Company A to prepare a letter with "false and malicious" charges against Colonel Coleman. This letter de Villiers placed in an envelope addressed to Brig. Gen. William S. Rosecrans and, in the Virginia House, handed it to Brig. Gen. Jacob D. Cox.

An unusual turn of events in all this legal maneuvering was de Villiers's dispatch to General Cox on February 5 of a letter entirely in French. After the usual salutations, the colonel began, "Pardonné la liberté que j'ai prende, pour adresser ses quelques Lignes, si j'ai perdû votre amitié, au moin donnéz moi votre justice, et je suis persuadéz que vous est conût; pour celâ partout, Captain Lain. . . ." (Please excuse my taking the liberty of addressing a few lines to you. If I have lost your friendship, at least give me your justice. I am persuaded that you understand what is happening, Captain Lane. . . .) His point seemed to be that Cox should put Lane under arrest, as had been done to de Villiers.

De Villiers argued his case passionately. His final statement to the court may be of interest to students of analytical philosophy, oration, and debate, as it contains at least two separate errors in formal logic.

> The history of the world reveals but few men who did not possess some blemish of character, some weak point, that a critical, fault-finding cynic might justly condemn. Had others been as willing to conciliate and pardon, as they have been to censure and blame, I should not be this day required to stand at the bar of this honorable court. I confidently submit a soldier's honor and future reputation to the keeping of my peers.

His peers found him guilty of six of the thirteen specifications and sentenced him to be "dismissed [from] the service of the United States and forfeit all pay and allowances. And, the Court orders his property to be seized by the commanding officer of his post and held, subject to future and legal disposition."

The findings were reviewed and approved, with the exception of the forfeiture of property. That was referred to the U.S. district attorney for action. Two final entries bring de Villiers's records to a close. On March 15, 1862, a William Keaney wrote to the major of the 11th Ohio: "We have searched Colonel de Villiers' baggage and found items taken from Mr. Fisher." In April 1862, General Cox wrote his superior, "De Villiers is still under arrest. His relations to his regiment are most lamentable, and his return to his regiment would undoubtedly destroy its efficiency. His general reputation is that his statements are not to be relied upon, owing to a vivid imagination."

Today, the Gauley and New Rivers are meccas for whitewater rafters and other out-of-doors enthusiasts. Clad in white crash helmets and bulky orange lifevests, the water lovers squeal with delight as huge waves toss their rubber boats into the air. Above them, from the railing of the world's longest single-span steel arch bridge, skydivers leap into space and float toward the ground. One hundred thirty-five years ago, danger was a necessity, not a recreation, and not the least of the dangers were thieves and liars like Colonel de Villiers. Sadly, his capacity for fabrication and dissimulation, which served him so well in a Confederate prison, was turned toward less noble ends in his position as a commander.

Chapter Thirty-One

"Unceasing and Tyrannical Abuse"

COL. JAMES FAIRMAN

James Fairman, a thirty-seven-year-old New Yorker, spent his brief Civil War career at the center of several apparently self-generated storms. He joined the 10th New York Volunteers as a captain of Company B in late April 1861. Four weeks later he was discharged. He spent the rest of that year trying to raise the 4th Excelsior Regiment for Dan Sickles, but failed in his recruiting efforts. He then turned his attention to the 96th New York, which, under the name of McComb's Plattsburg Regiment, was organized in early March 1862, and, after three weeks of training, joined McClellan's Peninsular Campaign, with Fairman as colonel.

The spring of 1862 found the 96th New York at every step of that long and ill-fated march up the Peninsula: Yorktown in April, Williamsburg in May, Seven Pines as June began, Richmond as June faded into July, then Malvern Hill, then a miserable month huddled at Harrison's Landing. But a perusal of Colonel Fairman's court records, where there is no mention of these battles, might give the casual reader the impression that the major conflict was within the regiment, rather than with the Confederates.[1]

The court-martial record contains four charges and thirteen specifications, and was apparently held during the siege of Yorktown, thus tying up thirteen senior officers while the men of the 96th squabbled.

Under the heading of "conduct prejudicial to good order," Fairman was charged with suspending Capts. C. H. Burham, Alfred Weed, and Joseph H. Nichols from the command of their companies "without right or cause." He was also charged with suspending from rank and duty Lt. Thomas M. Newman "without right or cause." In the case of Newman, the colonel was charged not only with suspending the lieutenant, but with expelling him from the camp of the 96th and throwing his baggage after him.

The second charge, "contempt and disrespect toward his commanding offi-cer," was based on his public statements about Brig. Gen. William H. Keim, who Fairman described as a "Pennsylvania Dutchman, who knows nothing, and got his appointment through political influence." The third charge, "breach of arrest," reflects Fairman's behavior after being put under arrest by General Keim and ordered to stay within the boundaries of the camp of the 96th, which was then near Young's Mills, Virginia. Fairman left his camp and stayed out all night.

The charge of "conduct unbecoming an officer and a gentleman" contains a half dozen specifications. The colonel called Capt. D. L. Lockerby "a fool" while the captain was drilling his company, and called Capt. Davins Parsons "a jackass" while Parsons was similarly occupied. At another public gathering, Fairman "in a loud voice," called both Parsons and Capt. Hiram Eldridge "jackasses." Other charges included Fairman urging Lt. John E. Green to prefer false charges against Captain Nichols, and giving Lt. John S. Hurdie fifteen minutes to either resign his commission or be put before an examining board.

The testimony on these points occupies seventy-five pages and is often tedious, but a few citations will give the tenor of the Fighting 96th.

Lieutenant Newman was sick and missed dress parade. The colonel suspended him from rank but restored him the next morning, without explanation. On another occasion, the lieutenant, who had a pass, was two hours late in returning, having been lost in the woods. On arriving at camp, he stopped at Captain Burham's tent, but the captain was under arrest and could not speak to Newman. Next, Newman reported to Captain Weed, who said that he was under orders not to recognize Newman as an officer and to put him out of camp, along with his baggage.

After being cast out, Newman then went to brigade headquarters, where he stayed two days, until General Keim ordered him back to the 96th. Fairman refused entry to Newman, stating that his commission was invalid, even though it had been signed by the governor of New York.

Many witnesses testified that the turmoil and emotional uproar had a bad effect on the morale of the enlisted men and that many of them were deserting. Other witnesses described Fairman's orders at parade as hard to understand, and deplored his custom of calling the troops "jackasses" if they got in a muddle while drilling.

It seems that Captain Burham was very popular with his company and, when Colonel Fairman suspended the captain, the men refused to draw their rations. Fairman subsequently said to the acting company commander, "Tell Sergeant Hill to go and draw the rations, and if he refuses, shoot him on the spot."

A multitude of witnesses confirmed the original charges, though other witnesses contradicted them. The final decision of the court was that the colonel was guilty of none of the charges, but was guilty of the fifth specification of the first charge (expelling Lieutenant Newman) and of the sixth specification of the fourth charge (throwing the lieutenant's baggage out of the camp), but "attached no criminality to either and therefore not guilty." Having found Colonel Fairman not guilty, the court then sentenced him to be reprimanded by the brigade commander.

The case was reviewed by Brig. Gen. Silas Casey, who was quick to note the logical inconsistency in such a decision and commented, "These words of the Court are disapproved, as guilt and a certain degree of criminality are always co-existent. This is a contradiction in terms. Inasmuch as the accused was found guilty of no charges, the Court was unauthorized in pronouncing any sentence. Colonel Fairman will be released from arrest and returned to duty."

This decision settled nothing, and the ill will, if anything, grew worse. Later in April, a petition to remove Colonel Fairman, signed by eight captains and fourteen lieutenants, all of the 96th, was submitted to General Keim. "The colonel abuses us upon battalion drill in the presence of our men, using language and epithets both ungentlemanly and unofficerlike." The petition went on to cite the forced resignation of two lieutenants, the troops' dissatisfaction and frequent desertion, the demoralizing effect of suspending officers while they are drilling their men, and, finally, of Fairman's boasting to the brigade commander of the proficiency of his regiment, when, because of having had only ten days to drill with arms, the men were still quite inexperienced, and they knew that they were. Further complaints included Fairman's sleeping out of camp without authorization and his "unceasing and tyrannical abuse." The petition concluded, "We beseech of you that we be relieved of his command."

The record does not reflect the events of the next four months or whether the petition had the desired effect, but on September 25, 1862, Colonel Fairman was discharged from the army. By then, the regiment was at Fortress Monroe, recovering from the effects of Robert E. Lee's tactical brilliance, and from its own internal dissensions. Fairman did not apply for a pension, and his life after 1862 is absent from the military records.

Chapter Thirty-Two

"Annoyed to Death by Old Soldiers"

COL. JOSIAH HARLAN

Having a regiment named after oneself is no guarantee of a quiet term of office. Harlan's Light Cavalry, organized at Philadelphia under the authority of the secretary of war in September 1861, was commanded by Col. Josiah Harlan. Only four months after he assumed his new post, he was court-martialed on five different charges. The first was "habitual neglect of duty," in which it was charged that he had never attended a dress parade, that he had been at only one regimental inspection, and that he had never instructed any of his officers or men in any aspect of military science or tactics. Further, he had failed to see that entries were made into the Regimental Letter Book.[1]

The second charge was violation of the 45th Article of War. The specifications were that he had been too drunk to perform his duty on November 18, 19, and 20, and December 18, 1861. On December 24, he "exposed himself in a state of intoxication to the officers and enlisted men in his command."

The third charge was conduct unbecoming an officer and a gentleman. It was alleged that Colonel Harlan had told the regimental quartermaster, S. H. Jacobs, that Quartermaster Tallmadge was "a liar," and that Harlan had said of Lt. James D. Mahan, "Oh, yes, he is the damned fool that cannot pronounce his own name, 'tis Mahone, not Mahan." On another occasion, he said to Capt. William H. Seip, "Now, sir, if another horse gets loose from your line, you had better have a rope around your neck," while a few days later he had words for Maj. George Stetzel, when that man reported for orders as field officer of the day. "What in hell do you report to me for? What is your American way of doing business in camp? I know all about the English service, but nothing about your American way of camp service."

When Capt. Robert B. Ward reported for duty as officer of the day, Harlan was reported to have said, "What do you report to me for? As an old officer, you ought to have better sense. Why in hell don't you report to Major

144

[Noah] Runyon? All of you are damned fools. Am I to be annoyed to death by old soldiers? You have turned out to be as big a fool as the rest of them."

The fourth charge was violation of the 39th Article of War. Capt. John B. Loomis had returned from recruiting duty and presented a bill for $350 for expenses. Harlan said, "Take this bill back and make it out at least $200 more," "thereby persuading the said Loomis to embezzle or misapply."

The fifth and final charge was violation of the 53rd Article of War, in which Harlan had given the watchword, "to six different persons not entitled to receive it, said persons being officers, servants, citizens, and Negroes."

The trial record contains a most unusual document, addressed to the colonel and signed by the lieutenant colonel, two majors, nine captains, and sixteen lieutenants:

> Charges and specifications of a most serious character are about to be preferred against you by the officers of the regiment. Although we have no doubt as to the result of a court martial, we are satisfied it would have the desired effect, viz: your removal. But sir, as it is not our desire to heap upon you any further disgrace than is necessary to the accomplishment of our purpose, we hereby afford you the opportunity of tendering your resignation, and we hereby apprise you, that your conduct toward us and toward the men has been such, as to force us to leave no stone unturned to remove you from the Regiment. With the expression of the hope that our reasonable request will be speedily acceded to, we subscribe ourselves below, etc. etc.

In addition to this document, there were 157 pages of additional testimony, including a description of a mass meeting in which the officers held nominations for the posts to be filled when the colonel departed and the officers would have a chance to move up the promotion ladder. Much of the recorded proceedings is a wearisome belaboring of the points raised in the charges originally listed, punctuated by testimony that borders on low farce.

Samuel A. Morehead, farrier (horse shoer) for the regiment, was called for the defense.

> Q. [by Colonel Harlan] During the three days of the march, 18th through 20th November, 1861, through Washington City to Annapolis, did you often see me through the day?
> A. I did.
> Q. How did I appear to be employed during the march?
> A. You were employed seeing that the regiment was getting along as well as it could, part of the time in front of the regiment and part of the time in the rear.
> Q. Did you think I was drunk at any time during the march?

A. No.

Q. Do you think you could have known if I was drunk?

A. I think I could.

Q. Are you acquainted with Lieutenant James D. Mahan of your company?

A. I am, since he joined the company. Not before.

Q. Since you have been in the company together, do you know of anything against his character?

A. He told me one day that he had had a yellow girl with him during the night.

Q. Has Mr. [sic] Mahan ever talked with you about inviting me to dinner?

A. He told me that he had made a dinner and had invited Colonel Harlan there to make him drunk, to show the officers he would get drunk, so that they could prefer charges against him.

Q. [by the court] Who was present at the conversations with Lieutenant Mahan?

A. No one but him and myself.

Q. How came you to be engaged in this conversation with Lieutenant Mahan?

A. I went into his tent and he told me he was afraid he was burned and asked me what would be a remedy.

Q. When did this conversation occur?

A. About the 16th of December.

Q. Is he accustomed to talk with you familiarly and confidentially?

A. He has frequently.

Q. [by Colonel Harlan] Are you the farrier or the horse doctor?

A. I am the farrier.

Q. [by the court] What did you understand Lieutenant Mahan to mean when he said "he was afraid he had been burned"?

A. I understood him to mean that he was afraid he had contracted a venereal disease.

Q. Does your practice as a farrier include that of venereal diseases?

A. No, it does not.

After the conclusion of the testimony and statements by the accused, the court-martial board found Harlan guilty on about half of the specifications and sentenced him to be suspended from rank and pay for six months.

The trial record was then reviewed by Maj. Gen. John E. Wool, who was greatly distressed by what he saw. "In reviewing these proceedings, it was discovered with regret that a combination was formed . . . with a determination and persistency . . . seldom, if ever, witnessed in the Army of the United States, to remove their colonel from his regiment." Wood further noted:

The dinner given to him by Lieutenant Mahan, one of the principal witnesses against him, to get him intoxicated, so that charges might be pressed for intemperance, a combination of officers, whose conduct was no less insubordinate than dangerous to the discipline of the army . . . would not fail to subvert every rule and principle . . . that should govern a man of honor.

The sentence of the Court is disapproved and remitted. Colonel Harlan will reassume command of his regiment. It is not to be understood that it is intended to encourage neglect of duty, harsh treatment to officers or intemperance; on the contrary, the object is to prevent a greater evil: the combination of officers who would leave no stone unturned to force commanders from the service. Had the officers in question made themselves acquainted with the Rules and Articles of War, it is not believed they would have ventured upon so perilous a course and so dangerous to themselves and to the discipline of the regiment.

General Wool was kind enough not to invoke the 7th Article of War, which states that any officer or soldier who begins or joins in a mutiny shall be put to death.

Colonel Harlan may have escaped the wrath of his colleagues, but not the effects of bacteria. In July 1862, a Surgeon's Certificate described him as debilitated from diarrhea. He was mustered out of the army the following month at the age of fifty-seven.

Chapter Thirty-Three

Bad Water or Bad Faith?

COL. GEORGE S. HAYS

The trial of Col. George S. Hays, of the 8th Pennsylvania Volunteer Infantry, was a tortuous search for the truth. Even today, readers may differ as to whether it was found. He was charged with neglect of duty: "On the march from Tunstall's Station to Dispatch Station, along the Richmond and West Point Railroad, he did allow his regiment to become scattered and disorganized in defiance and contempt of written orders and repeated instructions." The trial was in early June 1862.[1]

The brigade commander was Brig. Gen. John F. Reynolds, who, in September 1861, had been placed in command of the 1st, 2nd, 5th, and 8th Pennsylvania Volunteer Regiments. As an old regular, he was disgusted by the pillaging by his troops at Dranesville, Virginia, in October 1861, and he hoped to have the offenders hanged. In December 1861, he wrote to his family of his despair over making volunteers into soldiers. In late May 1862, Reynolds marched his men from Falmouth into Fredericksburg and for two weeks was its military governor. His tight control over his troops won the begrudging respect of the citizens. Reynolds was not a man to be trifled with. The prosecution opened with his testimony.

> The route of march was along the railroad tracks. I observed many of the 8th Pennsylvania Volunteers sitting by the side of the road playing cards. Stragglers so numerous I thought something was wrong with the regiment. They were mixed in with the other regiments. I rode to the head of the column, or what I could find of it. I could find the colonel nowhere. I did find Lieutenant Colonel [Duncan] Oliphant with a few of his men around him. I learned that Colonel Hays had preceded his regiment to Dispatch Station. I sent my adjutant general to find Colonel Hays and place him under arrest. I then halted the brigade and got the regiment together in something like order. My written orders regarding this march were totally disregarded by Colonel Hays.

Appearing next for the prosecution was Capt. Charles Kingsbury.

We overtook the 8th Pennsylvania and could not find the colonel. We were told he was in the rear. I went about half a mile and found the adjutant, the only officer I could find to deliver an order to. He also thought the colonel was in the rear. I still could not find the colonel, but I did find Captain Gallope with 15 or 20 men and I sent him forward to put a guard across the road until we could get the regiment together again. A mile further on, I found Lieutenant Colonel Oliphant with about 50 men. When I found Colonel Hays, he told me he was not well and had come on ahead. He stated that he had placed Colonel Oliphant in charge. The regiment was scattered over four miles. I saw six or eight officers walking together with hardly an enlisted man near them. Later, Colonel Oliphant got them together as much as possible.

The third witness was Lieutenant Colonel Oliphant.

Colonel Hays said he was going to General Reynolds' headquarters. He told me to carry out any orders that might arrive. Soon orders came to move out and I put the regiment into the line of march behind the 1st Regiment. When they halted, we were halted, too, but in a place without shade or water. Colonel Hays said he was unwell and asked me to repeat his orders to the men as it affected his head to speak in a loud voice. The regiment became very scattered. I assumed that the colonel was along the line of march. I did not understand that the regiment was turned over formally to me. Colonel Hays gave no actual orders. He did not inform me that he was going to leave.

Four more witnesses spoke for the prosecution. Sergeant Major [J. Lind] Ingraham stated, "I fell out of the line of march, but the colonel said nothing to me." Sgt. Robert Minor recalled, "I was lying by the side of the road. The colonel asked if I was sick. I said I had a headache. He said not to hurry myself, as someone of my build could have sunstroke." Pvt. J. Greishaber testified that it was very hot but that he was able to march. "The colonel saw that I was behind and told me to take my time." Pvt. T. S. Wells stated, "Two of us were sitting by the side of the railroad. The colonel said if a train came along to get on it and catch up with the rest of the regiment." Here the prosecution rested, and defense witnesses appeared.

Dr. Lewis Read stated, "Colonel Hays had been sick the night before and looked unwell on the day of the march. As soon as we got to the camp, I prescribed for him." Pvt. Reuben Hand remembered, "I heard Colonel Hays tell Lieutenant Colonel Oliphant, 'If I am not back in time, take over the command.'"

Dr. F. S. Williams testified: "The day before this march, we had been on a long march with the cavalry. Many of the men had diarrhea from the heat and from drinking too much water. Nearly half the regiment had diarrhea. I told the colonel not to march them fast in the heat. They can't take it."

Lt. Col. Henry McIntire of the 1st Pennsylvania stated, "It was a hot day. In the railroad cuts it was as hot as I have ever seen it. The men straggled from fatigue and not for any other reason."

Colonel Hays defended himself as follows. "I did not consider myself in command that day. I was very unwell. Any orders I gave were not from any military duty, but from my professional knowledge and a view to nursing the men along. I believe I succeeded admirably, judging by how few went to the surgeon the next morning."

The court-martial board found Colonel Hays not guilty. His verdict was reviewed by Brig. Gen. Truman Seymour, who strongly disagreed: "The proceedings of the Court in the case of Colonel G. S. Hays, 8th Regiment PRVC, are disapproved. There is abundant evidence that his regiment was in a state of disorganization on the march from Tunstall's and for that condition the colonel of the regiment should be held responsible."

Second-guessing, which is the privilege of students of history, suggests that the regiment probably had a bacterial dysentery from drinking contaminated water the day before (certainly common in most wars), and that rapid marching in high heat, while dehydrated from diarrhea, could indeed have been harmful. On the other hand, Colonel Hays did not clearly relieve himself from duty, nor directly procure a Surgeon's Certificate to do so, and Reynolds's despair at enforcing discipline in volunteers had a real basis in experience.

Chapter Thirty-Four

Friends in High Places

COL. MICHAEL K. LAWLER

At the age of forty-seven, Col. Michael Kelly Lawler, commander of the 18th Illinois, was still handy with his fists. In January 1862, he was tried on some remarkable charges, with an even more remarkable result. The trial, held at Cairo, Illinois, concerned five charges with a total of twelve specifications. "At Camp Mound City, Illinois, Colonel Lawler did, on the second day of October, 1861, knowingly permit Private Robert Dickman, of Company G, to be taken by the soldiers of his command, and, without trial or sentence by a general court-martial, or other competent authority, to be hung by the neck until dead."

This apparent aiding and abetting of a lynching only began the litany. On August 28, 1861, Colonel Lawler compelled Corp. Thomas Day and Pvt. Edward Burns to fight a fistfight, while the colonel stood by with drawn sword, "to prevent interference with said fight, which was a most brutal and demoralizing affray." On September 10, 1861, several of Lawler's troublemaking soldiers were in the guard house. He sent them a present: a bottle of whiskey, laced with ipecac, a powerful emetic, which caused intense vomiting and "dangerous and severe illness." Around September 15, 1861, Colonel Lawler did "strike and beat with his fist, Private Allen Brock, of said 18th Regiment, and other soldiers of his command."

In early October, Colonel Lawler's troops became troublesome to the citizens of Cairo. Lawler ordered his officers to police the streets of the city, "and bring to their quarters all soldiers belonging to said 18th Regiment, and to knock down all those who refuse to come peaceably." The same day, Capt. S. H. Wilson was having some trouble with Pvts. Patrick Wilson and John Dwyer. The colonel told the captain to knock them down. The captain argued with Lawler, who then offered to knock the captain down.[1]

On payday at the end of August 1861, Lt. M. B. Kelly had a rude shock; he found that his colonel had marked him on the muster roll as "resigned, intending thereby to fraudulently deprive said lieutenant of his office and pay."

While at Bird's Point, Missouri, in June 1861, Colonel Lawler caused to be placed on the roster of Company H, the names of Pvts. John F. Hopkins,

William Hawkey, Edward Farr, John Filkey, and Andrew T. Finnell, "when, in fact, to the said Michael K. Lawler's knowledge, the said privates had previously mustered into the United States service, May 28, 1861, in Company G."

On November 4, Lt. Scanlan, with a loaded pistol in his hand, compelled Private Rice, also of the 18th Illinois, to "dance, mark time and perform other compulsory movements, and threatened to shoot him if he failed to obey said tyrannical orders." It was charged that Lawler watched these proceedings with approval. In December 1861, Lawler appointed his own son-in-law, Patrick Lawler, as captain of Company D, when he knew Patrick Lawler to be "notoriously incompetent to perform the duties of said office."

In June 1861, as the regiment was forming, the majority of the officers petitioned that one Reverend Babbitt, a Protestant, be appointed as chaplain. Instead, Lawler, without consulting any of his staff, placed Father Louis Lambert, a Catholic priest, in that post. What was the background of this colonel, who, from the charges preferred against him, seems to have run the regiment as an Irish fraternity? He was born in County Kildare and came to the United States when he was age two. The family settled in Gallatin County, Illinois, where, in time, Michael Lawler married the daughter of a large landowner and was farming on a considerable scale by 1850. During the Mexican War, he distinguished himself as a captain of the 3rd Illinois, in the march from Vera Cruz to Mexico City. After the hostilities, he returned to Shawneetown, the county seat, where he added a general store to his holdings. In 1861 he and his regiment were mustered in by Capt. Ulysses S. Grant.

The court-martial board seems to have had little comment upon the "lynching." While it was true that Dickman was hanged, it was for the murder of William Evans; the irregularity was that the hearing and sentencing was by a regimental court-martial, not a general court-martial, in clear violation of the regulations. On the other issues, however, the court was less sympathetic to Lawler; it found him guilty of several of the charges and dismissed him from the service. The case then went to Maj. Gen. Henry W. Halleck for review. He took a different view of these matters.

> The evidence shows that irregularities have occurred in mustering, and in the way of drunkenness, punishments, et cetera; also, that through probable fear of a mob, certain improprieties were not stopped, and no efforts were made by Colonel Lawler, either for aid and support from other stations or turning out his own command to put down insubordination.
>
> Colonel Lawler was improperly charged and found guilty of violating the 87th Article of War. The accused objected to his being tried upon said charge, but the Court overruled said objection, tried and found the accused guilty of violating said Article of War, which refers exclusively to the powers of courts-martial.

Col. Michael Kelly Lawler sent a gift to the drunks in his guard house: a bottle of whiskey laced with ipecac, a violent emetic. MASSACHUSETTS COMMANDERY MILITARY ORDER OF THE LOYAL LEGION, U.S. ARMY MILITARY HISTORY INSTITUTE.

Halleck raised further objections, which, from a vantage point 130 years away, seem more like quibbling over legal fine points. He thought there was not enough evidence to sustain the "drawn sword" and "knocking down" charges. He held it "highly improper" for charges to be accumulated over a five-month period and pointed out that charges should be tried promptly or not at all.

Halleck was even more concerned that the court read most of the charges and specifications to the witnesses, as it could have coached them regarding time and details and "instructed them in the matter upon which they had been called to testify." He also noted that the records failed to account for the absence of seven members out of thirteen during the course of the trial. Halleck disapproved the sentence of the court and restored Lawler to duty.

Perhaps Halleck had noted that war was fighting, and that Lawler was a fighter. Whatever his reasons, Halleck sent Lawler back to his regiment where, a few weeks later, he was wounded at Fort Donelson. The ball passed through his left forearm, cutting the muscles so badly that he could not hold a hairbrush. Since he was left-handed, his ability to hold a sword or a pistol was greatly impaired. Furthermore, the cannonade at Fort Donelson left him permanently deaf, and, according to later pension records, "softened his brain." Lawler returned to Illinois and, after only two months of recuperation, was back on duty at Shiloh.

An exploding shell barely missed him at Champion Hill. Soon afterward, he was breveted a brigadier general, but illness plagued him. In July 1863, he had hepatitis and diarrhea, and the doctor prescribed a month's leave. In December 1863, he was sent home for two months because of "fever." In January 1864, he was declared unfit for duty because of tonsillitis and bronchial inflammation.

In spite of the wear and tear on his body, he served brilliantly at the siege of Vicksburg, capturing 1,100 Confederate soldiers, and was employed in brigade and divisional command in Louisiana and Texas.

After the war, he wrote in his memoirs, "I have come home to Illinois to await the last roll call," but seventeen years passed before his final summons, years that he filled with buying and selling horses, always his personal passion. In early 1882, he began to fail and in July of that year, his wasted body was wrapped in a winding sheet, the traditional shroud of his Irish ancestors, and taken to the Hickory Hill graveyard near Equality, Illinois, where he awaits the final reveille.[2]

Chapter Thirty-Five

Baa Like a Sheep

LT. COL. HENRY L. POTTER

Dan Sickles's famous command was the Excelsior Brigade, composed of the 70th through 74th New York Volunteers. The 71st Regiment was raised by George B. Hall and Henry L. Potter, and it was the thirty-five-year-old Lieutenant Colonel Potter who was court-martialed in March 1862 on three charges and thirty-two specifications. The first charge, "conduct prejudicial to good order and military discipline," contains such misbehavior as permitting his quarters to be the scene of excessive drinking, being in an altercation with his own officers, issuing improper orders, being unable to command, breaking arrest, causing a riot and bloodshed, calling a subordinate "a god damned whorehouse pimp," and assaulting a sergeant with his sword. The second charge, being drunk on duty, contained the same specifications as the first charge.[1]

Conduct unbecoming an officer and a gentleman included such mischief as grappling with two of his officers, violent and profane language, causing a riot that resulted in broken bones, inciting a mutiny, and failing to quell a mutiny. The full text of the charges covers many pages and lays out, in painful detail, a wild night of rioting—by officers. The charges were preferred by Col. William Dwight of the 70th New York and by Lt. A.M. McCune of the 71st.

After the charges were read before the court, Colonel Potter challenged six members of the court-martial board. The first six challenges were somewhat routine, based on the officers' being of inferior rank to Colonel Potter. Thus, Capts. E. G. Jackson, J. F. Littlefield, J. N. Oakley, and Majors J. D. Moriarty and Williams Stevens withdrew. Potter then challenged Lt. Col. Charles Berteese for "personal differences and unfriendly feelings." He, too, withdrew. After the trial board was filled again, Potter then objected that the three charges and thirty-two specifications were "vague and ill-defined." The court was unimpressed, overruled his objection, and began testimony. Maj. John Tolen recalled the night of the uproar.

> I went to bed early. The assistant surgeon came to me and said, "There is a row among the officers and someone will be killed." I called out

the men and formed companies. When we arrived at the commotion, Captain [Edward] Power announced that he was in command as he was Officer of the Day. Colonel Potter announced that as colonel, he was in command, and I announced that I was in command since the colonel was indisposed and I outranked Captain Power.

I ordered everyone to their quarters; I dressed the companies back in column by platoons, marched them up the street and back in retreat. Colonel Potter, Captain Power, and Lieutenant [Thomas] Leigh were in a fresh altercation, and I ordered them to their tents. I then met the Officer of the Guard, who was drunk. I sent him to his tent, under guard, and appointed Lieutenant Claftin as Officer of the Guard.

The defendant, Colonel Potter, now cross-examined the witness.

Q. Could it not have been nervous excitement and fatigue, rather than drunkenness?
A. I might have been mistaken.
Q. Are there officers in the regiment who are unfriendly to me?
A. I think so.
Q. What has been my character for sobriety?
A. Better than most of the officers. I have seen you drunk on only three occasions in these ten months.
Q. Was there any disturbance earlier?
A. Only loud speeches, as a sword was presented at the door of Colonel Potter's tent.
Q. Had there been previous difficulty?
A. Colonel Potter was already under arrest by order of General Sickles.

Next, Capt. Thomas Glover testified.

There was a large crowd and I saw Colonel Potter chasing Lieutenant [Alexander] McCune. I grabbed them both and said, "For God's sake, stop this!" I took McCune to Colonel Hall's tent and thrust him in. I then returned to Colonel Potter and told him, "This is disgraceful and must be stopped. I will assist you." Colonel Potter answered, "I'll show who commands the regiment, [Colonel Hall was apparently absent.] and it's not that little whorehouse pimp" I was then knocked down by a blow which loosened five of my teeth.

When I got to my feet, Captain Knowland's company was there, there had a stabbing, and everyone was very excited. Colonel Potter ordered Lieutenant Leigh to go to his tent, but Leigh replied that he had been ordered to go to the beach. [The regiment was camped at Sandy Point, Maryland.] Colonel Potter began shouting,

"I'll show those God damned sons of bitches who is in command!" and then he ordered a company to charge into the crowd, but Major Tolen stopped that.

I then went to Dr. [George] McAllister's tent to see about my face. He was gone. Then I went to Dr. J. J. McGowan, but he was under arrest, and sent me back to Dr. McAllister. I then went to my own tent and tended to my own face. It was the colonel's orderly who loosened my teeth.

I thought Colonel Potter was drunk. I have never seen a man so excited. Sweat ran from every pore. His clothing was thrown off so that the underclothing showed. Whether it was excitement or drunkenness I cannot say, but he was unfit for duty. The witnesses to this brawl were about eight officers and 300 men.

The next witness was Captain Paul Bradlee.

When I arrived, Colonel Potter had his hat off. There were swords out and Colonel Potter was shouting, "Cut him down, God damn him, cut him down!," referring to Lieutenant Leigh. Major Tolen, Colonel Potter and the Officer of the Day were all claiming to be in command. Major Tolen then appointed me Officer of the Day and I spoke with Colonel Potter.

Captain Power believed that the colonel had cut Power's son and also one of Power's soldiers, even though the affair was between officers. I made Captain Power and Colonel Potter converse, to clarify these matters.

Now it was the turn of the defrocked officer of the day, Capt. E. W. Power, who began:

At 7:00 p.m., I attended a presentation of a sword to Lieutenant [Benjamin] Franklin, by his command; things were quiet. About 10:00 p.m. I heard a noise; I went toward it and when I arrived, I heard Colonel Potter shout at Captain [William] Greene, "You know it is not so, God damn you!" Then Lieutenant McCune appeared and Colonel Potter called him "A God damned son of a bitch little whorehouse pimp." McCune began to run and Potter chased him; then McCune fell over a tent rope and Potter fell on top of him. McCune began to shout, "Take him off me." I lifted the colonel, but my sabre caught between my feet and I fell on the colonel.

The colonel then got hold of my sword and I grappled his arm, so he could not strike with the sword. Then his orderly knocked me down. I sent for Major Tolen, who relieved me as Officer of the Day. I saw Colonel Potter order Lieutenant Leigh to his tent and I saw five officers with drawn swords about to attack Lieutenant Leigh. I saw three men wounded in the commotion: my son, who was pierced with a sword point; Sergeant [Edward] Conway, whose face was slashed; and a corporal who was hit in the head. The men were angered and were loading their muskets.

Lieutenant Colonel Potter did not quell the riot, in fact, he was one of the principal rioters. There were ladies in the colonel's tent. All the officers drank whisky after the presentation of Lieutenant Franklin's sword. Lieutenant Franklin was staggering drunk by 9:00 p.m. and I helped him to his tent. I have since resigned the regiment. A man's life is not safe in this regiment, with these officers.

Lt. A. M. McCune next took the stand and recalled, "I heard a noise. I put on my overcoat and went out. There Colonel Potter saw me and called me a 'whorehouse pimp.' The colonel tried to punch me but missed. I had been sick, so I ran, but I fell and the colonel fell on top of me. I think he was upset because I had previously preferred charges against him." Lt. T. J. Leigh told the court:

I was headed for my tent, when I heard James O'Brien, the colonel's orderly, yelling that Captain Glover was a "God damned old white-haired son of a bitch." I felt it was my duty as an officer to admonish him. As I did so, Colonel Potter came up, missing his hat, and said that I was under arrest, and placed a guard over me. I told Colonel Potter that that was not customary with an officer. He yelled, "I'll be God damned if I don't have the whole regiment under arrest!" Six officers approached, and Colonel Potter ordered, "Charge bayonets on Lieutenant Leigh." One of the officers pointed out that officers do not carry bayonets. "Well, then," he roared, "charge swords!"

One of the officers presented his sword point at my breast, and Colonel Potter seized my throat from behind. Then someone knocked Colonel Potter flat on his back, where he lay yelling, "Run him through, run him through." Major Tolen told me, "Leave now—they are all drunk and they will murder you." I left and went into Colonel Hall's tent.

Someone outside the tent made a noise like a sheep—"baa." I ran outside and found that Colonel Potter made the "baa." I said that was disgraceful and he said, "So what?"

Further questioning showed that Lieutenant Leigh was already under arrest by General Sickles for some previous contretemps.

Surgeon J. J. McGowan next took the witness stand. "I was already under arrest by Colonel Potter. The night of the riot, I heard a noise and went out of my tent. Someone told me that Sergeant Conway had been cut by Colonel Potter, who was very drunk and waving his sword." Assistant Surgeon McAllister had a different opinion. "Colonel Potter was under the influence but not drunk. I examined Captain Glover. His gums looked contused but his jaw was not fractured or dislocated. The captain was very drunk. I also examined Sergeant Connaly; his face was cut and he said that Captain Power did it. I think part of the problem started when a New Jersey lieutenant colonel called Colonel Potter 'an old scoundrel.' The Officer of the Guard and the Officer of the Day were both very drunk and were slashing at the crowd until they were disarmed."

Further witnesses were called and the picture became more confused rather than less. Lt. F. B. McAvey said, "I was there the whole time. Colonel Potter was not drunk. He was well behaved. He did not curse and he did not even hold a sword, nor did he order a charge. Colonel Potter tried to quell the riot. I think it was all a plot by some of the officers. I recall the events clearly, as I do not drink."

Lt. J. J. Lowentrout had yet a different recollection. "Captain Power was Officer of the Day. He was noisy and drunk, and he slashed right and left until his own son took his sword away and ran off with it. Captain Greene was crazy drunk at the sword presentation and worse later. He had been drinking all afternoon at the sutler's." When Captain W. H. Greene took the stand, he stated that he had "taken the pledge," and was therefore not drunk.

Sergeant Edward Conway stated that he was sober the night of the riot. "Colonel Potter was waving Captain Power's sword, and got me across the face. The colonel denies that he cut me—but he did." Chaplain J. H. Twitchell disagreed with many of the witnesses. "Colonel Potter was not drunk and he was fit to command. He is a temperate officer."

Now the defense witnesses appeared. Pvt. Nelson Blackmore identified the slasher: "It was Captain Power who cut Sergeant Conway. The sergeant cursed Captain Power all the way to the hospital where he had his face done up. I think the sergeant was drunk."

Major Tolen had strong views on the politics of the fracas. "There are two hostile groups in the regiment: those that favor Colonel Potter and those that favor Colonel Hall." When asked his views on Captain Power's character, Tolen replied, "I'd rather not answer that question." The recipient of the presented sword on the night of the riot, Lt. Benjamin Franklin, addressed the subject of the booze supply: "Colonel Potter brought one bottle of gin and I brought four bottles of whisky."

The trial record contains dozens of pages of additional testimony, all of it conflicting. At the end, the court found Colonel Potter guilty of some of the charges and sentenced him to be suspended from command for fifteen days, to receive no pay for thirty days, and to be reprimanded in General Orders. The case was then reviewed by Brig. Gen. Joseph Hooker: "After patient examination of the evidence . . . the commander finds it impossible to arrive at any decided conviction as to innocence or guilt. The disgraceful proceedings in the

Second Regiment of the Excelsior Brigade are regarded as a sentence of more severity to an officer jealous of his reputation . . . than one a court martial is likely to inflict. The proceedings are confirmed."

In the record of the rest of his life, the story of Colonel Potter still contains puzzles and contradictions. In June 1862, at Burnt Chimneys, near Fair Oaks, Virginia, he was wounded in the left leg below the knee. He was wounded again at Bristoe Station, Virginia, in August 1862; a musketball shattered the bones of his left wrist. After healing, the wrist was inflexible, and the fingers immovable.

At Gettysburg, where he was a full colonel, he was wounded a third time. A few months later, a surgeon certified, "General weakness, secondary to chronic diarrhea, acquired at Chickahominy. He is unfit for field duty, but would be suited for garrison or invalid duty." The record shows that Potter was "dismissed" in December 1863, usually a punitive measure, but that order was revoked and he received an honorable discharge, to date from July 30, 1864.

In 1869, General Hooker described Colonel Potter as "a gallant and meritorious officer . . . entitled to generous consideration." In 1875, a Surgeon's Certificate described "atrophy of the tibialis anticus and gastrocnemius muscles," and awarded a pension of $30 a month. The next year, another doctor certified that Potter's sicknesses were "not due to immoral habits but were all secondary to field service."

A third doctor's report in 1880 described him as suffering from "spasmodic attacks of asthma, which leave him utterly helpless, choking and coughing black matter from his lungs." Another report described his lung problems as not service-connected, but a 1907 doctor's letter stated, "His severe asthmatic bronchitis and pain in the chest is secondary to falling off his horse in the War; also chronic sinuses and ulcers in his leg, secondary to unhealed bullet wounds."

Colonel Potter's first wife died in 1892 and, seven years later, he remarried to one Eliza, who continued to receive a pension after Potter's death in 1907. The old soldier was seventy-nine years old when he died. Whether his drunken sword-waving was real or a creation of perjury, the record is clear enough that his shattered hand and the chronic infection in the bone marrow of his left tibia were wounds that he carried to his grave, marks of combat still present forty-six years after the Great Conflict.

As a postscript, it is worth noting that Lieutenant A. M. McCune was also court-martialed in relationship to the same 1862 riot. The charges included knocking out three of Colonel Potter's teeth—one real and two false. McCune was acquitted.

Chapter Thirty-Six

The Russian Thunderbolt

COL. JOHN B. TURCHIN

The Civil War was filled with flamboyant characters, but few could match Ivan Vasilovitch Turchinoff, born in 1822 in the Russian province of the Don, ancestral home of the Cossacks. He graduated from the Imperial School of Artillery in 1841, fought in Hungary and in the Crimea, rose to the rank of colonel, and served on the personal staff of the crown prince, later Czar Alexander II.

In 1856 he immigrated and was soon employed as an engineer with the Illinois Central Railroad, with the Americanized name of John Basil Turchin. In 1861, with the coming of the war, he was commissioned colonel of the 19th Illinois Regiment of Infantry. He used European methods of discipline with his troops, which soon produced an efficient and tightly run fighting unit. It was also a unit that followed the European tradition in that to the victors belong the spoils—the losers could expect pillage and plunder.[1]

In the spring of 1862, the 19th Illinois was, successively, at Bowling Green, Kentucky; Nashville and Murfreesboro, Tennessee, and Huntsville, Tuscumbia, and Athens, Alabama. In July 1862 Turchin was court-martialed for neglect of duty, in that he allowed his troops to plunder the town of Athens, rape female slaves, and set free male slaves, who committed further crimes. The facts, the fury, and the myths of this event were not soon forgotten. In 1940 a Mrs. H. W. Hobson wrote to the War Department, asking for a copy of the Turchin trial, adding that her mother's diary said of Turchin, "He does not ride well. He looked like a fat bug and bounced."

At the trial, Turchin not only pled innocent, but demanded that the secessionist witnesses against him take the Oath of Allegiance, arguing that the Athenians were trying to have it both ways: treason toward the United States while invoking the protection of the laws of the United States. The court declined to honor his request.

One of the many witnesses against him was John Haywood Jones. He recalled that Turchin's troops entered the town on May 2 and that two companies of Col. Geza Mihalotzy's regiment were then quartered in the Jones home. Mihalotzy reserved one room for the Jones family, "but then he cursed me and said I deserved the inconvenience, as I was a damned Secesh." Jones took his family to a neighbor's home, rather than endure the sight and sound of his Yankee boarders. Later that day, an artillery company under a Capt. Warren Edgarton arrived and was quartered in the parlor of the Jones home, where it stayed ten days.

Testified Jones, "My house and furniture were damaged considerably. Mahogany sofas, divans, chairs and bureaus all injured. A valuable carpet was destroyed by dirt and grease. All of my [silver] plate, valued at about $1,000, was gone, except for a few pieces so large they could not be carried and these were damaged."

Jones further recalled that the soldiers used an axe to chop up bacon on the hall floor and piled forty pounds of meat on the piano. When the soldiers departed, his library was missing fifty volumes and all of his food was gone— flour, pickles and preserves. It rained heavily in early May, and officers and men damaged the Jones bed linen by lying down with their muddy boots still on.

"Captain Edgarton seemed sorry to quarter his troops there and said he had been ordered to do so. He took from me two valuable sporting rifles, saying his orders were positive regarding firearms. He said I would get them back, but I have not; one cost $175 while the other one cost $100 [a total of about $6,000 in 1996 money]."

Another citizen-witness said he had heard soldiers say "Colonel Turchin allows us to go in," and further recalled, "I saw soldiers and Negroes carrying all sorts of goods from the stores, on both streets leading north from the square. Citizens told me that Colonel Turchin's headquarters were at the hotel of Mr. Davison, close to the depot, but I hardly ever saw the colonel." This witness obtained protection for his home from Col. Timothy Stanley of the 18th Ohio, after he had had Capt. William Edmiston of the same regiment to dinner. There was further testimony that the Union soldiers had stolen forage, fodder, jewelry, cash, hams, photograph albums, and financial records. In all, there were 203 pages of testimony.

In his defense statement, Turchin opened with a description of the role of the *état major,* an intelligence force that collected and prepared maps, interrogated citizens, and made lists of supplies, roads, and bridges. In Russia he had been a colonel of the Etat Major of the Imperial Guard. Here in the United States he was forced to do such staff work himself, which left him little time to attend to peripheral matters.

He reminded the court that shortly before he arrived, Federal troops had been driven out of Athens, with many Union men killed or captured. The Confederates had burned the railroad bridge and citizens had insulted the soldiers as they withdrew. Further, the Union men had abandoned their knapsacks in their retreat and that Turchin's forces, on reoccupying the town, had found these knapsacks in homes all over Athens, proof of civilian complicity in secessionist activity. Turchin added:

I issued strict orders for no depredations. The men were to stay where they are assigned, and no stragglers. Some of the citizens of Athens joined the Rebel cavalry and fought against us. The citizens should have stayed in their places of business. I know of no depredations as they made no complaints to me. Being among an unfriendly and disloyal population, and considering the good of the service a paramount duty, I could not accommodate the citizens of Athens and fulfill my military duties at the same time. I had over 3,000 loyal lives entrusted to my care and, in comparison therewith, I did not care much about the inconveniences of Secessionists.

What is clear from Turchin's thirty-three-page defense statement is his Old World view of warfare. Rather than the courtly fictions of Sir Walter Scott, with their intimations of chivalry and gracious treatment of professed noncombatants, Turchin's eye beheld the civilian secessionists as traitors, grist for the mills of more hardheaded conquerors such as Genghis Khan, Tamerlane, and Ivan the Terrible. His view might be summarized as: "If you don't like war, don't start one." In this, he prefigured the campaigns of William T. Sherman against the Southern economy and the assaults on national will seen in the bombings of London, Dresden, and Hiroshima. Whether Turchin was cruel, or merely pragmatic, is a task for the philosophers of history. It is obvious that Turchin had little use for Victorian sentimentality toward the vanquished rebels, who fired on his troops and then retreated to the sanctuary of their parlors to complain of soiled carpets.

The court found Turchin guilty and sentenced him to be dismissed, but added the following request for clemency: "The undersigned members of General Court-martial before which was tried Colonel J. B. Turchin, respectfully submit that in view of the fact that the finding of the Court acquits Colonel Turchin of any personal dishonor, and believing that his offenses were committed under exciting circumstances and was one rather of omission than of commission, we would respectfully recommend him to the favorable consideration of the Reviewing Officer."

The court-martial board was not the only entity recommending clemency. Turchin's wife, Nadine, who had accompanied him on the Huntsville–Athens campaign (Turchin was severely criticized for bringing her on campaign), urgently pressed President Lincoln to not only set the verdict aside, but also promote Colonel Turchin to brigadier general of volunteers. Nadine was a formidable person in her own right, a vigorous defender of her husband, and her entreaties to the President were entirely successful. Turchin, who had been violently ill throughout the trial with fever and headache, was triply relieved by his remittal and promotion, as well as by his medical improvement.

Lincoln's confidence in Turchin was well rewarded. Turchin successfully commanded a brigade of Gen. Joseph J. Reynolds's division at Chickamauga (where he acquired the sobriquet "Russian Thunderbolt"); at Missionary Ridge, one of his regiments was one of the first to the top; in the Atlanta Campaign, his superior, Absalom Baird, praised Turchin's "soldierly and patriotic" performance.

What the Confederates could not do, the hot southern sun did. In July 1864 his surgeon wrote, "I have examined this officer and find from his peculiar organization that he is peculiarly susceptible to solar influences, producing violent pain in the head, approaching coup-de-soliel, and that this tendency is much heightened by his continuance in this climate." In October 1864 he resigned because of ill health.

From 1865 to 1872 he was solicitor of patents in Chicago. In 1873 he founded a Polish colony in southern Illinois at the town of Radom. Turchin was active in the Grand Army of the Republic, and was a prolific writer on his favorite subject. In 1865 he published two editions of *Military Rambles,* a series of reminiscences. His 295-page study of Chickamauga was published in 1888, and in 1895, he produced a pamphlet as part of a lawsuit denouncing the commission of the Chickamauga and Chattanooga Military Park. The issue was the design of the monuments, which in his opinion did not sufficiently glorify the Union effort. Many people disliked Turchin, which troubled him not at all.

In the late 1890s, he was overcome by senile dementia, and in 1901 he died at the Southern Illinois Hospital for the Insane. He is buried in the National Cemetery at Mound City, Illinois.

Chapter Thirty-Seven

"In the Hands of a Clique"

COL. EMIL VON SCHOENIG

The legal problems of Col. Emil von Schoenig of the German Rangers began innocuously enough. He was mustered in during the early days of October 1861, and a few weeks later, arrived by train in Washington, D.C., accompanied by his brother Oscar, a captain in the same regiment. The pair strolled up Pennsylvania Avenue admiring the sights and were immediately arrested by the provost guard for not having passes from the brigade commander.

At the court-martial, presided over by Brig. Gen. Silas Casey, the prosecution witness was Lt. A. Sheridan, who testified that on November 7, 1861, as "Officer of the Patrol Provost Guard of Washington City," acting under the authority of Brig. Gen. Andrew Porter, through General Order No. 2, he had arrested the two officers for being without passes.[1]

Colonel von Schoenig defended himself, noting that his regiment, the German Rangers (later the 52nd New York Infantry), which he had raised himself, was still on Staten Island, that he had just gotten off the train at Washington, and that he knew nothing of Porter's General Order No. 2, which required passes for all officers.

The court considered the charges and concluded that the facts were "proven as stated; but, under the circumstances attach no criminality thereto." He was acquitted, but that was not the end of his troubles.

On November 13, 1861, the German Rangers arrived to defend the capital and were posted to Camp California, near Alexandria, Virginia. The ground was swampy; the air was cold and damp. Soon, von Schoenig had the chills and fever of malaria, rheumatism that crippled his right leg, and an ear infection that left him deaf on one side.

But being deaf, lame, and racked with fever was again not the end of his troubles. His obvious lack of military capacity led to a court of inquiry.

Maj. Charles Freidenburg gave his evidence. "Emil Schoenig claims to be Emil von Schoenig, but is not. [In German, "von" connotes aristocracy or nobility. The unwarranted addition of this prefix suggests pretention bordering on fraud.] "He claims to have been an officer in the Prussian Army, but is an imposter. He is a weak character, speaks poor language, and is a mere tool in the hands of a clique of the lowest orders of society."

Freudenburg went on to comment upon Oscar Schoenig: "Colonel Schoenig gave command of a company to his brother, a worthless individual who has been in court for assault and battery, and is a bankrupt. The colonel pockets the money that is intended to feed the recruits, and is so notorious in this in New York City that the German Society has disowned him. He is a fraud."

Questions about von Schoenig's skills in military science caused him to appear before a board of examination. The chairman, Brig. Gen. Oliver O. Howard, recorded the findings of the board in mid-January 1862: "Colonel von Schoenig's deficient knowledge of tactics and his lack of grasp of English language wholly unfit him for the command of a regiment. Further, we are of the opinion that he knows nothing of Prussian tactics either. He uses sickness as an excuse. We recommend that he be mustered out as totally incompetent."

Indeed, von Schoenig was a civilian again after only three months of service. He was sent home as sick, corrupt, and incompetent, while his regiment went on to lose a total of 350 men—one-third of its number—through battles such as Fair Oaks, Gaines Mill, Savage Station, White Oak Swamp, Antietam, Fredericksburg, Spotsylvania, and Cold Harbor, as well as through the ravages of disease. His brother, Oscar, resigned March 3, 1862.

In 1882 Emil von Schoenig reappears, this time in the records of the pension office. Dr. Alexander Hugart certified that von Schoenig still suffered from malaria every spring. The colonel was awarded a pension, which he drew for three years until his death from "sudden cerebral hemorrhage." His widow Pauline lived on until 1904, when the von Schoenig connection with the Federal Treasury came to an end.

Chapter Thirty-Eight

Five Cartridges per Man

COL. NELSON G. WILLIAMS

The Hannibal and St. Joseph Railroad runs straight across the upper quarter of Missouri, a distance of two hundred miles. In the summer of 1861, four companies of the 3rd Iowa Infantry were stranded in Monroe, just west of Hannibal, surrounded by a Confederate force under the command of Thomas Harris.

The rest of the 3rd Iowa was near Chillicothe, Missouri, one hundred miles to the west, under the command of Col. Nelson G. Williams. Numerous telegrams urged Williams to load his troops on the train, speed east, and rescue his comrades. The route was straight, the rails intact. At twenty-five miles per hour, they could be there in four hours. The story of Colonel Williams's action, or inaction, at this dramatic moment is the story of this court-martial.[1]

Nelson Williams was born in upstate New York in 1823. He entered West Point at age sixteen, but withdrew after a year because of deficiency in mathematics. He then labored fifteen years in the importing business in New York City; six years before the Civil War, he moved to Iowa, where he tried his hand at farming and running a general store. With this martial background, he was appointed colonel of the 3rd Iowa Infantry on June 26, 1861; his call to action at Monroe arrived July 10th, 1861, just two weeks after assuming the awesome responsibilities of his new profession.

In December 1861, he was court-martialed for the events of July and September. The charges were cowardice, conduct prejudicial to good order, neglect of duty, and drunkenness on duty. The details occupy many pages, which may be summarized as follows.

On July 10, 1861, Colonel Williams was notified that four companies of his command were surrounded by "an overwhelming force of the enemy and in imminent danger" at Monroe, Missouri. He did not use due diligence in going to their rescue, "through fear of meeting the enemy." Having started, apparently from Utica, Missouri, a town now gone from most maps, he made a stop of several hours at Chillicothe "on the pretense of looking for secessionists, but actually out of fear." Arriving at Macon, two-thirds of the way to his destination, he stopped there for twelve hours, though he was still receiving frequent telegrams urging him to the rescue. While stopped at Macon, he told his officers that the Rebel commander, Thomas Harris, was a West Point graduate, "a splendid officer," and commanded a large contingent of cavalry, infantry, and artillery, which words "disheartened" Williams's staff.

Upon reaching the vicinity of Monroe, he stopped at Salt River Bridge and proceeded with "unnecessary slowness" toward his besieged comrades. When his command reached Monroe on July 12, as soon as the first shots were fired, Colonel Williams went to the rear and did not appear again until he was informed that his troops occupied the town.

Later charges of cowardice arose from events in September. Early in that month, his regiment was attacked by a "band of Rebels under one Martin Green." In this battle, at Shelbina, Williams reacted by retreating "in a hasty and precipitous manner," leaving his wounded and a large amount of government property in the hands of the secessionists.

Three days later, Williams's superior was too drunk to give orders, so Williams put his command back on the train, holding the conductor and engineer at gunpoint, and took them west again, to Brookfield, abandoning a scouting party that had been sent toward Shelbina, though "no force of the enemy was within 20 miles."

The next charge contains more details: Williams had "recourse to intoxicating liquors at various places along the line of the Hannibal and St. Joseph Railroad, on July 10, 11, and 12th." On those same days, he rebuked Capt. Matthew Trumbull for issuing cartridges to the men, and excoriated Lieutenant Clark for not issuing cartridges. Amid this confusion and urgency, Williams stopped everything, and ordered the quartermaster to cook him a ham for breakfast.

The third charge, neglect of duty, states that on July 20, he left Companies E and F at "an unhealthy station along the railroad without tents or equipment, and failed to send them supplies when they were available." Five days later, learning that two of his companies were about to be attacked, he warned them, but sent neither reinforcements nor ammunition.

The final charge preferred against Colonel Williams was that on September 2, 1861, at Paris, Missouri, he was too drunk to command his detachment. The court-martial was held at Benton Barracks, Missouri, and occupied the time of a dozen colonels for two months.

Capt. Matthew M. Trumbull, Company I, 3rd Iowa, was the first witness. He described the scene on July 10, soon after the urgent telegram had been received. "All the men of Companies E and I were on the train west of Chillicothe. There was firing in the distance and suddenly Colonel Williams appeared frantic with fear. He shouted to the officers to fill their hats with cartridges. I had started to distribute cartridges, but Williams had screamed at me to stop. A few minutes later, the colonel was screaming at the quartermaster to issue cartridges faster, and threatened to cut the quartermaster in half with his sword."

In a few minutes, it was learned that the firing had been Company C, discharging their weapons before boarding the train. With the crisis passed, the available portion of the regiment proceeded down the tracks and reached Chillicothe at 9:00 P.M. and picked up Company B, about ninety men. It took three hours to load the men, as Colonel Williams ordered men off and on the train. They traveled all night and arrived at Macon at dawn. Trumbull also recalled that the colonel seemed intoxicated. Trumbull was then cross-examined by the accused.

Q. How do you know that my canteen contained whisky?
A. I drank from your canteen. You went about with it slung over your shoulder saying, "Take a suck of my titty."
Q. How much did you drink from my canteen?
A. Very little. The liquor was not good.
Q. Was my function to command impaired?
A. You did not post a guard at night. I thought that was negligent.

Captain Trumbull's statement continued: "Colonel Williams told us the Confederate force was larger than ours, very well equipped, commanded by a splendid officer, and that we would be cut to pieces. He was trembling."

Several companies of the 3rd Iowa had only five cartridges per man, while Captain Patrick's company had plenty of ammunition. It took the colonel a long time to decide what to do. "Finally, we all had ten cartridges per man."

Maj. William M. Stone added his recollections: "When the troops were boarding the train in Utica around nightfall, Colonel Williams seemed confused and excited. His orders were frequent and incoherent."

After days of testimony describing terror and drunken incompetence, there were days of rebuttal, with witnesses describing Williams as calm, coherent, effective, and cold sober.

William H. Dulaney, a tobacco merchant of Paris, Missouri, had dinner with Colonel Williams on September 4, 1861. "He was in excellent command of his 700 men. He was entirely sober. Lieutenant Colonel [Charles] Blair of the Second Kansas was also at dinner and he got drunk. Colonel Blair was carried out by two soldiers. Some citizens confused the two colonels in the dark. Later, I saw Colonel Williams at Shelbina, when the Confederates attacked with 1,000 men. A cannonball hit near Colonel Williams, and Captain McClure's foot was torn off, but the colonel stayed calm. I saw no cowardice."

Harmon Tisdale, age twenty-seven, was the engineer on the train that withdrew the Union troops after their defeat at Shelbina on September 5, 1862. "My conductor went out on the prairie and got captured by the Rebels. That was not Colonel Williams' fault. When the Union troops left, the Kansas men went first. The officers from Kansas demanded to leave first. Then the Iowa troops loaded up. Colonel Williams was the last man on the train. Colonel Blair of Kansas came to me and said, 'Get started. Leave Colonel Williams for the Rebels.' Colonel Williams looked sober to me."

Brig. Gen. Stephen Hurlbut testified that he had ordered Williams to hold Shelbina, but his investigation had shown that Lieutenant Colonel Blair and Major Cloud had both insisted on retreating. "I had the Kansas men put it in writing. They assumed responsibility for the retreat. They felt themselves relieved from military duty, and their discipline was bad."

Capt. Frederick Loring of the 22nd Missouri testified that his fifty-six mounted men were attached to Williams's force at Paris. "I saw him every few hours all night. While others slept, he was in the saddle. I consider him a prudent and watchful officer. I know he was not drunk: he had a very spirited horse and only a sober man could control it. I was also at the action at Shelbina. It was the Kansans who wanted to leave. Colonel Williams is no coward."

The final result of all this testimony was complete acquittal. Colonel Williams resumed his sword and his command in mid-February 1862.

Seven weeks later, his military career was over. At Shiloh (Pittsburg Landing), he commanded a brigade in Hurlbut's Division. A cannonball passed through his horse, killing the animal instantly and hurling its body on top of Colonel Williams. The double shock produced effects that never fully left him. Concussion of the spine paralyzed him for weeks. He had severe pain in both ears, lost half the sight of his right eye, and suffered permanent prolapse of the anus (a protrusion of the lower part of the intestine). Rheumatism, deafness, diarrhea, and jaundice, acquired in the spring of 1862, plagued him all his life. In the weeks following Shiloh, Maj. Gen. William T. Sherman had his own personal physician attend to Williams, but not much could be done.

Williams resigned his commission on November 29, 1862, since he was incapable of further duty. His appointment as a brigadier general was refused by Congress, as he had left the service. He returned to his Iowa farm for seven years.

Then President Ulysses S. Grant, a former classmate at West Point, made Williams a deputy collector of customs in New York City. This bit of political largesse sustained Williams for twenty-eight years. He died in Brooklyn in 1897 of hypertrophy of the heart, with edema of the legs, combined with bronchitis and cirrhosis of the liver. He had been in pain for thirty-five years.

PART FOUR

Cowardice

Chapter Thirty-Nine

"I Have Been Ruptured!"

COL. HENRY AMISANZEL

The 1st Virginia Cavalry, later the 1st West Virginia Cavalry, after having been mustered at Wheeling, had already seen action at ten sites and been at considerable disadvantage from the lack of a veterinarian when the skirmish at Bloomery Gap embroiled its thirty-year-old colonel in a bitter dispute and subsequent court-martial. The location was the hills between Cumberland, West Virginia, and Winchester, Virginia, south of Paw Paw. The date was February 14, 1862.[1]

At the court-martial, four days later, Col. Henry Amisanzel, commander of the 1st Virginia Cavalry Regiment, was charged with "misbehavior before the enemy." The president of the court was Col. Erastus B. Tyler of the 7th Ohio.

The opening statements illuminate the geography of the dispute: a road winding east through the hills, from Romney to Winchester. Just before passing through Bloomery Gap, a narrow declivity in the mountains, a road branched north toward Paw Paw.

There had been reports of Confederate officers in a house about half a mile east of the gap, and of fortifications and a train of Confederate supply wagons about six or seven miles farther east, toward Winchester.

The commander of the Federal forces that morning was Brig. Gen. Frederick W. Lander, who had already distinguished himself in prior years by surveying the Northern Pacific Railroad, serving as an aide to General McClellan, and receiving a wound at Edwards' Ferry. He was forty-two years of age.

The first witness for the prosecution was Lt. J. J. Cannon of Russell's Company of Independent Cavalry. Before dawn, a small knot of mounted officers gathered in the ribbon of mud that was the Romney-Winchester Road. Present were General Lander, Colonel Amisanzel, Lieutenant Cannon, and Captain Carman of the 1st Virginia Cavalry. Cannon recalled, "When we first arrived, General Lander had me take a lantern and ten men and see which way the enemy had gone—north toward Paw Paw or east toward Winchester. I took my men up the road about a mile, found that the hoof and wagon marks went toward Winchester, and reported back to the general. He ordered me to send Colonel Amisanzel toward the enemy. When I reached the colonel, he was already underway." Russell's men had no cartridges for their pistols and did not advance, since the Confederate force was reported to be three hundred men.

Col. Samuel S. Carroll of the 8th Ohio gave his testimony: "Colonel Amisanzel commanded 400 cavalry. General Lander ordered them to charge through the gap and surround the two houses that were said to have Confederate officers in them. When we charged the houses, I didn't see the colonel until we had both houses surrounded. Most of his regiment didn't keep up; I don't think they tried their best."

By the time the two houses were surrounded and found to contain no Rebels, daylight had arrived. The next action was a skirmish with Confederates in the bushes on the hillsides on either side of the road, about a mile east of the gap. Lieutenant Cannon recalls General Landers saying, "Why are you staying here? Follow me." Only Cannon, Carman, and one other man followed the general. "It was a four-man charge." This small Federal group captured six Confederates—four privates and two officers, including a colonel.

Capt. Irvin Redpath of Morehead's Cavalry recalled that the ground on either side of the road was very rough and that the enemy was up in the hills. "An officer rode up to me and asked, 'Why in hell and damnation don't you charge!' I referred him to Colonel Amisanzel, who was just ahead of me. When General Lander ordered the charge, some went one way, some went another. I charged into the hills, where I could see the smoke from the Rebel guns."

Union attention now shifted to the supply wagons and fortifications said to be up the Winchester Road. The beginning of the advance was not auspicious. Maj. John B. Farthingham of the 6th Virginia and aide-de-camp to General Lander, recalled that Lander ordered the cavalry to "advance and capture the secesh wagons. He repeated the order several times before anyone moved. The general said he'd shoot them if they didn't move, and fired a charge from his pistol. Then Colonel Amisanzel and some of his men went east."

Wagonmaster Samuel B. Fuller of the 8th Ohio, was called upon to give his recollections. "When the 200 cavalrymen were ordered to advance, only about 15 men went as far as the wagons. I was one of them, and so was Colonel Amisanzel. I remember his wearing his glasses." Fuller continued that there were too few Union forces at the end of this advance to capture the Confederate wagons, and that the colonel sent for reinforcements, which never arrived. Fuller felt that they were surrounded by a superior force. "One man's dun mare was shot and the colonel told him to cut a horse out of the enemy train. I saw no cowardice in our group."

As the small force retreated back toward the gap, Colonel Amisanzel's horse slipped in the mud and fell. Col. Nathan Kimball testified, "I met the colonel on the Winchester Road. He looked in pain and was covered with mud; he said his men had been repulsed." Colonel Kimball, apparently in doubt, rode two miles east, saw no enemy and returned.

Major Farthingham also saw the mud-soaked colonel: "He told me the Confederate fire was so heavy it reminded him of Paris during the Revolution." Colonel Caroll added his own observations: "After the skirmish, I met Colonel Amisanzel. He was covered with mud and said he'd been ruptured." Carroll rode eight miles toward Winchester, "to examine the supposed Rebel fortifications. There were none."

The final witness was Capt. Nathan D. Menkin of the 1st Ohio Cavalry. "The cavalry had sufficient equipment to meet the enemy: Enfield rifles, Sharp's carbines, sabres and pistols. I felt a want of confidence in Colonel Amisanzel."

The colonel, as part of his defense, introduced a hand-drawn map, which is still in the Federal archives. His sketch showed the major features of the hills and valleys and the location of each event.

The court then considered the specifications of the charges made against Colonel Amisanzel, specifications which seemed quite damning. It was claimed that he had "wholly neglected and failed to make an attack" when he outnumbered the enemy eight to one, and then when ordered to further advance, he "halted his men after proceeding a short distance, and sent back word that the roads were fortified and the hills were black with men." The court then considered the lengthy and contradictory testimony, which by now filled thirty-six pages, and found Colonel Amisanzel not guilty.

General Lander did not fare as well. After a day of exhorting laggardly men to do their duty, he wrote in his report on the Bloomery Gap action that "my health is much too broken to do any severe work," and he requested to be relieved of his command. No relief arrived, and, on March 1, 1862, he was stricken with a "congestive chill" and died the following morning in spite of energetic treatment by his physician.

In July 1862 Surgeon William C. Bennett reported that Amisanzel had an inguinal hernia as a result of the skirmish at Bloomery Gap and was unable to endure long marches. A week later, the colonel's letter of resignation concluded, "I deeply regret the state of my health and I will do whatever I can for the cause." The command was then assumed by Lt. Col. N. P. Richmond, who was promoted to full colonel.

Amisanzel's subsequent life is a mystery. He made no application for pension, and local historians can find no record of him.

Chapter Forty

"For God's Sake, Don't Skedaddle"

COL. ROBERT C. MURPHY

Ske-daddle, intransitive verb; *skedaddled,* past tense. Meaning: to leave in a hurry, to run away. [Colloquial; etymology unknown.]

In his sixteen months in the volunteer army, Col. Robert C. Murphy, commander of the 8th Wisconsin, set a record for positions lost and reproofs received. He was mustered in with the rest of the 8th Wisconsin at Madison in September 1861. In the spring of 1862, the regiment was active in operations at New Madrid and Island No. 10, Missouri, and in the May siege of Corinth, Mississippi. For two months of this time, Colonel Murphy was absent in St. Louis, for reasons not reflected in the record, but May 1862 found him back with his regiment and commanding the Second Brigade, Second Division, Army of the Mississippi. His records show little in the way of remarkable events until September 1862, but then three fateful days in the northeast corner of the state of Mississippi started his downhill slide. His court-martial was based upon two specific charges.[1]

The said Colonel R.C. Murphy, 8th Wisconsin Volunteer Infantry, at Iuka, in the State of Mississippi, on the 14th day of September, 1862, when threatened with an attack by the enemy, did omit and refuse to give the enemy battle, and run away from the enemy, and withdraw his troops from the town of Iuka, and hastily retreat with his troops before an inferior force of the enemy, and did continue to retreat with haste to the town of Farmington, without making a stand or attempting to check the pursuit of the enemy.

The said Col. R. C. Murphy, having been placed in command of the town of Iuka, Mississippi, then occupied by United States troops as a military post, by his commanding officer Brig. Gen. W. S. Rosecrans, with orders to hold the same until the Commissary and Hospital Stores had been removed, did disobey said orders, and did shamefully abandon said post, and withdraw the troops under his command from said post, before said Commissary and Hospital Stores had been removed, and did neglect to destroy said stores, but abandoned them to fall into the hands of the enemy.

176

His court-martial files contain the principal on-the-spot record of these crucial events, in particular a series of telegrams. They are handwritten, mostly in pencil, which leaves some margin for error in interpretation, and are dated but not timed. Thus, the seven telegrams of September 12 are puzzling as to their exact sequence. Beyond that, there is a certain inexactness in the phrasing, which seems to have confused both the sender and the receiver in 1862. This can be equally puzzling to the contemporary reader. However, with these caveats, a reasonably clear picture emerges. The authors of the telegrams are Colonel Murphy himself and his commander, General Rosecrans. Murphy is in Iuka; Rosecrans is in Corinth.

From Rosecrans: "I supposed that the 43rd Ohio was with you as I intended. I just learned you have only two regiments. Stay at Iuka with both regiments until further orders, but be ready to move by railroad at short notice."

From Murphy: "I have just arrived [at noon]. Received your dispatch and orders—will act accordingly. I am too sick to do more just now. I must go to bed."

From Murphy: "Have but one section left. Will send the 5th Minnesota, with a section of Dee's Battery [Battery C, First Michigan Light Artillery] to Burnsville tonight. Tomorrow, the 8th Wisconsin will march. I am quite done up myself. Two large trains of stock [supplies] here yet."

Another telegram from Murphy may be paraphrased as follows, "No one tells me what to do. I was ordered to send a regiment and a battery to Burnsville and the other regiment tomorrow."

From Murphy: "Intended to send 5th Minnesota with section of artillery to Burnsville, as ordered, and march after them in the morning with the 8th Wisconsin. The railroad train was offered to move the 8th Wisconsin. I did not embrace the offer. Have asked for orders more plainly as there seems to be some mistake somewhere."

From Rosecrans: "Dispatch received. For God's sake, don't skedaddle any more. Look at your orders. Is there not a section of a battery from Eastport at Iuka served by a detachment? One regiment and a section of six companies of cavalry were ordered to remain at Iuka. If you are wanted, we can send for you by railroad. No hurry."

From Rosecrans again: "Happy to get word from you. The cavalry has been ordered to cover your front. The stores must be sent to Corinth. You may move when that is done. A [telegraph] office will be opened at Burnsville. Give me particulars where the [Confederate] troops appeared. The exact position and what they did. I hope in future you will set ambushes for cavalry. Order your men to hold their fire and hold the fellows until you can spring a trap on them."

The following day, September 13, Murphy sent this telegram: "Tried to reach you by telegraph and courier. My force is on the hill, 8th Wisconsin and two guns. Were attacked from the south by [Brig. Gen. Frank] Armstrong's brigade of cavalry, said to be 2,000 strong. Our cavalry was slow getting ready. Our officers behaved well, the men very poorly. The 8th Wisconsin and the rifled gun of Dee's Battery repulsed attacks for one and a half hours. They attacked again on my left,

Brig. Gen. William S. Rosecrans telegraphed to Col. Robert C. Murphy, "For God's sake, don't skedaddle," but he did nevertheless. At Holly Springs, Murphy was captured still in his pajamas. Maj. Gen. U. S. Grant had Murphy arrested. MASSACHUSETTS COMMANDERY MILITARY ORDER OF THE LOYAL LEGION, U.S. ARMY MILITARY HISTORY INSTITUTE.

but our pickets and Dee's Battery drove them off. No problem since, but Rebel prisoners tell us [Maj. Gen. Sterling] Price's army will arrive tomorrow. If reinforcements are sent, must be sent by dawn tomorrow." Apparently anticipating criticism, on September 15, Colonel Murphy asked for a court of inquiry.

On September 23, Colonel Murphy submitted a nine-page explanation of his abandonment of Iuka. This paraphrasing reflects the principal points:

On September 12th, at 12:00 o'clock M [noon], I entered Iuka with the 8th Wisconsin, seven companies of the 5th Minnesota, one section of Dee's Battery and three companies of cavalry. Five companies of cavalry were left behind by mistake and joined me on the morning of the 13th. During the day of the 12th, I examined roads and placed the 8th Wisconsin and Dee's section on the hill, the 5th Minnesota in the town and the cavalry on the roads leading south and southwest. On the evening of the 12th, I received a series of telegrams from headquarters, which led me to believe that an attack was expected at any moment on Corinth and that General Rosecrans thought we were under strength. ["Attack on Corinth" and Rosecrans' concern about "under strength at Iuka" do not seem to be mentioned in the telegrams now in the file.]

On the morning of the 13th, my pickets were driven in and captured, but we drove them back. We took two prisoners who told us that this was an advanced force of 2,000 Confederates. Now our telegraph was out and the railroad was blocked. I sent couriers and telegraph repairmen, but never saw them again. I saw many enemy signal rockets. A courier that I sent to the garrison at Burnsville returned at 8:00 p.m. and told me there was not a single Union soldier there. I was now cut off and surrounded by a superior force. At 9:00 p.m., I notified Captains Simmons and Mott to prepare the stores for destruction. I awaited orders to hold Iuka, at all costs. I sent orders to destroy the stores at daylight and evacuate the town. Captain Webster, then commanding the cavalry, was ordered to form a rear guard and to burn our supplies as we moved out.

When we were four miles out of the town, enemy forces in superior numbers pressed our rear and my cavalry came up informing me that they had been surprised and unable to burn the stores. As we neared Burnsville, I deployed my forces [here he gave considerable tactical detail] but found no enemy at Burnsville. My scouts reported sharpshooters [Federal? Confederate?] in Burnsville. We turned towards Farmington. A few enemy shot at us from a swamp. Captain Webster asked me to move my columns so that he could get at the snipers. We arrived at Farmington without losing a wagon or a man. One of my men who had been wounded in the initial skirmish and released by the Confederates reported that the enemy has at least 3,000 cavalry and believed that I had 17,000 men.

General Rosecrans, who had had Murphy arrested on September 14, was not very impressed by these explanations and replied, "I think extreme fright and a want of judgment of Colonel Murphy so manifest as to need no comment. For example, he says that he formed a line facing westward expecting a fight at Burnsville, and when he learned that two companies of sharpshooters were there, he still remained in order of battle over one hour, until Captain Webster requested that Murphy get out of the way. Murphy never went to the telegraph office, nor did anything to know if his retreat was not sufficient, nor did he wait for further orders. He got out of the way of Captain Webster and got prosperously into Farmington."

After several days of testimony, the court-martial board, headed by Brig. Gen. John McArthur, found Murphy not guilty of both the charge of "misbehaving himself in the face of the enemy," and that of "shamefully abandoning a post which he had been commanded to defend." Rosecrans reviewed the findings and made the following comment:

> The General Commanding, with much regret, feels compelled to disapprove the findings of the Court. The evidence shows fully the abandonment of the post and public stores without pressure from the enemy. It shows a rapid retreating march, without the show of anything deserving the name of pursuit. The forming of a line of battle, faced to the rear, without a shadow to justify it. It shows a colonel in command of a covering column, retreating without feeling of the enemy's advance, which had subsequently to be done; leaving to fall into the hands of the rebels, public stores which he was bound by the first principle of military caution to have seen destroyed, and that he could have remained three hours later to accomplish this without seeing a Rebel infantry soldier to interfere with him. But when seven miles distant, and behind a defile, he forms a line of battle faced, not toward, but from the defile, and pressed forward to Farmington, some ten miles, leaving at Burnsville, without heed or notice, the telegraph operator and two companies of sharpshooters, for a garrison to meet the enemy from whom he was retreating.
>
> The General Commanding, having himself a high personal and official regard for Colonel Murphy, considers that to pass over such conduct with nothing but the announcement of an honorable acquittal, would be to sanction that which would ruin the service. Colonel Murphy is released from arrest and will report to Brigadier General [David] Stanley for duty. The General Court-martial, of which Brigadier General J. McArthur is president, is dissolved.

Whatever the nature of Colonel Murphy's illness at Iuka, in early November his surgeon submitted a certificate, affirming that the colonel needed thirty days off duty because of "chronic inflammation of the liver."

By early December, Murphy appears to have recovered from both the shadow cast by his court-martial and his liver troubles, and was the object of the following order by General Grant, dated December 13, 1862. "The Territory from and including Cold Water on the north, to and including Oxford on the south, will constitute the District of the Tallahatchie. Colonel R. C. Murphy, 8th Regiment Wisconsin Infantry Volunteers, is assigned to the command of same, and will with the force under his command, guard and protect the railroad through his District." Seven days later, Colonel Murphy surrendered the town of Holly Springs, Mississippi, to the Confederates, including all of its vast store of Federal military supplies. A few days later, he was paroled and headed north, but that was not the end of his problems. On December 28, 1862, Grant sent the following telegram to Maj. Gen. Stephen A. Hurlbut, commanding the District of Memphis: "Arrest and detain Colonel Murphy of the 8th Wisconsin. He is a paroled prisoner, now on his way out by my authority. He will not be permitted to leave Memphis until again authorized from these headquarters."

What General Grant had in mind for Colonel Murphy was revealed in General Orders No. 4, dated January 8, 1863, Headquarters, Department of the Tennessee. He began by expressing pride and satisfaction in the Federal garrisons at Cold Water, Davis Mills, and Middleburg for "the heroic defense of their positions on the 20th, 21st and 24th of December, and their successful repulse of an enemy many times their number." Grant continued Section 1 of these General Orders by naming the specific regiments, which he commended for their valor and discipline. However, Section 2 of the General Order was much different.

> Colonel R. C. Murphy of the 8th Regiment Wisconsin Infantry Volunteers, having, while in command of the post at Holly Springs, Mississippi, neglected and failed to exercise the usual and ordinary precautions to guard and protect the same, having after repeated and timely warning of the approach of the enemy, failed to make any preparations or defense, or show any disposition to do so, and having with a force amply sufficient to have repulsed the enemy and protected the public stores entrusted to his care, disgracefully permitted him to capture the post and destroy the stores—and the movement of troops in the face of an enemy rendering it impractical to convene a court martial for his trial, is therefore dismissed [from] the service of the United States to take effect from the 20th day of December, 1862, the date of his cowardly and disgraceful conduct.

Murphy himself was hardly unaware of his position after Holly Springs. Earl Van Dorn and his Confederate raiders had destroyed about a million dollars (in 1862 money) worth of Federal supplies after coming undetected through Murphy's pickets. The *Mobile Register and Advertiser* reported that Murphy had been found under his bed, and was brought to Van Dorn still in his night clothes. The *Official Records* contain Murphy's views: "My fate is most mortifying. I have wished a hundred times today that I had been killed."

At this point Colonel Murphy disappears from the Federal records. He did not apply for a pension and certainly was not eligible for one. Sadly, the second thoughts he may have had after Iuka did not inspire him to anything better at Holly Springs.

Chapter Forty-One

"The Worst Colonel I Ever Saw"

COL. FRANCIS QUINN

With these ringing words, Austin Blair, governor of Michigan, summarized the career of Col. Francis Quinn of the 12th Michigan Volunteer Infantry. The nation's political system for selecting volunteer officers produced a few winners, a mass of competents, and a few true losers. Quinn and his immediate subordinate, Lt. Col. William H. Graves, set a classic example of how not to lead a regiment, and, at Shiloh, in their first battle, the regiment was so filled with internal conflict that it split into two noncommunicating segments, each fighting separately.[1]

Quinn was an Irish immigrant who had achieved small-town success in Niles, Michigan. He was active in Republican politics, which rewarded him with the postmastership of Niles. He had no military experience. Graves also was a Republican but had some combat experience, having been wounded at Bull Run while serving as a captain in the 1st Michigan Infantry.

Even before the 12th Michigan left its state, the relationship between Quinn and Graves had deteriorated from active dislike to virulent hatred. They fought over every detail of regimental organization. Each put forward a different candidate for quartermaster. They finally agreed upon Graves's selection, but as soon as the train left Niles for St. Louis, the governor, who owed political favors to Quinn, removed the just-appointed quartermaster and substituted Quinn's selection. The schism between the colonel and the lieutenant colonel deepened.

From St. Louis, the 12th Michigan traveled on the steamer *Meteor* to Cairo, where they picked up a new division commander, Brig. Gen. Benjamin M. Prentiss, and proceeded to a sleepy stop on the riverbank—Pittsburg Landing. In a day or so, the 12th was camped at the far left of the southern boundary of Grant's command, as part of Col. Everett Peabody's Brigade, which included the 21st and 25th Missouri and the 16th Wisconsin.

It is estimated that 60 percent of the men around Shiloh Church that week had never heard a shot fired in anger, and thousands had never been taught to load a rifle. The officers were little better. Even the senior men seemed to lack the caution taught by experience: no entrenchments had been dug, no fields of fire cleared, no distant pickets sent out. The Confederate commander, Albert Sidney Johnson, was far away at Corinth, Union reinforcements 25,000 strong under Don Carlos Buell were arriving from Nashville, and there was nothing to worry about.

Of course, the Confederates were on their way, moving an entire army undetected up to the very edge of the Union position. In spite of skirmishing on April 4 and 5, Grant, Sherman, and Prentiss all remained convinced that danger was far away. A few men, even a chaplain, thought differently.

The Rev. Andrew J. Eldred of the 12th Michigan noted that Prentiss had sent pickets no farther out than 1500 yards and had dug no rifle pits. But who listens to a chaplain? Three line officers, however, displayed both alertness and initiative: Col. Everett Peabody and Maj. James Powell of the 25th Missouri, and Lt. Col. Graves of the 12th Michigan. On April 5, Powell had seen a dozen Confederates peering out from the underbrush; he conferred with Graves, who was officer of the day. Colonel Quinn himself seems to have been relatively invisible throughout. Powell and Graves convinced Prentiss to send out several patrols, who returned at 7:00 P.M., having found no Confederates. At 8:30 P.M., a long line of Confederate campfires could be seen in the distance. The sounds of Rebel bugle calls drifted through the evening air. These were reported to General Prentiss, who felt little concern. Graves and the man who had seen the campfires went to Prentiss again, who again told them not to worry. That same evening, Peabody had recommended a state of alert, but Prentiss dismissed this as well. On his own initiative, Peabody sent out five companies at 3:00 A.M., with orders to look for the enemy.

All through the afternoon and night of April 5, Graves and Quinn had no discussion of these events, and Quinn seems to have taken neither interest nor initiative on the issue of the approaching Confederates. His only contribution during the evening was to shoot a hole in his own left hand while sitting in his tent.

At 5:00 A.M., the scouting parties skirmished with the enemy and Union wounded began to come in. This seems to have finally convinced Prentiss that something was up. He sent out a party under Col. David Moore; Arkansas infantrymen quickly shot Moore and most of his officers out of the saddle.

Without waiting for orders from Prentiss, Peabody ordered the drummer boy to sound the "Long Roll," calling all his men to arms. By now, the battle was on, and Colonel Quinn finally appeared. He called for Graves, who responded slowly, probably from having been up all night. In his report, Quinn attributed Graves's slowness to cowardice.

The full force of the Confederate attack now reached all of Prentiss's division, who finally were ordered "To Arms." There was retreat and rout everywhere. Only the arrival of a force under Brig. Gen. Stephen A. Hurlbut allowed Prentiss to regroup and form the now-famous defense of the Hornets' Nest. Meanwhile, the 12th Michigan continued to suffer from the Quinn-Graves feud. Graves commanded most of the regiment, though a handful under

Quinn fought entirely independently. Between 4:30 and 5:30 P.M., the final Confederate assault collapsed Prentiss's position and he surrendered. Graves, Quinn, and two hundred of the 12th Michigan escaped the Hornets' Nest, reunited, and fought together the second day, when Grant's reinforced army drove the Confederates back.

Shiloh was over, but the Quinn–Graves battle was growing in fury. Each accused the other of cowardice. In his official report, Colonel Quinn noted, "About daylight, the dead and wounded began to be brought in. The firing grew closer and closer, till it became manifest that a heavy force of the enemy was upon us. [Quinn does not seem to notice the self-indictment in his narrative.] The division was ordered into line of battle by General Prentiss." Quinn's report goes on to say that after about thirty minutes of fighting around the regimental camp, the entire division was driven back, scattered and broken.

What Quinn failed to mention in his report was his shooting himself in the hand, his having no part in the detection of the approaching force, his having had no communication with his own lieutenant colonel, and his spending the night of April 6 warm and dry on a steamboat while Graves and the other men of the12th Michigan camped in the rain.

Internal dissension and demoralization rose to a crescendo. Maj. George Kimmel, who had run at Shiloh, resigned to avoid a court-martial, but not until he had filed charges against Quinn, which led to a military commission, which arrived at no conclusion and took no action.

The Quinn–Graves battle spread to the newspapers and to the governor's office. The *Niles Inquirer* favored Quinn, lauded his bravery in a May 14, 1862, article entitled "Headquarters Regiment Michigan Infantry." The article accused Graves of cowardice, while the rival paper praised Graves. Both men wrote to the governor, denouncing each other. The reputation of the regiment was such that when Maj. Gen. John A. McClernand was ordered to move his command to Washington, D.C., he asked if he could leave the 12th Michigan behind. No one wanted them.[2]

The governor asked Quinn to resign, which he did in July 1862; the regimental surgeon was so eager to see his colonel gone that he filed an exaggerated report, claiming that only a permanent change of climate could save Colonel Quinn's life. But Quinn wasn't gone yet. He changed his resignation to a request for a thirty-day medical leave and after claiming a week later that his health had been suddenly restored, withdrew his resignation. It was too late. The governor had had enough. Blair telegraphed Secretary of War Edwin M. Stanton, urging that Stanton accept the original resignation. In this message, Blair declared that Quinn was the "worst colonel I ever saw and has made me more trouble than all the rest put together."

On September 1, 1862, the officers of the 12th Michigan preferred charges of neglect of duty, cowardice, and incompetency against Quinn, and requested a court-martial. Quinn avoided the trial by mailing off a new resignation and left his regiment without either saying good-bye or asking permission to go. He took with him nearly all the regimental papers.

Quinn failed to remove his own military service records, which are still in the National Archives and contain the charges that he escaped by resigning. In their full form they occupy twelve pages. Even in summary, they are a damning litany:

> Shamefully deserted his command on the battlefield of Shiloh . . . at Pittsburgh Landing . . . in a cowardly manner deserted his command . . . treats officers in a very ungentlemanly and discourteous manner . . . has never given orders regulating the proper disposition of the sick . . . gave highly improper [drill] commands, showing thereby that he was incompetent . . . used a solder as his private cook . . . removed a sick man from the ambulance to make room for his personal cook . . . unnecessarily moved sick men two miles in the rain . . . would not allow the chaplain to see a dying man . . . tied a solder to a tree over the objections of the man's commander . . . used a pass to engage in illegal cotton trading . . . caused to be written a letter to the Niles <u>Inquirer</u> praising his own "bravery and daring" . . . [and] delivered a negro to a man who claimed the negro as his slave.

Seventeen witnesses volunteered to testify against Quinn.

Quinn returned to Niles a ruined man. At the first postwar reunion of the 12th Michigan, a resolution was passed branding Quinn as a liar. He did not attend future reunions. He moved to a suburb of Chicago and entered the livestock business. In 1874 his wife left him. Two years later, he fell dead in a steam bath, a victim of "rheumatism of the heart." A government-issue gravestone stands over his remains in the Niles Silverbrook Cemetery. His deadly rival, William H. Graves, promoted to colonel, restored the morale of the 12th Michigan and led it ably through the siege of Vicksburg and on to its final mustering out in early 1866.

Chapter Forty-Two

Hiding Behind a Tree Stump

COL. DAVID H. WILLIAMS

Col. David H. Williams, commander of the 82nd Pennsylvania Infantry, studied civil engineering as a youth, and at age eighteen became a railroad surveyor, first in Michigan and later in Pennsylvania. He served in the Mexican War, though the details remain obscure.

In Pittsburgh, his militia activity was a springboard to a colonelcy when war came. The 82nd Pennsylvania was organized at Philadelphia as the 31st Regiment of Volunteers (a designation it kept until mid-1862) and served at Washington and Manassas until it joined McClellan's Peninsular Campaign. It was there, at the Battle of Fair Oaks (Seven Pines), that Williams's qualities came into question.[1]

His trial on August 10, 1862, was under the presidency of Brig. Gen. William H. Emory. The charge was misbehavior in the face of the enemy. There were five specifications.

Colonel Williams ordered Capt. Charles Williams and his company to skirmish through the woods near Fair Oaks Station, and while these men were out, he moved the rest of the regiment away. As a result, he left Company A without support, orders, or even any notice "whereby the said Company A and officers was nearly surrounded by the enemy, the said Colonel David H. Williams allowing himself to be so overcome by fear as to forget that the said Company A was absent, until informed by Major John M. Wetherall, this at Fair Oaks, Virginia, on the 31st day of May, 1862."

On that same day the Confederates had advanced to within ten paces of Colonel Williams's regiment when he ordered his men to cease firing. This was not because of any surge of humanitarian impulse, but because the colonel was lying on the ground behind a stump at the extreme right of his position, unable to see the center of his own line. He had previously been ordered directly by his superior officer, Brig. Gen. Darius Couch, to take the usual position of a regimental commander, but did not.

On June 22, Williams demonstrated another failure of command. At the Williamsburg Road, he failed to post his pickets properly so that there was a considerable gap between his left and the right of the next regiment. When the

Confederate pickets entered the gap, confusion and panic ensued. This emotion spread to Colonel Williams, who "became so much frightened as to give several orders countermanding each other, and was so confused as to be unfit for duty."

On July 1, 1862, near Turkey Creek, Virginia, Williams was ordered to defend a certain sector. He ordered his troops to open fire, commencing on the left, "front rank first," when at least two of his companies noticed that the troops in front of them were not Confederates at all, but were instead, men of the 61st Pennsylvania. The order to fire was countermanded by Major Wetherall, who explained the situation to the colonel. Williams persisted, and again gave the order to fire, whereupon his troops cried out, "Come out from behind that tree, you damned coward and see for yourself."

On that same day, Williams placed a portion of his command where there was no enemy to engage. The principal danger to his troops was from Union batteries, which were firing over them, wounding several of Colonel Williams's own men. When Capt. Joseph Rudolph of Company H and Capt. Charles Williams of Company A went to the colonel to protest, the reply was, "Keep your companies where they are or I will shoot you." This also was at Turkey Creek.

The fifth specification referred both to the events of June 22 and of July 1, and charged that Williams "gave way to fear and trembling in the presence of the privates of his regiment, to such an extent as to be unable to attend to the duties of his command. His fear was to such an extent as to excite the contemptuous remarks of the private soldiers while under fire, saying, 'Come out from behind that tree, Stumpy Williams, you coward, you are not competent to command,' and such like language."

In the prosecution testimony, Maj. John Wetherall stated, "I thought the colonel had been wounded, as I had not seen him for some time. I finally found him on the extreme right, lying down behind a tree stump. The men were calling out to him, 'Come out from behind that tree stump, you damned coward.'"

Capt. Joseph Rudolph had also observed the colonel's subarboreal position, and remarked further on the occasion when his men were under Union fire: "My men were being wounded by our own canister, so I pulled them back. Colonel Williams collared me violently from behind and criticized me harshly."

The court, after much testimony, returned a surprising verdict: not guilty on all specifications except the one relating to his own men being under Union artillery fire. "The Court finds the accused guilty of the facts alleged, but attaches no criminality thereto, as Colonel Williams was placed in that position by superior authority, with orders to hold it, and he took prompt and proper means to inform his superiors" of the problems of that position. The court went further than that, taking the colonel's part against the officers and men of his regiment:

> The Court deems it their duty to notice the evidences of a mutinous spirit and want of harmony and discipline in the regiment commanded

by Colonel Williams, which the testimony exhibits. It appears by that testimony that men were allowed to apply opprobrious epithets in the ranks to their commanding officer and, except in one instance, no effort was made by the officers to suppress it, but on the contrary, the practice seems to have been made a merit of, and exhibited in the charges and the testimony with a prominence which shows that some of the officers and men of that regiment are insensible to the first requirements of discipline.

This view of the regiment as a willful and mutinous lot was supported by the reviewing officer, Maj. Gen. Erasmus Keyes, an old West Point man, who wrote, "The foregoing proceedings are confirmed. Colonel Williams is released from arrest and will resume his sword and return to duty. The Major General commanding the corps regrets to perceive in the foregoing proceedings and the testimony the evidences of a want of discipline in the 31st Regiment of Pennsylvania Volunteers. This fault will at once be corrected."

Williams kept his command. Many of his men who survived Turkey Creek died at Malvern Hill. Williams survived Antietam and, just before Fredericksburg, was promoted to brigadier general of Volunteers. Someone must have had some doubts about Williams, as his brigadier's commission was never forwarded and his colonel's commission expired on March 4, 1863. This effectively discharged him from the army.

He returned to his civilian profession of engineer, but bad health cut short this career. He was still able to write, however, and he turned out dozens of magazine and newspaper articles. He died of apoplexy on June 1, 1891, at Allegheny, Pennsylvania, and was buried in the cemetery at 4734 Butler Street in Pittsburgh.

PART FIVE

A Miscellany

Chapter Forty-Three

Sense Enough to Come in Out of the Rain

LT. COL. EDWARD F. ELLIS AND COL. WILLIAM M. WHEATLEY

Two colonels, one from Illinois and one from Indiana, were both charged with the grave offense of "conduct grossly unmilitary and dangerous to the safety and discipline of his command."

The first defendant was Lt. Col. Edward F. Ellis, a married banker, age forty-three, who had been appointed to command the 15th Illinois Regiment of Volunteer Infantry by Gov. Richard Yates. In the first week of January 1862, he was temporarily in command of the First Brigade, First Division of the Army in Central Missouri, encamped at Lamine Cantonment.[1]

A severe winter storm swept the state that month, with rain, sleet, and bitter cold. Colonel Ellis chose not to mount brigade guards, as there were no tents for the guards, cold weather clothing was woefully inadequate and, in the colonel's opinion, his men were in greater danger from the cold than from the Confederates. For this, he was court-martialed.

The first witness was Lt. C. F. Barber, of the 15th Illinois, who described the weather as "stormy, cold, raining and disagreeable, dangerous to the men." Maj. William Goddard testified that brigade guards had never been mounted until December 28, when a mule had been stolen and Col. Alvin Hovey (usually commanding) had feared that more stock would be stolen. "The night Colonel Ellis took the guard off, no man could stand it without being frozen."

Colonel Ellis spoke in his own defense:

> The charges are inappropriate. To truly defend against enemy approach, far outlying pickets would be needed, not brigade guards, who would be too close to sound an alarm. Further, when I took command, I found no order for a brigade guard. I simply followed my predecessor's practice. I console myself with the reflection that the charges against me are for humanity, for sympathizing with soldiers,

destitute of every proper accommodation . . . exposed to the severe storms of midwinter.

Colonel Ellis was acquitted, but the coming of warm spring weather did not bring good fortune. On April 6, 1862, he was killed at the battle of Pittsburgh Landing in Tennessee.

Col. William M. Wheatley had been a lumber dealer before his appointment as commander of the 26th Regiment of Illinois Volunteer Infantry. In the third week of January 1862, he commanded the same brigade at the same location as had Colonel Ellis, and was also charged with "conduct grossly unmilitary and dangerous to the safety and discipline of his command, and did, on the pretext of cold weather, take off guards, both internal and external.[2]

Maj. C. E. Hines of the 24th Indiana was the first to testify. "The weather was very bad. We requested guard tents, but none arrived. Any guard posted would have been frozen." Colonel Wheatley gave this defense:

Under Colonel Hovey, we camped many weeks at several locations— Springfield, Tipton, Otterville, and Sedalia—without a guard being posted. In Colonel Hovey's absence, I posted a guard until the night of January 16th, when the weather turned bad again. Captain Mankin, who was Officer of the Day, came to me and said that even with changing the guard every hour, the men were being frozen. Several of the men have required amputation.

Colonel Wheatley was also acquitted, but for him the future held another court-martial. At Springfield, Missouri, in August 1862, in a trial presided over by Col. Clark Wright of the 6th Missouri Cavalry, Wheatley was charged with absence without leave, fraud, and disobedience of orders. The specifications were that he had gone beyond the limits of the camp without permission, that he had connived with the blacksmith in making a private brand and using it on a horse stolen from a citizen of Missouri, and that he had refused to discharge one Pvt. Thomas McLoughlin in direct violation of the orders of General Halleck. Further, it was charged that he had permitted men, in particular Principal Musician E. G. Collins and Sgt. George Buchanan, to be absent in violation of general orders.

On the charge of being AWOL, the first witness was Lt. J. B. Roath, who had no information regarding Wheatley's travels. The second witness, Lt. S. M. Bannister, did not know where the colonel was at Christmas, but had heard, secondhand, that the colonel had been in Indianapolis with Gen. John W. Turner's permission. Capt. N. A. Logan, also called as a witness, had no relevant information.

The second day of the trial, it was begun *de novo,* as Lt. Col. John Pound was unable to continue and a new member had to be sworn in. The same three witnesses testified once again that they knew nothing.

On the charge of fraud, John W. Robertson, the regimental blacksmith, said that he had been ordered, by the wagonmaster, to make a brand, with "US" on it, but had not branded any horse, had no knowledge of the horse that was branded, and knew of no connection between Colonel Wheatley and either the horse or the branding iron.

Regarding the charge that Colonel Wheatley had failed to follow orders in discharging Private McLoughlin, or in permitting the sergeant and the musician to be absent, there were two witnesses. Maj. John Clark testified that McLoughlin had, indeed, been discharged as ordered, and that the papers ordering his discharge had been lost. Capt. C. E. Whitsell added his evidence: "Private McLoughlin has been discharged and received no pay at the last muster. I know of no evidence that Colonel Wheatley created a false muster."

Wheatley was acquitted. In his review of the proceedings, Brig. Gen. Egbert B. Brown commented:

> The commanding general disapproves of this futile attempt to injure a superior officer by bringing charges of a frivolous character, sustained by not a particle of evidence. If the officers in the command would devote themselves to the faithful discharge of their duties, instead of attempting to destroy the influence of their commanding officers, they would provide a useful service to the country, and such a service as is expected from them at this time. The findings are approved and Colonel Wheatley will resume his sword and take command of his regiment.

Perhaps Wheatley had had enough. He resigned his commission in the month following the second court-martial. He served again, briefly, during the Morgan Raid scare, as captain of a militia unit assembled at Indianapolis.

In 1907, at the age of eighty-two, he applied for a pension. The doctor's affidavit described the colonel as six feet, one inch in height, with grey eyes, suffering "the infirmities of age," and living with his daughter in Los Angeles. He was awarded $20 a month, increased to $24 in 1912. Wheatley lived another five years, passing from this earth as America entered another great war.

Chapter Forty-Four

In the Middle of the Forehead

COL. JONAS P. HOLLIDAY

The trial of Col. Jonas P. Holliday was a court of inquiry, rather than a court-martial. The board of six officers met in early April 1862 near Harper's Ferry to investigate what had happened to the commander of the 1st Vermont Cavalry.

The regiment had been mustered the previous November at Burlington, Vermont, and four weeks later was sent to Annapolis, Maryland. There they remained until the move to Harper's Ferry in late March 1862. Now, these six officers had a mystery to be solved—how to explain the events that took the life of their commander.[1]

The first witness to give evidence was the regimental adjutant, Edgar Ritkin.

> The colonel was upset the last time I saw him, very concerned about an order given to Captain [Lemuel] Platt. The Chief Bugler came to me and said that the colonel wished to see me on the Stone Bridge. I could not imagine why there; I rode there and saw him in the distance. When I arrived, the colonel's horse was hitched to the bushes. I called out, "Colonel!" but received no reply. I dismounted and went to the river and saw him lying in the water. When I took him out, he was still warm and breathing, but soon stopped breathing. His orderly arrived and we turned him over so that the water might not strangle him. I unbuttoned his shirt and put my hand on his heart, but it had ceased to beat.
>
> I recall that he had worn a pistol for the first time that morning. I think he did it to himself. The cause is clear to me—an alteration of the mind or a low despondency. I saw no one around the spot. When help arrived, I notified Lieutenant Colonel [George] Kellogg.

P. H. Calwell, quartermaster sergeant of Company I explained what he saw.

> I saw him ride down the road about 50 rods [825 feet] away. He went out of sight. Then I heard the report of a pistol. I set off down the road with another soldier. We met the adjutant, who called out that the man

with the swiftest horse should go for the surgeon. My companion went off and the adjutant and I went to the riverbank. The adjutant said that the colonel had been shot. I saw no one lurking around the area. We found the pistol in the mud. One chamber had been fired. We took the body to Regimental Headquarters in an ambulance. I think he died by his own hand.

L. H. King, quartermaster sergeant of Company C testified, concurring with Calwell. Captain E .B. Sawyer saw the pistol and confirmed that only one chamber was empty. "After I examined the pistol, I gave it to Lieutenant Colonel Kellogg."

The regimental surgeon, Dr. George S. Gale gave his evidence.

No post-mortem was done but I feel certain that death was occasioned by a bullet wound received in the brain, about the center of his forehead. The ball would appear to be lodged in the brain, as there is no appearance of it having come out the other side. There was a slight discoloration about the wound, which might have been from the gunpowder.

The colonel had not been well during his time with the regiment. He had been nervous and excitable. On the march from Annapolis to Poolsville, he did not rest well. At his request, I once used chloroform to calm him. [Chloroform is a liquid which, when inhaled, can be used as a general anesthetic, and in small doses by mouth can relieve pain and spasm. Chloroform and ether were the chief anesthetics for surgery at the time of the Civil War.] I let him have a bottle of chloroform, but I took it away as he was using too much.

He had no symptoms of delirium. He refused to use stimulants, though I had suggested them. [A typical stimulant would have been brandy.] All the business of conducting a regiment agitated the colonel. I persuaded him to rest at a house in Harper's Ferry, and he insisted that I stay with him. He was afraid to be alone. He told me, "If I can't get some sleep, I will go insane." His sighs and groans convinced me that the suffering and privation of the men, both now and in the future, distressed him. He had had not more than two hours of sleep a night in the past month, but I saw no reason to fear suicide.

Having heard the evidence, the six-man court issued its conclusions. "The deceased came to his death from a bullet wound made by some person or persons unknown, but from the evidence adduced, the Court is of the opinion that the act was committed by his own hand."

In terms of today's psychiatric terminology, the label of major depression with agitation might be applied. Persons with this condition have extreme insomnia, feelings of worthlessness and hopelessness about the future, and cannot imagine any improvement. In extreme cases, their bodies as well as their minds are agitated and they will pace back and forth, wringing their hands and speaking of what a disappointment they have been to others.

Unlike the volunteer colonels, it was not a lack of familiarity with military life that had unhinged Holliday. He had graduated from West Point in 1850 and successfully completed eleven years of active service before the war, with posts in New Mexico, Texas, Kansas, and the Dakota Territory. In theory, he was prepared to lead. Nevertheless, psychiatric speculation about someone who died 130 years ago must have limited validity. What is known is that no surviving family member applied for a pension in the years that followed.

Chapter Forty-Five

Sick at Astor House

LT. COL. JULIUS C. KRETSCHMAR

History has not been kind to the lieutenant colonel of the 103rd New York Volunteers. The organization of his unit is confused in the records, the spelling of his name seems entirely dependent upon whatever orthographic frenzy seized the scribe, he was accused of unauthorized absence when he seems to have been sick, and many of his pension files are lost.[1]

The 103rd had its origin in the winter of 1861–62. Its organizer, Col. Baron Frederick W. von Egloffstein, named the infant regiment after William H. Seward, Lincoln's secretary of state. Elsewhere in New York City, Col. Casper Schneider was raising his 3rd Regiment of German Rifles. Neither Schneider nor von Egloffstein found enough men to fill a regiment, but the two groups combined were sufficient to make the new 103rd New York Volunteers, which in April 1862 arrived in New Bern, North Carolina, where they stayed for the next four months.

They were engaged in the skirmish at Gillett's Farm, on April 13, and at Haughton's Mills, both in North Carolina, two weeks later. In July they were back on shipboard, headed for Norfolk once again and in August were in Fredericksburg.

The lieutenant colonel in question must first be properly named. He appears in the records variously as Tul. C. Crutchmar, Julius C. Kretzchmar, Julius C. Kretschmar, and Julius Kretchman. It may be easiest to simply name him by an initial.

Colonel K. was age thirty-four when he enrolled at New York City on February 3, 1862. The following day he was mustered as major and on April 4, promoted to lieutenant colonel. In June 1862 he was listed as absent due to illness, and a Surgeon's Certificate dated August 5, 1862, recommended that he be sent north for his health.

For reasons unclear in the record, he is listed as absent without leave for July and August of that year, in spite of a second surgeon's letter, this one in late August, certifying that Colonel K. was sick with typhoid fever and dysentery and unable to do duty. The certificate, still in the records, was attached to

197

a letter penned by the colonel himself, written at Astor House Hotel in New York City, where he was recuperating. Sadly, his signature on the letter is not easily deciphered.

In spite of his letter and the certificate, he was still carried on the books as AWOL in September 1862. In October he submitted his resignation. On November 4 the records show him as being discharged from the army at Washington. The files of the New York State Adjutant General's Office show November 1862 as the end of his military career.

To further illustrate the confusion and complexity of uniform data gathering regarding court-martialed colonels, no actual trial record has appeared, but he appears in two different long lists of dismissed officers, once as "—Kretchman, Lt. Colonel, 103rd New York," and in a different printed list of dismissed officers as "Tul C. Crutchmar, Lt. Colonel, 103rd New York Volunteers."

His being dismissed, under whatever name, would seem to end the saga, but how then to explain a document dated March 1863, at Dry Tortugas, off the tip of Florida, which revoked his "dismissal?" Tortugas, a maximum security prison, was hardly the place for a New York colonel with typhoid, and "dismissed" most commonly signified a punitive discharge from the army.

Equally puzzling is this note sent by Abraham Lincoln to Marsena Patrick, provost marshal of the Army of the Potomac, on November 12, 1864: "Please oblige me by seeing and hearing the bearer, Lt. Col. Kretschmar, who is well vouched to me as a most worthy gentleman, and who wishes to see you on business."[2]

The few scraps that remain of his pension record indicate that he received a pension after the war and that following his death, his widow, Ambrosia, received further payments, but the records that have survived do not state his illness or how it might be service connected.

The clichéd "mists of time" have certainly covered the tracks of Colonel K., leaving even the spelling of his name in confusion. Did his chance for a glimpse of fame at Gillett's Farm cover him with momentary glory, or was he even then staggering from his bed to the privy, his intestines inflamed and ulcerated? Why was he at Dry Tortugas, Florida, one thousand miles from home? Did he bring the chronic and contagious typhoid bacillus home to his Ambrosia? And why was he dismissed instead of being allowed to resign? All these questions are apparently without answers.

Chapter Forty-Six

"Low and Bawdy Engravings"

COL. EBENEZER W. PEIRCE

Three hundred years before the Civil War, Pieter Brueghel painted *The Fall of Icarus*. The scene is a landscape. In the foreground, peasants carry on the routine of agriculture; beyond them lies the ocean. In the far distance, almost unnoticed, is a tiny splash, marking the end of the man who dared to fly so high. The peasants regard their labors as central, while the historian, with a longer view, might be drawn to the tragic aeronaut in the distance.

A scene of equally misplaced emphasis was played out by the officers of the 29th Regiment of Massachussetts Volunteers in March 1862. What they had witnessed out on the waters near their camp changed history: the first duel between ironclad ships—the clash of the *Monitor* and the *Merrimac*. But what seemed to preoccupy this regiment much more was the taste in literature and song of their colonel, Ebenezer W. Peirce.[1]

The 29th Massachussetts was organized at Newport News in December 1861, assembled from the fragments of several other units; the new regiment stayed at Newport News until May 1862, when it moved a few miles to Norfolk.

In the court-martial, Colonel Peirce faced five charges, with eleven specifications, beginning with "the said Ebenezer W. Peirce, Colonel of the 29th Massachussetts Volunteers, did send for certain privates of said regiment, to sing to him certain improper, vulgar and indecent songs. This at Camp Butler, Newport News, Virginia, on or about the tenth day of February 1862." The next specification was that two days later, he again requested a concert of "low, vulgar and indecent songs, and did listen to same." The third specification is identical with the others, except that it notes that Colonel Peirce "did laugh and encourage them while singing."

Other offenses alleged in the charges preferred included: leaving camp after dark without a pass on March 21, 1862; using a false and assumed name while on his nocturnal stroll; remaining out until a late hour; reading indecent and immoral literature; looking at "low and bawdy" pictures and engravings; assaulting Pvt. John H. Spears without justifiable cause; failing to drill and discipline his regiment;

and failing to instruct his officers. The fifth charge, "incompetency," was dropped by the court, which concluded that it had no jurisdiction over such an issue.

The reader today may be tempted to conclude that there was not enough to occupy this command, since the following testimony reflects the high points of an eight-day trial, eight days in which thirteen officers and at least one scribe were fully employed.

The first witness for the prosecution was Adj. John Collingwood, who described Capt. Charles Richardson's tent as the venue for the offensive singing. "Colonel Peirce summoned the men to sing. Some songs were very good, while others, such as 'The Farmer's Daughter,' were very vulgar, and the colonel seemed to be enjoying the singing." Lt. George H. Taylor recalled that "The songs were low, dirty and vulgar." When asked by the judge advocate to define "vulgar," he replied, "Having connexion with the other sex. The colonel liked that song and laughed out loud."

Capt. S. H. Dotin was equally scandalized. "Yes, the colonel laughed at the dirty songs. Also, he has failed to instruct us in our duties as line officers. It was understood that Colonel Peirce would resign if, after a month's trial, the officers did not like him. Lieutenant [Ezra] Ripley said we would not press charges if the colonel would resign."

Lt. Thomas Mayo told the court that the songs in question had been sung by four enlisted men and that the subject was "something about a gentleman putting his hand where the curly hair grows." Mayo was cross-examined by Colonel Peirce: "Was it curly hair or curly locks?" Mayo replied, "Curly locks, I think. It was the song called 'The Farmer's Daughter.'"

The next prosecution witness was Pvt. William McFarland, Colonel Peirce's orderly. "I saw the colonel reading a book called <u>Frances Hill</u>. It had bawdy pictures. It was in a closed drawer in the colonel's desk." The judge advocate asked, "Did you ever see any other obscene books or immoral literature in the colonel's quarters?" He had not.

The man allegedly struck by the colonel's sword, Pvt. John Spears, was next to testify. "We were in battalion drill, and I was coughing. I could not help it. The colonel struck me over the head with his sword, and sent me to the guard house. I was wearing my hat, but I could feel the blow." Capt. Libbeus Leach shed some light on the subject of coughing: "The colonel thought there was too much coughing in the ranks, and he held the captains responsible."

The next subject to be explored was the colonel's midnight foray, said by some to be a visit to "nigger wenches." Preliminary testimony had established that beyond the picket lines was the farm of a Mr. Parish, with three houses, one of which was occupied by several black families. To the soldiers, the latter building was the "Parish house," and its inhabitants included, in their opinion, "nigger wenches and squaws." Lt. William Pray commanded Picket Post No. 5. "About 2:00 in the morning, the colonel and another man came in. They had the countersign, but we were under orders to report anyone entering before sunrise. Colonel Peirce made no attempt to disguise himself." Four other men confirmed Lieutenant Pray's story. A "colored witness" for the prosecution was deemed inadmissible because of his race.

The "other man" with Colonel Peirce at 2:00 A.M. was twenty-one-year-old Lt. Freeman Taber, who testified under oath that "We were wet and visited the Negro house to dry our feet, and we were there about 15 minutes. At no time was the colonel alone with the Negroes. Nothing untoward happened." Lieutenant Taber had a few other things to say, which were of little help to the prosecution. "I was there when the singing happened in Captain Richardson's tent. There was nothing indecent, nothing at all. Lieutenant Ripley told me that if I testified 'the right way' the charges would be withdrawn."

On the seventh day of the court-martial, the subject returned to singing. Capt. Charles Richardson had this to say. "The singing was in my tent. Colonel Peirce asked that my sergeants sing. They are known for their good voices. They sang 'The Indian Warrior,' 'Yankee Maiden,' and 'Faded Flower.' They also sang 'The Farmer's Daughter.'" The court asked if there were vulgar words in the latter. "I should say not. Lieutenant Ripley, who now objects, was there. He clapped his hands and showed delight at the songs." The court continued its interest in "The Farmer's Daughter," asking, "What kind of a song is 'The Farmer's Daughter?'"

"It might be called a comic song."

"Does it not suggest the idea of something indecent?"

"With a little variation, it might have made a vulgar song."

Lt. Ezra Ripley, who seems to have been the colonel's nemesis, had much to say.

> Our drill is full of errors and the colonel does not correct them. I have seen him holding his sword in his left hand. I have seen half the regiment at shoulder arms, with the other half at support arms. Also, there are frequent errors when the regiment receives the order "By the right of companies to the rear into column." Colonel Peirce has posted only two written orders, one about passes for officers and one requiring target practice.
>
> When I spoke to Colonel Peirce, he agreed to resign in a month if the officers did not approve of him. The colonel also denied to me that he had connexion with the nigger wenches at Parish House.

Capt. Thomas Clarke took a different view of drill. "The colonel attended nearly every parade and battalion drill except when he was sick or on other duty. We have never been instructed by him, perhaps because my company was drilling correctly."

Now, a whole different light was shed on the colonel's alleged possession of pornography. Musician James Boothe had this to say: "I am Colonel Peirce's orderly now. William McFarland, the previous orderly, was dismissed for having brought a vulgar book, *Frances Hall*. It is a vulgar book. I have not read it, but I saw a picture in it when Private [Daniel] Blazedell had the book. The picture showed a woman with her legs open. She was all bare. Private McFarland also had a book called *Memoirs of a Lady of Pleasure*."

Further testimony showed that there were two groups of officers: "old" and "new." The old would not associate with the new, "even after they had been introduced." The old objected to Colonel Peirce, because they had heard that his conduct at Big Bethel was not good. The old officers "hooted" at the new.

After deliberation, the court found Colonel Peirce guilty of three of the charges and sentenced him to be dismissed from the service, but added a request for clemency. The proceedings were reviewed by Maj. Gen. John Wool and not approved. After analyzing all the parts of the findings, he concluded:

> There being no evidence before the Court to justify its decision, the sentence is remitted, Colonel Peirce is released from arrest and will resume the command of his regiment.
>
> The commanding general cannot forego calling attention to the fact, as presented by several witnesses, that a combination was formed by a portion of the officers, some of whom were witnesses on the part of the prosecution, to remove the accused from the regiment. Meetings were held and conditions prescribed, on which he was to retain his position.

Wool, who had previously served in the War of 1812 and the Mexican War, was deeply distressed by these evidences of collusion, insubordination, and subversion. He admonished the members of the court "to be more careful in the discharge of their grave and responsible duties, and by their proceedings show to the Army what they should be—the true conservators of its discipline and subordination."

General Wool was right, of course. The imperfectly perceived Icarus was, for the 29th Massachussetts, not only the change wrought by the ironclads, but the coming enormity of three more years of bitter fighting. Their regimental flags would soon reflect Fair Oaks, Seven Pines, Gaines Mill, Malvern Hill, Antietam, Fredericksburg, Vicksburg, Jackson, Blue Springs, Cold Harbor, and Petersburg—graver events, indeed, than who introduced what book into the colonel's tent.

Whatever may have been Peirce's shortcomings at Big Bethel, his physical courage could hardly be questioned after an examination of future events. A month after his court-martial, he was at Nelson's Farm, White Oak Swamp, Virginia, where he was "struck by a cannon ball from a Confederate battery, tearing off his right arm near the shoulder." On November 10, 1862, he wrote to his commanding general that his wound was still unhealed, and "although convalescent, still suffers great inconvenience from the hardship incident to service in the camp," and requested assignment to recruiting duty. His signature is a pained and awkward scrawl, done with his left hand. It is easy to imagine the other difficulties caused by a missing right arm: buttoning a frock coast, mounting a horse, even saluting.

In March 1863, he described his wound stump as "healed," and requested return to active service. Burnside gave him command of a post at Paris, Kentucky. Five months later, he assumed command of the Second Brigade, First Division, Ninth Army Corps. In March 1864 sickness took its toll: his surgeon certified Peirce as "suffering from bilious remittent fever [probably malaria] and unable to travel," and Peirce again requested recruiting duty. In July another surgeon's report described severe anemia, "the result of a long attack of intermittent fever." The next month, Dr. Thomas Bump described "vertigo, so severe he is unable to walk or even sit up more than a few minutes," and added the diagnosis, the following month, of "piles in their worst form." In early November, a further report stated that Colonel Peirce was totally disabled because of "General Nervous Debility from Miasmatic Diseases." The next week, Peirce resigned.

By now, his nemesis Lt. Ezra Ripley lay deep under Mississippi's fertile soil, having died of disease at Vicksburg on July 28, 1863.

Chapter Forty-Seven

"Goddamn Dutch Hounds"

LT. COL. GEORGE W. ROBERTS

If it was possible to be nattered to death, Lt. Col. George W. Roberts of the 42nd Illinois would have been dead in 1861. His misfortune was to be stationed in the very heartland of Missouri, at Smithton, a small village ten miles east of Sedalia. His *bete noir* was a small town merchant, whose chief stock in trade was indignation and possible secessionism.[1]

The 42nd Illinois was organized in Chicago in July 1861, and assigned to the Department of the Missouri from September until early 1862. The colonel of the regiment was a shadowy figure in these records, apparently very sick and, in practice, Colonel Roberts commanded the regiment much of the time.

In December 1861, based upon various citizen complaints, Colonel Roberts was accused of conduct unbecoming an officer and a gentleman. The first specification was that he "after receiving and reading an order from Colonel T. J. Turner, to give William Beck, a citizen, and his family, ingress and egress to his [Beck's] store, did refuse and fail to obey said order, and did in a violent manner force said Beck into his [Lieutenant Colonel Roberts'] tent, and say to Beck, 'You are an infernal liar, a damned liar, if you stated to Colonel Turner that you were not permitted to go into your store by the guard.' This at Smithton, Missouri, on or about the seventeenth day of December 1861."

The second specification accused Roberts of preventing Mrs. Beck from entering her husband's store "for the purpose of getting necessaries for home use, on the sixteenth day of December." The third specification accused Roberts of stating that he would pay no attention to Colonel Turner's order and "did further say to William Beck and to William Loewer, citizens, without just cause or provocation, 'you are infernal Dutch hounds,' and did violently shake William Beck and say to him, 'You are a damned thief, a damned liar, and if you say one word I will mash you to atoms.'"

Colonel Roberts pled not guilty to these charges, and asked to have the trial delayed because of insufficient notice. He filed a statement that said, "I have had no notice of this charge until 5:00 P.M. yesterday. I am commanding a post under orders of Brigadier General Pope. The third specification sets forth two distinct offenses under the Article of War Nos. 9 and No. 83. This makes the plea therefore double and cannot be pled to. Please see as my reference DeHart, page 289." He then added that the first specification was also a double plea and therefore could not be pled to. The court considered these objections, did not sustain them, and called the first witness.

This was William Beck himself, who stated that he had received a written order from Colonel Turner in Sedalia that he and his family should have full access to their store in Smithton. Beck says that he presented this order to Colonel Roberts, who then called him "an infernal liar." Mr. Beck was there with another German merchant, William Loewer, and Colonel Roberts told them both that there never had been a problem about entering Beck's store, but Mr. Beck claimed that his wife had been stopped from entering by a sentinel with a bayonet. Beck recalled that Colonel Roberts remarked that he and Loewer were both "God damned Dutch hounds, who only want to make money out of my soldiers." Roberts apparently also said that the order that he had received was from a man only one rank higher than himself.

Following Beck's initial testimony, there was a great deal of confusion revolving around examination and cross-examination about who said what to both General Pope and to Colonel Turner. The difficulty seemed to center around the word "storehouse," and its German equivalent. In the process of translation, it seemed to mean either a home or a store when, in fact, it meant neither.

The next witness was Mr. Loewer, who told the court that Colonel Roberts had hurt his feelings, but had done him no physical harm, and under cross-examination admitted that Colonel Roberts had given both him and Beck passes to come and go freely from the town of Smithton.

Col. Thomas Turner of the 15th Illinois was then called as a witness for the defense. He recalled that Mr. Beck had gone to Sedalia and spoken to General Pope, who had then ordered Turner to issue the access order to Mr. Beck. Turner, who seemed quite familiar with the situation in Smithton, noted that many other buildings at Smithton had been occupied by Federal troops and added that Mr. Beck had complained to him that he had been refused entrance to his own store by Colonel Roberts. There seemed to be an issue as to whether there was liquor in Mr. Beck's store, and Colonel Turner recalled that "I told Mr. Beck that Colonel Roberts had an undoubted right to prevent the sale of liquor or the congregation of soldiers in any store. Mr. Beck then claimed that he only wished to sell goods to the citizens of Smithton, not to the soldiers."

As he recalled these incidents, Colonel Turner's emotions seemed to warm. "When I spoke with Mr. Beck, he was very excited and talked rapidly in a mixture of German and English. I gave the pass to Beck and told him I did not want to see him again as I found him very annoying. I don't know what his basis for complaint is because when I saw him later, he mentioned nothing of ill treat-ment but said that he had moved away from the town of Smithton."

Mr. William Combs, a local citizen, was duly sworn in and stated that Beck had removed large portions of his goods from his storehouse when the regiment came to Smithton. The Federal troops occupied ten of Combs's houses, which was agreeable to Mr. Combs, and he added "I know from experience that Mr. Beck is a man of little veracity. He will treat his fellow man well for his money, but cares nothing further for him. Colonel Roberts' treatment of our town of Smithton is not at all oppressive, and as for Beck, I would not believe him if he swore under oath."

Capt. William Boomer of the 42nd Illinois also came to the defense of Colonel Roberts. When he was officer of the day, he gave orders that Mr. Beck was to have full access to his store, but that soldiers were to be kept from loaf-ing about the premises or going in the store. Boomer recalled that when the 42nd Illinois arrived in Smithton, Mr. Beck suggested many places where the men might be quartered but made no mention of any of his own houses.

Dr. E. Powell, the surgeon of the 42nd Illinois, recalled that the weather was very bad when the regiment arrived at Smithton and that there was a great deal of pressure and confusion finding adequate shelter for the troops. "Colonel [William] Webb could not assist at all as he was very sick, and, in fact, has since died. Colonel Roberts was also very sick, with chronic diarrhea and I advised him to stay in bed, but he stayed up and tended to his duties, caring for the troops."

Capt. Leonard Norton of the same regiment recalled to the court that he had received orders to specifically protect Mr. Beck's property, including a pile of coal in Beck's back yard. "Mr. Beck is very excitable. He insulted me the first time I saw him and he also wrote an article in a German newspaper denouncing Colonel Roberts." Norton further stated that the officers had exercised great care in assigning houses in Smithton so as not to inconvenience the citizens, and emphasized that two of the companies were still camped in the snow at the time of the court-martial, unable to find shelter under a roof. "Mr. Beck had already moved nearly all of his goods to the town of Sedalia and his Smithton store was nearly empty, yet he would not allow soldiers to be sheltered there. It is true that the sentinel stopped Mrs. Beck from entering once, only because he did not know who she was."

Capt. Edgar Swain of Company D noted that his men were camped in the snow and that Colonel Roberts had given Mr. Beck several days to vacate his store so that the troops could be sheltered. "Mr. Beck was very uncooperative, very slow to move his goods, refused us the key to the building and complained a great deal." Captain Swain had received information from a firm in St. Louis that Mr. Beck owed them money, was considered financially unreliable and that he did not want the soldiers quartered in his store so that he could remain open for business. "Beck told me that he could make three dollars for every dollar he spent."

Capt. Nathan Walworth also spoke in Roberts's defense: "Mr. Beck's property has not been injured in any way. Every little thing angers him. His article in the German newspaper, which Lieutenant [A.F.] Stevens translated for me, said that Smithton was under 'tyrannical rule.'"

The court considered all the evidence and voted for acquittal. Maj. Gen. Henry Halleck agreed with the verdict and ordered that Lt. Col. Roberts be released from arrest and resume his sword.

In January 1862, there were again difficulties between Roberts and the citizens of Smithton. The colonel wrote to his immediate superior stating, "I have been court martialled once before and acquitted, and now they are at it again. The citizens of Smithton have continued to slander me, especially a Mr. Bird Smith, whose letter is false in word and spirit. I believe that Smith is a Rebel sympathizer and is using this means of injuring our cause." This new file contained a considerable flurry of letters about who had used the stove in a church in Smithton. Neither the stove nor the church appears to have been damaged and a close reading of the correspondence suggests much ado about nothing.

Perhaps the citizens wore him down or perhaps his dysentery recurred, but Roberts was absent from duty in May and June 1862 because of sickness. However, his health appears to have improved and his military services found valuable because in September 1862, he was commanding the First Brigade of the First Division of the Army of Missouri.

Smithton and its citizens may have been unpleasant but combat itself was far worse. On December 31, 1862, Colonel Roberts was killed at the Battle of Stones River.

Chapter Forty-Eight

Firing Into the Suburbs

COL. JOHN H. TAGGART

The case of Col. John H. Taggart tells of sociological matters incomprehensible in today's economy, of another battle in a peach orchard, of musical penny-pinching, and of behavior which, on first reading, sounds like senseless brutality.[1]

Taggart's regiment, the 12th Pennsylvania Reserve Infantry (41st Volunteers) was organized in August 1861 and, after only ten days of training, was placed on a passenger train and sent to the defenses of Washington at Tennally Town. Taggart's trial began with charges related to the train trip. The president of the court was Brig. Gen. Edward O. C. Ord.

The one charge was "conduct unbecoming an officer and a gentleman," and contained four specifications. The first was that on August 11, 1861, Colonel Taggart "shamefully beat, choked and kicked one Minor Moyer, a private in Company B of the 12th Regiment PRVC [Pennsylvania Reserve Volunteer Corps] in a car on the Washington branch of the Baltimore and Ohio Railroad." The second specification was that on that same day that Colonel Taggart "did brutally beat and threaten Private George Davis, Company C, 12th Regiment PRVC, at a water station on the Washington branch of the Baltimore and Ohio Railroad."

The third specification related to an event on August 30, 1861, in which it was alleged that Colonel Taggart "used blasphemous and threatening language toward one George M. LeBarr, Teamster of Company B and did continue to threaten said George M. LeBarr, at Camp Tennally, District of Columbia."

The fourth specification was that on the evening of December 27, 1861, Colonel Taggart "obtained money from the company officers of his regiment by false promises and by agreeing to conditions with which he afterwards refused to comply."

There was another charge, "signing a false certificate for rations for himself and a servant," which the court declined to press. The court's reasoning for not pursuing the prosecution of this alleged false certificate sheds an interesting light on the economic and sociological differences between our century and the previous one. The court stated, "Officers travelling alone or far from home and far from most of their servants, are called on to give a minute and detailed description—color of eyes, color of hair, height, weight and so forth—of their servants, while the latter are being changed without any possibility of the officer becoming minutely acquainted with their persons. The officer hires servants on the road, or before the enemy, when he cannot obtain a scale of feet and inches to measure them."

This remarkable description of a bygone world in which the upper-middle class acquired and dismissed servants, either at a distance through managers, or casually without even glancing at the personal appearance of the new hire, continued with the following statement. "It is generally understood in the army that these allowances [of salary for servants] are intended to cover the expense officers are at for the servants at home, as well as in the field, and the certificates are looked upon as a mere formality—since the officer is compelled to furnish himself with servants."

Having thus disposed of the false certificate charge, the trial opened upon the charge and four specifications described above. The proceedings began with Colonel Taggart objecting to the presence of Col. Elihu B. Harvey as a member of the court, stating, "Colonel Harvey entertains a prejudice against officers from Philadelphia." Having disposed of the acceptability of Colonel Harvey, the prosecution produced its first witness, Pvt. Charles A. Meeker, of the 12th Pennsylvania. He testified that, "Colonel Taggart jerked Minor Moyer off the car, struck him twice and shoved him behind the car. Minor had fired his gun in the car. I had not heard that there was any order prohibiting firing guns in the cars."

Colonel Taggart swiftly disposed of this witness by the following question: "Since you entered the service, and a gun was put in your hand, have you understood that you could fire it off when you pleased?" After replying, "No, sir," Private Meeker retired from the witness stand, certainly meeker and perhaps wiser.

The next witness was Pvt. Thomas May, who stated that, "Private Moyer fired his gun in the car. The colonel jerked him off the car and hit him a couple of times." Another witness, Sgt. Maj. Mason Parker stated, "Soon after we left Baltimore, Private Moyer asked me if it would be okay to fire off his gun. I said it would be all right if he was careful where he shot. I knew nothing of an order prohibiting firing guns in the railway cars."

Now the court moved on to the third specification, regarding the "blasphemous and threatening language." The witness was Private LeBarr, who recalled that the sergeant major had come to him for a horse and that he had replied to the sergeant major that the quartermaster had ordered him not to release any horses. The sergeant major went away and returned with Colonel Taggart, who said, "You God damned son of a bitch, why did you not give a horse to the Sergeant Major? I have a notion to knock you down. If you don't shut up your glab, I will have you in chains in less than five minutes."

The court now considered the battle of the peach orchard. Prosecution witness Pvt. Peter Hummel told the court: "A group of men were in a peach orchard taking the fruit. They had already been ordered to get out of the orchard. Colonel Taggart told Pvt. George Davis to drop his peaches. He did. Then the colonel struck him with his fist." Pvt. Abe Grove testified that the colonel had ordered the men out of the orchard once before and when they went back in, Colonel Taggart hit Private Davis three times with his fist, then drew his pistol and pointed it at Davis. There was considerable discussion about who had stood where among the laden peach trees. The court then moved on to the fourth specification, that of obtaining money through false promises. A great deal of testimony clarified the following story. At a meeting of the officers, money was collected to hire a regimental band. One officer was to be sent to York County to hire "the cheapest band available." This was followed by a long session of quibbling and dissention over who was to look for this band and who was to hold the money, given that the element of trust among these officers, whose regiment was only two weeks old, was at a minimum.

The second day of the trial, there was no quorum because of the expedition to Dranesville, Virginia. The third day rehearsed the themes of testimony heard on the first meeting. Following the closing of testimony, Taggart submitted his written defense. The high points are these: at Baltimore, he had formed the regiment into line at the depot of the Northern Central Railway. He reminded them of the difficulties that other Yankee troops experienced with the citizens of Baltimore, but added that the Baltimore police had assured him of a peaceful passage. Because of some earlier concern of a clash with civilians, the soldiers' muskets were capped and loaded. Colonel Taggart ordered the percussion caps removed and stated that no gun was to be fired unless he gave an order. The train left the station; only minutes later, while it was still proceeding through the suburbs of Baltimore, twenty-five or thirty shots were fired out of the windows. Shortly thereafter, the train stopped because of a broken coupling and the colonel went from car to car. He asked who had been firing, and every single man denied knowing anything about it. As he came to the last car, he saw Private Moyer (who does not appear to have been very bright) point his gun out the window and fire. Taggart went into that railway car, put Moyer under arrest, and ordered him to another car to be put under guard. Moyer refused to move, so the colonel boxed his ears once or twice with his open hand.

He further noted in his statement that he had been placed in command of nine hundred undisciplined men whose company officers exerted little or no control. He had no guard house, no leg irons, no handcuffs. He felt that if he did not make an example, he would have no control over these men, who did not have military training or the sense to stop firing their muskets. As to the teamster who failed to provide a horse, Colonel Taggart recalled that he had explained to the teamster that both he and the quartermaster were under the command of the colonel; the response had been "mutinous and sullen muttering." Colonel Taggart categorically denied using either the word "glab" or "son of a bitch."

Moving on to the subject of the battle of the peach orchard, Taggart stated that when the train stopped for water a man rushed into the cars and asked for the colonel. He found Taggart and told him, "There are 100 men in my orchard; I am a good Union man and I did not expect to be treated in such a way by Pennsylvania soldiers." Taggart drew his pistol and drove the men out of the orchard back into the cars. He told them there were plenty of provisions and instructed them not to disgrace the good name of the state of Pennsylvania. Five minutes later, four of the men had returned to the orchard and were stealing more peaches. Taggart called out. Three of the men ran away, but the fourth man, Private Davis, came toward him "in a leisurely manner, his blouse filled with fruit." Taggart went toward him to take away the fruit and, "Davis stepped back as if to strike me. I then used my fist and he staggered back. I told him men had been shot for lesser offenses. After that, the men behaved themselves."

After reviewing both the testimony and Taggart's statement, the court not only "honorable acquitted" Taggart, but gave their opinion that the charges against Taggart were "frivolous and vexatious."

The reviewing general, George B. McClellan, was in entire agreement with this acquittal. In his statement, McClellan is once again the eloquent disciplinarian.

The Major General Commanding is surprised that the charge and specifications against Colonel Taggart were ever brought to trial, resting as they do upon evidence which is so complete a vindication of his conduct. It appears that the men whom, in the enforcement of good order and military discipline, he was obliged to punish, were contumacious and insubordinate—were, some of them engaged in pillaging and pilfering, in which they persisted after admonition, and others were guilty of firing their guns in the car to the terror of the passengers, contrary to positive orders. In order to reduce them to obedience, it was necessary to act with promptitude and energy. They resisted his authority, and if much severer punishment had been necessary to restore order, it would have been fully justified. [Here, McClellan seems to suggest that Taggart would have been within his rights to start shooting the more insubordinate soldiers.] The proceedings of the Court martial are confirmed. Colonel Taggart will resume his sword and his duties.

On July 6, 1862, Colonel Taggart, now age forty-one, submitted his resignation, citing "considerations of a domestic and business character, imperatively demanding my attention."

This resignation was endorsed by Brig. Gen. Truman Seymour: "Colonel Taggart has rendered useful and honorable service during these last battles. At Mechanicsville, his regiment occupied the place of honor on the left and held the enemy firmly in check and behaved with great gallantry."

In this remarkably positive endorsement, Seymour continued, "At Dranesville, Colonel Taggart was conspicuously useful. His desire to return to render still greater services to the government, in organizing new levies [of troops] may be granted as a fitting compliment."

Taggart played another, and even more interesting, role on the stage of history. By 1863 the Federal government had set up boards to examine privates and sergeants, who were applying to be commissioned officers in the newly raised U.S. Colored Troops. The boards were quite strict, and were not approving enough men to fill the vacant officer slots. What was needed was an officer candidates school to prepare the men to pass their board examination. There was a partial precedent—the crammers courses in Britain, for those striving for junior officer posts. At the suggestion of Maj. Gen. Silas Casey, the Philadelphia Supervisory Committee for Recruiting Colored Regiments put together a faculty, published a prospectus, devised a one-month course of study, and opened for business the day after Christmas 1863. The Free Military School for Applicants for Command of Colored Troops was located at 1210 Chestnut Street in Philadelphia. Of the first ninety-four graduates, only four failed to receive a commission, and by March 1864 even the hypercritical Edwin M. Stanton, Lincoln's secretary of war, had kind words for the school. John H. Taggart was the preceptor for the school, and instrumental in organizing the country's first formal program for creating commissioned officers from the ranks.[2]

Taggart played this vital role as a civilian; he does not appear again in the military record and never applied for a pension.

Chapter Forty-Nine

"Damned Fool and Illiterate Whelp"

LT. COL. JONATHAN TARBELL

The theme of Charles Dickens's *Bleak House* is that of interminable litigation. The same might be said of the two commanders of the 91st Regiment of New York Volunteers: Col. Jacob Van Zandt and Lt. Col. Jonathan Tarbell.[1]

Tarbell was an upstate New York newspaper editor who in May 1861, at the age of forty, became a major in the 24th New York. Seven months later he resigned to take the lieutenant colonel's position with the 91st New York. At that time, his new regiment was stationed at Key West, Florida. Van Zandt had been colonel of the 91st since December 1861 and was age twenty-nine. The origins of their conflict are mysterious. It may have been the age difference; it may have been that Van Zandt was from an old New York Dutch family; it may have been a pure personality clash. But whatever the cause, by the time Tarbell had been with the 91st only three months, he was court-martialed, mostly on charges preferred by Van Zandt, charges which in their full, prolix form cover many pages.

The first charge was disobedience; listed under that were five specifications. On February 17, 1862, he was told to drill the regiment by wing and refused to do so. On another date, he refused to attend dress parade. On one occasion, he slept out of camp without permission and on two occasions, left the camp without the colonel's permission.

The second charge was the violation of the 42nd Article of War, which prohibits "lying out of camp without permission." This provision is intended to keep officers in close proximity with their men for better discipline and control. In Tarbell's case, it seems to be simply a restating of the third specification of the first charge. (At the time of the Civil War, the form of court-martial charges tended to be wordy and redundant.)

The third charge was that of mutinous conduct, in that Tarbell attempted to "incite officers by declaring that he would not obey Colonel Van Zandt's orders."

213

The fourth charge was neglect of duty, in that Tarbell had missed one dress parade. The fifth and final charge was conduct unbecoming an officer, with the specification that he had insulted citizens visiting the camp and that he had told his peers that Colonel Van Zandt was "a damned knave, a damned fool and [an] illiterate whelp."

It was customary after the witnesses had finished testifying for the defendant to submit a detailed defense. In his written statement, Tarbell rebutted the charge of "lying out of camp:" "Yes, it is true that I slept out of camp, in the town of Key West, on the evenings of February 15th and 16th, with the express consent of Colonel Van Zandt, and at the express request of the Curtis family, the only original, uncompromising, unconditional Union family in Key West, who had accused me of neglect in not previously accepting their offers of hospitality." Tarbell continued his statement, noting that this was the only occasion in which he did not sleep or eat with his regiment. "I was not only in conformity with regulations, but I did it as duty and as examples to the men." Regarding the charge of mutinous conduct, Tarbell presented this defense:

I was fully in charge of drilling the regiment. Colonel Van Zandt and his adjutant, from February 1, 1862, to March 26, 1862, did not attend a single drill. Then, on March 27th, the colonel ordered that the next day we would have target practice, when the men had not yet been instructed in loading and firing. This instruction had been delayed in deference to orders from the Department Commander. Target practice without instruction in loading and firing would be an utter waste of ammunition. As to my saying that I would not attend drill the next day, this was entirely concocted by false testimony, by Captain [John] McDermott, who told so many lies that others came to believe them.

The court concluded that Tarbell was guilty of ten of the specifications and acquitted him on five of them, leaving a verdict of guilty, accompanied by a very strong recommendation for remission.

A petition signed by fourteen of the regimental officers stated that "Lieutenant Colonel Tarbell was an excellent soldier and before Colonel Van Zandt returned to the regiment, Tarbell had parade grounds built, was the only drill officer and held drills before breakfast, twice in the forenoon, held an officer's school at 1:00 P.M., and a final drill in the afternoon, and our regiment's progress was unprecedented." The same fourteen officers also noted that "If Captain McDermott testifies on any subject, we would not believe him under oath."

In July 1862 the conviction was remitted by Brig. Gen. John M. Brannan. Van Zandt immediately appealed this decision to Washington, and received an opinion from John F. Lee of the judge advocate general's office: "General Brannan did not have the power to remit, only the power to suspend and refer to the President. On the record, the charges are grave and the sentence ought to be enforced."

Lt. Col. Jonathan Tarbell spent most of the war in litigation with his semiliterate commander Col. Jacob Van Zandt. MASSACHUSETTS COMMANDERY MILITARY ORDER OF THE LOYAL LEGION, U.S. ARMY MILITARY HISTORY INSTITUTE.

The nature of the quarrel at this point may be partially illustrated by a memo dated March 25, 1862, in the hand of Colonel Van Zandt himself. "To the Officer of the Guard. You will have all the Musick Boys know in the guard house placed of police and to be kept at woork the hole day. They will geather all the loose stones in the camp and on the paraid ground. Keep them at woork all day." Since Van Zandt could not spell simple words, and Tarbell was a newspaper editor, this may account for his denunciation of his superior as "an illiterate whelp." Analysis of the content of the memo shows Van Zandt more interested in having his bandsmen picking up the loose rocks on the parade ground than in their playing music.

On May 14, 1862, the acting adjutant of the 91st Regiment, a protégé of Van Zandt, wrote the following memo to a Lt. William Barker, who was apparently under arrest. "I am directed by the colonel commanding to say that the limits of your arrest are extended to include the sinks [latrine]." It is not stated where Barker was supposed to perform his bodily functions before the limits of his arrest were extended.

On June 23, 1862, eighteen officers of the 91st New York wrote to Edwin M. Stanton and to Edwin D. Morgan, governor of New York, a letter that concluded "without one thought of insubordination . . . we pray for the removal of Colonel Van Zandt."

In a second petition to Stanton, sent in September 1862, again from a group of officers of the 91st New York, they noted that when they arrived at Key West there were 953 enlisted men and even without combat, there were now only 440 fit for duty, due to the "negligence and incompetence of Colonel Van Zandt." They also complained that over the recommendations of the other officers, Van Zandt had appointed as sutlers, Peter Haus, an Albany tailor, and William Paff, "an immigrant paper-hanger." They further charged that Van Zandt, in collusion with the two sutlers, had enforced payment of exorbitant prices by threats of military disciplinary action.

In October and November, the energies of the 91st New York seemed almost entirely consumed with internal dissention and petition-signing. In early October, the men of Company C were circulating a petition on behalf of Tarbell when Captain McDermott confiscated the petition, called the men "liars and thick lubber-headed fools," and threatened to have them locked up in Fort Pickens. The unhappy men of Company C noted that McDermott was a chronic drunk who had had two episodes of the delirium tremens since arriving at Key West. Lt. A. J. Oliver of Company E filed a paper certifying that Colonel Van Zandt had put him under arrest without his supper until he agreed to give Van Zandt the petition that was being circulated in favor of Tarbell.

Among the many supporters of Tarbell was the noted historian, chaplain, and Jesuit, Father M. A. Nash of the 6th New York, who wrote to Tarbell, "The officers of the brigade have repeatedly spoken of you in the highest terms of praise." This was followed by a petition signed by fourteen officers of the 6th New York, in which they stated, "We bear testimony to the unvarying good conduct of Lieutenant Colonel Tarbell." In early November, Lt. Col. S. de Agreda of the 134th New York wrote, "It would afford me great pleasure to testify in your behalf, as no officer in Key West enjoyed a more enviable reputation than you, in everything pertaining to the character of a soldier and a gentleman."

This flurry of letters and petitions apparently reached the governor's office in Albany, and on October 29, Edwin Morgan wrote to Abraham Lincoln, vouching personally for Tarbell's character and conduct. It was the governor's impression that

Colonel Tarbell had the confidence and respect of everyone in the regiment, "with very few exceptions," and expressed his opinion that matters had been and could be straightened out between the colonel and the lieutenant colonel. The governor concluded, "I may respectfully ask that you will cause the papers in the case to be examined in connection with the personal statements and explanations of Tarbell and such papers and testimonials as he may produce."

Lincoln apparently referred the matter to Col. Joseph Holt, the judge advocate general of the army. Holt's specialty was unraveling difficult legal knots, a function he performed very well for the President. On December 20 he prepared an unusually long—four pages—opinion in which he reviewed the facts of the court-martial, the remittal by General Brannan, the report by Judge Advocate Lee and the dismissal of Tarbell. Holt's training in the law shines through in the report:

> The remission of the sentence was a nullity. The action of the War Department proceeded on the assumption that under the 89th Article of War, the sentence had been "suspended" by the commanding general, until the pleasure of the President could be known. This was a mistake. Instead of having been 'suspended,' it had been approved, and the attempt to remit it being a nullity, the officer was no longer in the service, and of course, the order of the 23rd of August was necessarily inoperative. Such being the condition of the case, the only question to be considered is whether the Department will assent to the reappointment of Lieutenant Colonel Tarbell by the Governor of New York.

Holt then reviewed the petitions and letters in favor of Tarbell, including the personal communication from the governor of New York, noted also the unanimous recommendation of clemency by the court-martial board and further noted the even more amazing fact that 580 of the 600 enlisted men in the regiment had petitioned for the restoration of Tarbell. "In their memorial, they speak of him in the warmest terms of praise, declaring that he was not only an efficient soldier and a kind-hearted officer, but one who had ever labored for their improvement and good, both individually and collectively, and that in season and out of season, he had been untiring in his efforts to make them proficient soldiers and good men."

Holt further noted that the charges against him when "examined in the light of the evidence" dwindled down to "petty irregularities, which, however grave in the judgment of a mere martinet, weigh but little against the virtues as a man, which this officer unquestionably possesses and displays." Holt concluded, "The Court martial was prompted by malign and unworthy influences." He strongly recommended to the President that Tarbell be restored.

After some further maneuvering, Tarbell returned to the 91st New York in June 1863, again serving as lieutenant colonel under Van Zandt. Five months later, he appeared as a witness for the prosecution when Van Zandt himself was being court-martialed. Van Zandt's legal status appears to have been in limbo from about August 1863 to February 1865, when Van Zandt was dismissed from the service. With Van Zandt's dismissal, Tarbell, who had been commanding the regiment for a considerable time as a lieutenant colonel, was finally elevated to full colonel.

In the meantime, Tarbell's duties had continued in spite of the prolonged litigation. In September 1864 he wrote to his divisional commander, "I have commanded the 91st New York without any field officer for a year, and I now have a competent major and I request a leave." The leave was granted. (Much of this time, he had been in command of the army post at Fort Jackson, Louisiana.)

It would appear that Tarbell's many claimed virtues were more than mere claims, and in March 1865 he was elevated to brevet brigadier general for "gallant and meritorious service." Colonel Tarbell was "highly commended" for his actions in the engagement at Gravelly Run, Virginia, March 31, 1865, when he held his command in their place while other Union units were retreating in the face of heavy fire. The report uses the words "coolness and daring."[2]

Four months later, with the war over, he was mustered out with his regiment, after having participated in the surrender of Lee at Appomattox Court House and in the grand review held in Washington, D.C., on May 23, 1865.

After the war, Tarbell pursued a career in law, served as a judge and, from 1880 to 1885, was deputy first comptroller of the U.S. Treasury. He died in 1888, and was buried at Arlington National Cemetery.

In spite of all the opinions rendered and testimonials presented, the one indisputable part of the written record that comes down to us is that Tarbell was a good speller and Van Zandt was not.

EPILOGUE

In this sample of fifty officers, the first fifty colonels and lieutenant colonels to be subject to court-martial or court of inquiry after Fort Sumter, we find ten with some military experience. Turchin served in the Russian Army, Mihalotzy in Austria, and Vigneur de Monteil in France. Harlan claimed British Army experience, and Irwin, O'Keefe, MacGregor, and D. H. Williams claimed to have fought in Mexico. Miles was an old army man, and Holliday a more recent West Point graduate. Carrington was given a commission in the regular army on the basis of political and bureaucratic successes. Of these ten, only Miles and Holliday had seen recent active service.

The other forty had entered the Union Army with no military qualification whatsoever. At that time, there were at least three routes to a volunteer colonelcy: raising and/or funding one's own regiment; being appointed by a state governor; or being elected by the officers of a newly organized regiment. The military service records available on these fifty officers are rarely complete enough to enable accurate comparison of the routes to colonelcy of most of these men.

One possible factor predisposing a colonel to court-martial was his immediate prewar occupation. Four men had been lawyers; five had a principally military background. There was one man from each of the following occupations: congressman, land agent, postmaster, surveyor, banker, lumber dealer, and editor. Sadly, for our purposes, review of the court-martial proceedings, pension records, and compiled service records of thirty-two of our fifty men failed to reveal their prewar civilian occupations, leaving insufficient data for analyzing the factor of civilian occupation.

As to men who rose through the ranks to the position of colonel, there are precious few. Where the service records are complete, the usual picture for a volunteer colonel was direct appointment to the silver eagles, with a few men entering as captains or majors, but jumping up to the colonelcy after several weeks, as the turmoil of mobilization created openings.

Regarding the important question of who preferred the charges in these courts-martial, here, too, the record is often silent. Sometimes light is shed during the opening challenges, before testimony begins, but in most trial records, the preferrer of charges was not detectable by this author.

What is clear is that only two of the fifty cases presented here are those of experienced U.S. Army serving officers. The rest are volunteers, with the wide spectrum of backgrounds that "volunteer" implies. The typical case was one of a colonel with no military background tried on charges preferred by officers of his own regiment. A close reading of these fifty cases will show no two exactly alike, but there are enough trends or patterns to establish five broad groups, as summarized in Table A (see page 236). Clearly, the most common charges were those of conduct unbecoming an officer and a gentleman and insubordination.

In the 1860s, these were more meaningful terms. A "gentleman," at least in the British sense, seemed to be a product of the union of several factors: some money, a nontechnical education, a circle of past and present associates with shared personal beliefs, a knowledge of sports and games, and a certain air of disdain mixed with *noblesse oblige*. Perhaps the best definition might be this: A gentleman is someone whom other gentlemen would accept.

"Conduct unbecoming" can be anything that brings disgrace upon the regiment, upon the service, or upon the officer himself. An officer was expected to drink, but not be drunk. If he had a woman, she was supposed to be his wife and to stay at home. If he had political beliefs, they should stay noncontroversial. It was assumed that his expertise in manly sports such as hunting or riding to the chase would qualify him for outdoor rigors. He was supposed to manifest a mixture of firmness, wisdom, and effortless nonchalance, which would solve the problems in the camp and become fearlessness in battle. In brief, he had to set a good example. Some men failed these tests, but few so badly as to face a court-martial.

The next most common flaw was that of insubordination. In a country founded upon revolution (and certainly George III considered the Americans to be insubordinate), there has been, and still is, eternal warfare between "freedom" and "discipline." This is only an extension of other national values: all men are created equal; show me that you are the better man; that is just your opinion; don't fence me in; step outside and we'll settle this, man to man. The European wilderness was tamed or at least explored by 500 B.C. The American frontier closed almost within living memory and its mark is with us yet, in cowboy movies, Western music, and rapacious attitudes toward forests, prairies, and mining claims. Colonels who in their civilian life dominated a small town government or owned a large business, were used to giving orders, not taking them. Obedience was a bitter medicine for them and many colonels could never choke it down.

The interplay between initiative and obedience always rests on judgment. A colonel who had spent years coming up the ladder in the regular army had many years to develop that sense of judgment and to find a balance between conflicting factors. The colonels who had been created overnight had to learn in a hurry. They were quick to resent even other volunteer colonels with a few days of seniority over them. To function, an army cannot be a debating society, but the colonels who had made their living in the law seemed especially vulnerable to insubordination.

Poor leadership was the third category of problem that led to court-martial. Leadership is many things, including the ability to inspire a following and the avoidance of capricious cruelty, which alienates most soldiers, especially those in a democracy. Some leaders were too strict and enforced a brutality that led to hatred and demoralization. Others were so lax that their camps resembled gatherings of half-naked homeless vagrants and drunken bums, rather than the camps of soldiers. It was the burden of the colonel to find a workable balance between strictness and flexibility. The touch needed would also vary from regiment to regiment. There were units composed mostly of schoolteachers, while many of those regiments recruited in New York City had large numbers of illiterate brawlers. What would suit one group might be wrong for another. Fortunately, most colonels achieved a functional middle path.

Cowardice, the fourth most common flaw of our colonels, requires some remarks. The Civil War combination of new weapons and old tactics had lethal effects. Many of the early trials during that war centered around whether an officer "showed fear." This fiction, that leaders felt, or at least showed, no fear was true for only a very small number of men, many of them quite peculiar. Marching in a straight line into the mouth of the cannon seems to make little sense today, and the approved maneuvers of 1865 would elicit a cry from today's soldier of: "Get down, you fool!" Perhaps the best definition of officer cowardice in the Civil War was an unwillingness to do what he had just ordered the privates and sergeants to do.

The remaining category, loosely termed "other," contains offenses too diverse to yield up either conclusions or meaningful statistics. We have seen examples of men court-martialed for keeping their troops from freezing to death, and men in conflict with their superiors because of high-quality training. A man who was sent home because of typhoid, and is next shown as present at Dry Tortugas, a man who shoots himself while under the influence of chloroform, and a man accused of reading pornography are certainly too diverse upon which to base generalizations or meaningful statistics.

It is of interest that more than half of the courts-martial of both colonels and lieutenant colonels yielded a verdict of acquittal, as seen in Table B (see page 237). Again, each case is different. In a few, a not guilty verdict is surprising and seems to fly in the face of the evidence, but in most cases, an acquittal reflected the pettiness of the original charges, the tensions in the regiment that gave rise to the charges, the political ambitions of the captains and majors, and the tendency to inflate personal grievances into chargeable offenses. However, the fate of those found guilty was a serious matter indeed. Almost two-thirds of them were recommended for dismissal from the service (the officer's equivalent of a dishonorable discharge), showing that the offense was considered quite grave.

What began as a trickle of courts-martial gradually swelled to a flood. Table C (see page 238) shows the rising volume of trials as the war progressed and the army expanded. The month of the firing upon Fort Sumter, the army held only twenty-seven courts-martial; by March 1863, the number was 1,362—a 5,000 percent increase. Table C and Graph A (see page 243) illustrate not only the great increase in courts-martial, but also a strong cyclic trend. Each winter, as the camps filled with bored and restless men, the Devil found the traditional work for idle hands. Drinking, fighting, and gambling all fostered conflict. Plaintive letters from freezing wives and starving children (the records are full of such missives) gave motivation for many desertions.

As spring sunshine dried the roads, courts-martial dropped steeply. The men found a new focus for their energies. The preparations for campaign and the movement of troops gave rise to a renewed sense of purpose. They began to fight the enemy instead of each other. The men had new hope that their sufferings and privations would now lead to victory, followed by peace, and a joyful homecoming. These factors form the basis for a plausible theory of the fluctuations in the number of trials.

Less clear is the pattern of legal entanglements of the colonels, as seen in Table C and Graph 2 (see page 244). While there is a strong increase in courts-martial in the winter of 1862–63, in the rest of the time for which there is data, the fluctuations seem almost random. An explanation may lie in the greater flexibility of an officer's life. He could resign if he didn't like army life; a private could not. An officer was allowed to order whiskey from the sutler; a private could not. He could often go home to tend to personal and business matters, while privates with dying wives and sickly children might beg in vain for a furlough. It would appear that the rank and file, tied strongly to the rhythmns of the army, responded directly to seasonal stresses, while ranking officers, with their wider social and financial horizons, responded in a more complex pattern.

There were differences in tendency to be court-martialed not only manifest from season to season, and rank to rank, but also in the place of origin of the soldier. The troops of some states seemed to generate more misbehavior than others. Table D (see page 240) shows clearly that not all states had the same representation at the bar of justice. New York furnished 16 percent of the Union troops, yet accounted for 27 percent of the colonels tried, 28 percent of the lieutenant colonels tried, and 20 percent of the men of all ranks who were court-martialed. The reasons are as yet unclear, but it is easy to speculate that in some cases the politically connected, but troublesome, men were products of New York City politics, with hoodlum voters and Tammany Hall ethics. The equally disproportionate number of Pennsylvania colonels may reflect the "Philadelphia lawyer" tradition of rancor, hair-splitting, and litigation, combined with the supercilious attitudes of the sons of the Main Line, but, again, this is only speculation, which future research may clarify or disprove. The troops of other states seem to follow a much more predictable pattern, in which the rates of court-martial almost exactly parallel the expected rates.

The most remarkable finding of this study is seen in Table E (see page 241). A full regiment had approximately 900 privates and one colonel. One might expect, with a study group of 16,044 court-martialed privates, that one would see 18 colonels being tried, a ratio of approximately 900 to one. Instead, we find 105 trials of full colonels, five times the expected frequency. How can this be explained?

There are several possible answers. The first possibility in explaining the excess of colonels is seen in the large number of cases involving pique, jealousy, trumped-up charges, ill will, and ambition. These might account for the approximately 50 percent acquittal rate. But even if half the cases were unfounded, that would still leave a court-martial rate for colonels more than twice what would be expected. A fuller explanation may take several forms. The vast majority of the colonels tried were almost completely inexperienced. They had been to no school for officers, they were often in combat a few weeks after receiving a commission, and below them were men equally inexperienced, undisciplined, and untrained. Above them were either U.S. Army regulars—impatient with unpredictable volunteers (John F. Reynolds said of his volunteers, "I almost despair!")—or volunteer brigadiers who had even more political pull than the political colonels. In brief, one explanation is that of inexperience. This compassionate view of the burdens of colonelcy should account for some of the colonels, men simply appointed far beyond their experience by state and Federal officials who had no better choices.

It would be a serious omission not to consider the role of alcohol in generating courts-martial. In the 107 trials of colonels, alcohol was mentioned in the transcripts of 23 percent; for lieutenant colonels the percentage was identical. Twenty percent of the trial records of privates mention alcohol as a factor; the same percentage is found in reviewing all 22,217 courts-martial thus far available for study. For practical purposes, these percentages are identical, since some degree of intoxication was widespread and there was little agreement among witnesses as to whether any defendant was "under the influence." Alcohol was frequently described as a form of medication, as a stimulant, and as part of the soldier's daily ration. The most that can be concluded from these records is that in roughly 20 percent of cases, the defendant was intoxicated enough that men, in a tolerant era, would consider it beyond the accepted norm. In this, the colonels seem little different from the privates.

Another possible explanation for the higher rate of court-martial of colonels is one which would fit such men as Colonels McCunn and Lord. The records portray one as litigious and arrogant, and the other as an excited drunkard used to having his own way. The power given to them exposed their worst features, and they used their army experience in ways that reflected the misuse of power. It is said that power corrupts. This is not uniformly true. Men of bad character, flawed with deceit, self-deception, and ill will sink to their own level when given power to do so, while other men rise to the occasion and surprise even themselves with steadfast and courageous deeds.

A very important factor influencing the performance of colonels lay in politics, and in the difference between Federal and Confederate policies regarding depleted regiments. When a Southern regiment became below strength, whether from wounds or from disease, it kept its identity and was replenished. In contrast, when a Union regiment was below strength, it was often left that way, and new recruits were diverted into newly created regiments. A new regiment meant a need for an new colonel. Such appointments lay within the powers of the Northern governors and were a source of political patronage.[1]

A governor could reward political supporters with a pair of silver eagles. A colonel's commission was not only an honor in itself, a title with the ring of manly virtue, but could be a stepping stone to the further prestige of a general's commission or to postwar political opportunities. Nathaniel Hawthorne anticipated these trends as early as 1862, when he wrote, "Every country-neighborhood will have its general or two, its three or four colonels, half a dozen majors, and captains without end . . . all with their campaign stories, which will become the staple of fire-side talk forevermore . . . military notoriety will be the measure of all claims to civil distinction. One bullet-headed general will succeed another in the Presidential chair." No governor could escape the arithmetic of creating new regiments. A regiment of 900 privates needed a single colonel; three regiments, each with only 300 privates, required three colonels—three opportunities to pay off political debts.

In any population, there is only a limited number of men who combine intelligence with noble character. Enlarging the number of colonels insured that the chances of any single colonel being a splendid fellow were seriously diminished. This policy of gubernatorial largesse almost guaranteed a plethora of colonels who tended to be less suitable than their Southern counterparts. Thus, through "colonel inflation," the Union contributed to a supply of unsatisfactory men.[2]

Yet another possible explanation to the already-noted excess of court-martialed colonels may be a statistical problem, generated by the theoretical size of a regiment, and the steady decline in actual size. With an assumed regimental size of 900 privates, there were five times the expected number of colonels tried. If regiments had only 450 privates, the ratio would fall to two and one-half times the expected numbers of court-martialed colonels, and if the average Union regiment had only 180 men, then the ratio would reach the expected relationship. Establishing this explanation would require a study of regimental strengths, month by month, an undertaking beyond the scope of this book.

Another explanation of the disparate colonel/private ratio might be that the broader stage, in the great drama of war, furnished to a colonel the opportunity to make a greater fool of himself. The private, certainly capable enough of mischief in his own right, was constrained by being, literally, "in the ranks," shoulder to shoulder with other men in the drill, moving as a small part of a larger unit. The colonel, in command, on horseback, looking down on "his" men, was given an arena in which to see himself in a magnified role, with an inflated sense of importance, an attitude that leads to the conflicts inherent in hierachies, where the officially sanctioned wielding of power can lead to an inaccurate sense of entitlement, with the attendant dangers of hubris. It is only from great heights that one can be thrown down.

Finally, it may be a combination of all these factors—the lust for power and glory, the self-delusion that military skill can be quickly learned, the hope for future rewards, the certainty that combat will highlight character flaws, and the excitement generated by gubernatorial recognition—that contributed to the remarkable abundance of court-martialed colonels.

Yet, it is easy to to be ungenerous to these colonels of the past, just as it easy to second-guess the commanders of years gone by. We can replay those battles and decisions, with the hindsight denied to our ancestors; we can pontificate on this man's loss of nerve, and that man's failure to get his troops to point B on time. Perhaps we might be fairer if we recall that 130 years ago, no one knew how the war would end or what the future would bring. In the midst of great battles, where the smoke hung heavy in the air and contact between commander and field was perilous at best, the outcome was less clear to the participants than it is to us today. Our fifty colonels, presented here with all their vices and virtues outlined in the unkind light of history, had little or no idea what would happen in the next month or the next year of the war. In spite of their privileges, they lived in an era of rampant infection, ignorant doctors, inadequate maps, shoddy equipment, and confused intelligence. The Everyman of 1861–65, whether his shoulders be spangled with stars or as barren as the desert, spent his years tired, hungry, and unwashed. The camps smelled like pig sties, littered with human waste. The vast majority of men of all ranks alternated between the sweats and the chills of malaria, all the while keeping one eye on the nearest bush in anticipation of the next bout of diarrhea.

Perhaps we should be governed by charity, compassion, and humility in assessing, or even studying, these long-dead colonels. Perhaps we should ask ourselves if we could do better, if we were to be suddenly blinded to all we know of the history of the war and cast into that fog of the immediate present, in which all mankind actually lives. Would we really do better? Are we without sin, to cast the first stone?

A very different view of our troubled colonels is offered by a mother superior in the novel, *Madeleine's Ghost*: "I'm afraid we don't think much of history here, Mr. Conti. History is for the vain, since the hand of God will sweep it all away in the end." While she may well be correct, the writer of history seems entitled to hope that reflection upon the past can be meaningful, and that meditation on lives gone by may be redemptive, not only for the reader and for the writer, but even for the the subjects of the study, to exorcise their demons and to resurrect their acts of virtue.[3]

APPENDIX A:
THE INDEX PROJECT, INC.

The colonels and lieutenant colonels described in this book were discovered in the process of preparing a computerized index of all 100,000 Union general courts-martial. This project, which began in 1994, is now conducted under the auspices of The Index Project, Inc., a California nonprofit corporation, the principal investigators being the author and Beverly A. Lowry.

The court-martial records during the Civil War were filed in the order that they were received. Thus, a trial record from Virginia might appear next to a New Mexico record of six months earlier, since one came across a single river, while the other may have traveled up the Santa Fe Trail by ox-cart, making for a tangled chronology in filing.

The only index of the Union general courts-martial now extant was prepared in the 1880s, and it is a name index, available on six rolls of microfilm. Much of the ink is faded and an hour's search may yield a name and a file number, a bare beginning for a researcher. There is no subject index, no way to search by rank, or by crime, or by state, or by regiment, or by any other dimension that might be of interest to researchers or historians.

All the records are handwritten by hundreds of different scribes. No known computer program or scanning device is currently capable of analyzing or indexing these documents. No optical character recognition program can look at the handwriting of those long-dead scribes—who were paid fifty cents a day—and make anything useful of the input.

The Index Project began with the court records filed the day of the firing upon Fort Sumter, and as of March 1997, 24,000 courts-martial have been summarized and entered into a computerized data base. The investigators anticipate that by June 1998 every Union general court-martial from Fort Sumter to Appomattox will be available for computer search.

These colonels are only the beginning of what may be a major new phase in Civil War historiography, based on records previously unused by writers because of the impenetrability of the records as they stood. This wealth of new, yet old, material will open the eyes of those who value truth over myth. There were hundreds of murders by Union soldiers, scores of rapes, dozens of horses mutilated or sexually abused by their riders, and thousands of men whose fulminations, blasphemies, and curses were meticulously recorded by the Federal government. There were bisexual colonels, raids by laughing privates upon the naked inmates of bordellos, and severe penalties visited upon twelve-year-old soldiers. There are whole ranks of quartermasters who embezzled, surgeons who ran boarding houses stocked with supplies intended for the wounded, boatloads of officers who grew rich from kidnapping bales of cotton and dined on duck and champagne while the soldiers beneath them perished of malnutrition. There are more than 20,000 deserters, many of whom fell by the wayside, consumed with disease, and were later charged with a crime which can carry the penalty of death.

It seems very possible that the opening of these records will inspire a fresh generation of authors, ready to go beyond the twice-told tales familiar to all of us, to create a whole new genre of entirely primary source material, and become the foundation for decades of theses, dissertations, books, and articles.

APPENDIX B:
THE ARTICLES OF WAR

THE ARTICLES OF WAR—1775

The Articles of War were approved June 30, 1775, and appear in their full original text in the *Journals of the Continental Congress,* volume II, page 111, U.S. Government Printing Office, Washington, DC, 1905. Here they are summarized.

1. Every officer and soldier shall subscribe to these rules.
2. All shall attend Divine Service and behave reverently.
3. Soldiers who curse shall be reprimanded or confined. Officers who curse shall be fined four shillings.
4. Contempt for the commander shall be punished.
5. Beginning or joining a mutiny shall be punished.
6. Failing to suppress a mutiny shall be punished.
7. Any man striking or disobeying his superior shall be punished.
8. Men who desert or go absent without leave shall be punished.
9. Advising another to desert shall be punished.
10. All officers have the power to quell disorders and must be obeyed.
11. Dueling and challenges to a duel are prohibited.
12. Every officer shall prevent abuses of citizens, or be responsible for the effects.
13. Any officer feeling abused by his colonel may complain to the general.
14. Any soldier feeling wronged by his captain may appeal to his colonel.
15. Wasting of ammunition or provisions shall be punished.
16. Any soldier over a mile from camp without a written pass shall be punished.
17. No officer or soldier may lie out of camp without permission.
18. Every soldier will retire to his quarters at the beating of retreat.
19. No officer or soldier may miss parade, or leave guard, without permission.
20. A commissioned officer found drunk on duty shall be cashiered [dismissed]. A soldier drunk on duty shall be punished.
21. A sentinel who sleeps or leaves his post shall be punished.
22. Any soldier or officer who creates a false alarm shall be punished.

23. Any soldier who leaves his platoon without permission shall be punished.
24. No officer or soldier shall abuse a provisioner.
25. During battle, anyone who shamefully leaves his post, shall suffer immediate death.
26. Anyone who betrays or changes the watch-word shall suffer death.
27. Any soldier who helps the enemy shall be punished.
28. Any person giving intelligence to the enemy shall be punished.
29. All captured supplies shall be for the use of the United Colonies.
30. Anyone who plunders during a battle shall be punished.
31. Anyone who compels a commander to surrender shall suffer death.
32. All sutlers are subject to these articles.
33. All general courts-martial shall consist of at least thirteen commissioned officers. The president shall be a field grade officer. He shall have the power to administer oaths.
34. [Gives rules for precedence and rank during courts-martial.]
35. Members of the court are to behave decently; lowest rank votes first.
36. Field officers may be tried by captains and above; trials will be held between 8 A.M. and 3 P.M., unless an immediate example is needed.
37. Regimental courts-martial may be conducted by any commissioned officer, and may inflict corporal punishment, but the colonel must confirm sentences.
38. Regimental courts-martial shall contain at least five officers.
39. The Commander of a fort may assemble courts-martial as though they were regimental.
40. Menacing words or disorder during a court-martial shall be punished.
41. Until court-martialed, officers committing a crime shall be under arrest; and soldiers shall be confined.
42. Such arrest or confinement shall be for no more than eight days, or until a court-martial can be conveniently assembled.
43. An officer of the guard must receive such a prisoner; the charging officer must submit the charges in writing.
44. An officer of the guard must not release a prisoner without proper authority, or allow that prisoner to escape.
45. The officer of the guard must notify his commanding officer, within twenty-four hours, of any prisoner held by him, the charge, and the officer preferring the charge.
46. Any arrested officer who violates his arrest shall be cashiered.
47. Any officer convicted of scandalous or infamous behavior, unbecoming the character of an officer and a gentleman, shall be dischaged from the service.
48. These same rules apply to officers and soldiers of the artillery.
49. If not enough infantry officers are available for a court-martial, artillery officers may be used.

50. Excepting capital offenses, all disorders and neglects which are to the prejudice of good order and military discipline, even if not mentioned in these articles, may be punished.

51. The death penalty may be used only in those crimes named in these articles. Regarding other crimes, punishments are limited to degrading, cashiering, drumming out, fines not exceeding two months pay, imprisonment not exceeding one month, or a maximum of thirty-nine lashes.

52. Any fines levied will be used to help the sick and wounded.

53. [Gives the form and manner of administering oaths to members of the court.]

54. Any witness refusing to give evidence shall be punished.

55. Every officer shall, when so ordered, muster his unit.

56. Every colonel or field officer may grant furloughs to his soldiers, but not to exceed twenty days in six months, nor more than two men absent at the same time from the same company.

57. At every muster, each officer shall account for all his men, and so report to the general and to the Congress, or be discharged from the service.

58. An officer who signs a false certificate of leave shall be cashiered.

59. An officer who signs a false muster shall be cashiered.

60. Any commissary who takes a gratuity on the signing of the musters shall be dismissed.

61. An officer who musters a man who does not do duty as a soldier shall be guilty of a false muster.

62. Any officer who makes a false return of his men or equipment shall be cashiered.

63. The commanding officer of every unit shall make a monthly report, accounting for all his officers and men.

64. No sutler shall keep shop or sell liquor after 9:00 P.M. or before reveille, or during Sunday Divine Service.

65. Every commander is responsible that sutlers provide wholesome provisions at a reasonable price.

66. Officers who profit from sutler's sales shall be cashiered.

67. The general may pardon persons convicted at general courts-martial; the colonel may pardon persons convicted at regimental courts-martial.

68. If an officer dies, the Major shall inventory his effects, pay any debts and burial expenses, and provide the remainder to the executors of the deceased's estate.

69. Company commanders will provide the same service for soldiers who die.

THE ARTICLES OF WAR—1861

All soldiers and officers of the U. S. Army were governed by a written code of conduct, the Articles of War. These were revised from time to time in the period between the Revolutionary War and the attack on Fort Sumter. At the time of the Civil War, the version used was the *Revised Regulations for the Army of the United State—1861*, and were published in 1862 by George W. Childs of Philadelphia. For purposes of brevity and easy reference, they have been paraphrased as follows.

1. Every officer shall subscribe to these rules.
2. It is recommended that all officers and soldiers attend Divine Service and shall behave decently.
3. Any soldier or officer who curses shall be fined.
4. Chaplains who shirk their duty will be fined or discharged.
5. Speaking ill of the President, the Congress, or any State Legislature will be punished.
6. Any soldier or officer who shows disrespect toward his superior will be punished.
7. Any officer or soldier who begins or joins in a mutiny shall suffer death.
8. Any officer or soldier who fails to suppress a mutiny shall suffer death.
9. Any officer or soldier who strikes or threatens his superior with violence shall suffer death.
10. Every soldier shall have read to himself these Articles of War and will swear allegience to the United States.
11. All discharges from the Army will be in writing, by competent authority.
12. Commanders of regiments and companies may issue furloughs not to exceed twenty days in six months.
13. Every commander is responsible for submitting muster rolls accounting for all officers and men.
14. Officers submitting false musters will be cashiered.
15. Officers who make false musters of men or horses shall be cashiered.
16. Anyone taking bribes for mustering soldiers will forever lose any Federal employment.
17. An officer who musters a soldier who is not a soldier is guilty of making a false muster.
18. Any false report regarding troops or supplies shall be punished by dismissal.
19. Every commander will submit a monthly report of all his officers and their whereabouts.
20. Officers and soldiers who desert will suffer death.
21. Being absent without leave will be punished.
22. No soldier shall enlist in one regiment before he has been discharged from another.

23. Any soldier or officer who advised desertion shall suffer death.
24. Any soldier or officer using provocative speech or gesture shall be arrested.
25. Officers engaging in a duel will be cashiered.
26. Anyone who knows of a duel and does not report it shall be punished.
27. Officers of any rank have full power to quell all quarrels and disorders.
28. An accusation of cowardice regarding dueling will result in punishment of the accuser.
29. Sutlers may not sell alcohol or stay open past 9:00 P.M. or on Sunday.
30. Commanders are responsible for the quality of the goods sold by the sutler.
31. No commander shall profit by the business of a sutler.
32. Commanders are responsible for any pillage or brutality committed by their troops.
33. Commanders shall assist in apprehending accused persons.
34. Any officer who thinks himself wronged by his colonel may complain to the commanding general.
35. Any solder who feels himself wronged by his captain may complain to the colonel. Groundless complaints will be punished.
36. Unauthorized sales of army property will be punished.
37. Any soldier who wastes ammunition shall be court-martialed.
38. Any soldier who sells or damages his horse or rifle shall be punished.
39. Any officer who embezzles money shall refund it and be cashiered.
40. Every captain is accountable to his colonel for lost or damaged material.
41. Any soldier more than a mile from camp without a written pass shall be punished.
42. No officer may lie out of his quarters without permission.
43. Any soldier who does not retire to his quarters at the beating of "Retreat" shall be punished.
44. All officers and soldiers will be prompt for parade or be punished.
45. Any officer drunk on duty will be cashiered. Any soldier drunk on duty will suffer corporal punishment.
46. Sentinels found sleeping shall suffer death.
47. No soldier may hire someone else to do his duty.
48. Any officer conniving at the hiring of duty shall be punished.
49. Any officer causing a false alarm shall suffer death.
50. Any officer or soldier who quits his place of guard shall be punished.
51. Any officer or soldier doing violence to any person bringing provisions shall suffer death.
52. Any officer or soldier who runs away or shamefully abandons his post in the face of the enemy shall suffer death.
53. Any person revealing the password will suffer death.
54. Persons damaging property on the line of march will be punished.

55. Whoever forces a safeguard shall suffer death.
56. Whoever supplies money or ammunition to the enemy shall suffer death.
57. Anyone providing intelligence to the enemy shall suffer death.
58. All captured enemy supplies belong to the United States.
59. If any commander is compelled by his officers or troops to surrender, they shall suffer death.
60. All sutlers are subject to orders.
61. An officer's date of mustering shall determine his rank within his own corps.
62. In a combined operation, the officer of highest rank shall command the whole.
63. Engineers need not perform duty outside their special profession, and are to receive every mark of respect.
64. A general court-martial shall consist of not less than thirteen officers, when that number can be convened without injury to the service.
65. Any general officer commanding an army may appoint a general court-martial. No sentence shall be carried out until he has reviewed the findings.
66. Every regimental commander may appoint a court-martial of three officers for trying noncapital cases.
67. Regimental courts-martial may not try officers nor imprison nor put to hard labor.
68. Officers of the Marines may be appointed to courts-martial.
69. The Judge Advocate shall prosecute but also consider himself as counsel for the prisoner.
70. A prisoner who stands mute will be tried as though he had pled not guilty.
71. A prisoner challenging a court member must state the cause of the challenge.
72. Members of a court-martial will behave with decency and calmness. The youngest officer votes first.
73. All witnesses will be sworn in.
74. Depositions are acceptable in noncapital cases.
75. If it can be avoided, no officer shall be tried by officers of inferior rank. Trials will be held between 8 A.M. and 3 P.M.
76. Persons disturbing a court-martial will be punished.
77. Any officer charged with a crime will be confined to his quarters and deprived of his sword. If he breaks his arrest, he shall be cashiered.
78. Soldiers charged with crimes will be confined until court-martialed.
79. A court-martial will be convened within eight days of confinement.
80. Any officer confining a prisoner must receive a written statement of the charge.

81. No officer shall release a prisoner without authority, or allow escape.

82. Every officer in charge of a confined person, shall inform the commanding officer of such confinement within twenty-four hours.

83. Any officer convicted of conduct unbecoming an officer and a gentleman shall be dismissed from the service.

84. An officer suspended from rank may also have his pay suspended.

85. In every case where an officer is convicted of fraud or cowardice, his crime will be reported in his hometown newspaper, and it shall be scandalous for an officer to associate with him.

86. Where there are not enough officers to form a court-martial, the officer commanding the department will order the removal of the accused and the witnesses to a suitable location.

87. A death sentence requires concurrence of two-thirds of the members of the court. No offender may receive more than fifty lashes. (Flogging prohibited totally 5 August 1861.) No person may be tried twice for the same offense.

88. If over two years have passed between the offence and the order for trial, the offender may not be tried, unless he had absented himself during the two years.

89. Any officer with the power to order a court-martial also has the power to mitigate a sentence except a sentence of death or cashiering. He may suspend sentence until review by the President of the United States.

90. The judge advocate of every court-martial shall send, as soon as possible, the proceedings to the Secretary of War, who shall file and preserve them, and make copies available.

91. A commander may order a court of inquiry, of one, two, or three officers, plus a judge advocate. They shall not give their opinion on the merits of the case.

92. The proceedings of a court of inquiry may be used in evidence in a court-martial. Courts of inquiry are prohibited unless ordered by the President or demanded by the accused.

93. (Gives the proper wording for swearing-in.)

94. When an officer dies, the major of the regiment shall inventory his belongings and send them to the War Department, for the executors of the deceased.

95. In the case of dead soldiers or noncoms, the company commander shall have responsibility for proper disposal of the dead man's belongings.

96. Engineers and artillerymen shall be governed by these same Articles of War.

97. Militia officers and soldiers are also governed by these rules, except that such courts-martial shall be composed solely of militia officers.

98. When regular officers and officers commissioned by their states, of the same rank, are together, regular officers shall take precedence, without regard to date of rank.

99. Any noncapital offense, not mentioned above, shall be tried as conduct prejudicial to good order and military discipline.

100. The President of the United State shall have power to prescribe the uniform of the Army.

101. The Articles of War are to be read to all soldiers—or those about to become soldiers—every six months.

Section 2. All persons not owing allegiance to the United States, who are found lurking near army encampments, shall be court-martialed and suffer death.

APPENDIX C: TABLES & GRAPHS

TABLE A
Themes of Charges at Court-Martial*

	Number	*Percent*
Insubordination	14	28
Conduct Unbecoming	13	26
Bad Leadership	11	22
Cowardice	4	8
Other	8	16

*Based on the fifty colonels and lieutenant colonels whose stories are narrated in this book.

TABLE B

Outcomes of Trials of Colonels*

	Number	*Percent*
Acquittal	60	58
Guilty	44	42
Sentence		
Dismissal from the army	27	63
Reprimand	13	28
Suspend from rank or pay	5	12

Outcomes of Trials of Lieutenant Colonels*

	Number	*Percent*
Acquittal	28	51
Guilty	27	49
Sentence		
Dismissal from the army	13	48
Reprimand	12	44
Suspend from rank or pay	2	7

*Based on 15,608 Union courts-martial.

TABLE C
Number of General Courts–Martial Convened per Month

	Colonels	Lieutenant Colonels	All Ranks
April **1861**	–	–	27
May	–	–	57
June	–	–.	117
July	2	–	126
August	1	2	143
September	1	–	310
October	–	–	182
November	1	–	411
December	4	3	541
January **1862**	5	2	939
February	5	–	492
March	2	1	483
April	8	1	386
May	1	1	372
June	3	1	469
July	5	1	615
August	5	–	336
September	5	3	433
October	6	4	692
November	11	6	691
December	5	5	608
January **1863**	2	3	882
February	7	4	1209
March	7	1	1384
April	2	6	888
May	4	3	803

continued

TABLE C
(continued)

	Colonels	Lieutenant Colonels	All Ranks
June	5	5	575
July	1	–	431
August	1	3	604
September	2	3	520
October	–	2	543
November	2	1	624
December	1	2	1042
January **1864**	2	5	1282
February	–	–	1016
March	1	4	749
April	1	2	883
May	1	1	203

N.B. Figures after February 1864 probably are not accurate, as transmittal and filing delays caused records to be filed in a manner only partly chronological. Thousands more records, to be indexed in coming years, will be necessary before a complete statement can be made about the patterns of Union court-martial during the Civil War.

TABLE D
CONTRIBUTIONS OF TEN STATES

State	Percent of all Union troops*	Percent of all men court-martialed, all ranks	Percent of all colonels court-martialed	Percent of all lt. colonels court-martialed
NY	16	20	27	28
PA	12	10	18	20
OH	11	7	9	10
IL	9	7	10	10
IN	7	5	6	4
MA	5	4	2	0
MO	4	5	3	3
WI	3	2	1	1
MI	3	2	3	7
NJ	3	2	3	1

*From Frederick Dyer, *Compendium of the War of the Rebellion,* vol. I, p. 11. The court-martial figures are based on the first 22,217 courts-martial following Fort Sumter, and reflect 105 colonels and 71 lieutenant colonels.

TABLE E
Number of Union Courts-Martial by Rank

Total (All Ranks)	22,217
Colonel	105*
Lieutenant Colonel	71**
Major	90
Captain	883
Lieutenant	1,468
Sergeant	689
Corporal	765
Private	16,044

*There were 105 trials of colonels; 83 colonels were court-martialed once; nine were court-martialed twice; and one was court-martialed four times.

**There were 71 trials of lieutenant colonels; 59 men were court-martialed once and six were court-martialed twice.

N.B. The table does not include less common ranks such as ensign, cornet, cadet, teamster, general, musician, artificer, surgeon, hospital steward, and civilian. The lieutenant category includes all grades of lieutenant. Sergeant includes only those simply called "sergeant" and does not include sergeant major, quartermaster sergeant, or ordnance sergeant.

TABLE F
Categories of Action That Generated an Entry in Record Group 153

	Colonel	Lieut. Colonel
Subject of a general court-martial, once	75	45
Subject of a general court-martial, twice	7	4
Subject of a general court-martial, more than twice	1	–
Subject of a court of inquiry	5	1
Avoided a proposed court-martial	1	1
Subject of a military commission	2	–

N.B. All these categories of judicial actions are found filed together in National Archives Record Group 153, the file holding general courts-martial. Apparent discrepancies in the total figures of courts-martial relate to these four different categories of action being filed together. In physical appearance the four different types of records are nearly identical.

Seasonal Changes in Courts-Martial: All Ranks

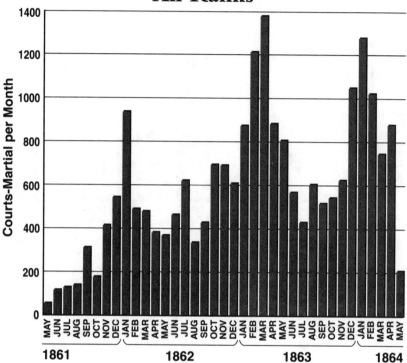

Graph A. *This graph, based on 22,217 courts-martial of all ranks clearly indicates a winter peak and a summer trough. The most likely explanation is the boredom and access to alcohol associated with winter camp, leading to conflict with peers. The summer trough is seen during active campaigning.*

Seasonal Changes in Courts-Martial:
Colonels & Lieutenant Colonels

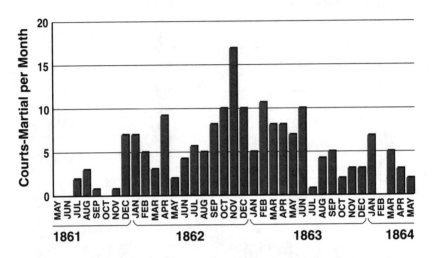

Graph B. This graph reflects 105 colonels and 72 lieutenant colonels. The winter peak, so prominent in all ranks, is prominent here only in the winter of 1862–63.

NOTES

Introduction: The Refiner's Fire

1. C. C. Brand, *Roman Military Law,* p. 27.
2. Ibid., p. 52.
3. Ibid., p. 82.
4. Ibid., p. 97.
5. Sylvia R. Frey, *The British Soldier in America,* p. 85.
6. National Archives Record Group 153: Pvt. Daniel Garrity, LL2700; Pvt. Amos Barbin, LL1109; Capt. James Cockefair, LL2656; Capt. Andrew Finch, LL2676.
7. Brand, p. 110.
8. Joseph DiMona, *Great Court-Martial Cases,* p. 97.
9. Harry G. Summers, *Los Angeles Times,* 3 Oct 1996, p. B-9.
10. Brand, p. 121.
11. Theodor Meron, *Henry's Wars and Shakespeare's Laws,* p. 75.
12. Frey, p. 34.
13. Ibid., p. 58.
14. Ibid.
15. Ibid., p. 62.
16. Ibid., p. 63.
17. Ibid., p. 67.
18. T. H. McGuffie, p. 96.
19. Francis P. Prucha, *Army Life on the Western Frontier,* p. 87.
20. Worthing C. Ford, p. 788.
21. James C. Neagles, *Summer Soldiers,* p. 67.
22. Luther C. West, *They Call It Justice,* p. 23.
23. G. Dearborn Spindler, "American Character as Revealed by the Military," p. 275.

Chapter 1

1. National Archives Record Group 153, Records of the Judge Advocate General's Office (Army), entry 15, Court-martial Case File, file II 412, cited as II 412.

Chapter 2

1. Thomas Kearny, *General Philip Kearny,* p. 316; E. M. Woodward, *History of the Third Pennsylvania Reserve,* p. 124.
2. KK81.

Chapter 3
1. Gerald E. Wheeler and A. Stuart Pitt, "The 53rd New York: A Zoo-Zoo Tale," *New York History,* October 1956, pp. 414–31.
2. II889.
3. National Archives pension file.

Chapter 4
1. 77th Article of War, 1861 version.
2. II584.
3. *New York Times,* 5 Mar 1878, p. 4, col. 6

Chapter 5
1. LL382.

Chapter 6
1. II855.

Chapter 7
1. II701.

Chapter 8
1. KK12.

Chapter 9
1. II405.

Chapter 10
1. II498, KK311.

Chapter 11
1. II427.

Chapter 12
1. KK233.

Chapter 13
1. II866.
2. Ezra Warner, *Generals in Blue,* p. 592.

Chapter 14
1. II573.

Chapter 15
1. II885.

Chapter 16
1. II455, II426.

Chapter 17
1. II408.

Chapter 18
1. KK193, KK194.

Chapter 19
1. II758.

Chapter 20
1. II680.
2. Kerrigan's advertisements, recruiting for the Brotherhood, appeared in several New York newspapers nearly every day, May 1 through June 7, 1866, and formed the basis for his arrest as a Fenian conspirator by Federal authorities June 7, 1866. Benedict R. Maryniak, personal communication, 1997.

Chapter 21
1. II895.

Chapter 22
1. II383.

Chapter 23
1. KK194.
2. Anton J. Heinlein, personal communication, Chickamauga National Military Park, 1996.

Chapter 24
1. II929.

Chapter 25
1. II813.

Chapter 26
1. LL247.

Chapter 27
1. LL706.

Chapter 28
1. LL1980, LL1982.

Chapter 29
1. Warner, p. 72.
2. "A Chapter on Complaints—Abuse in the Army." *Cincinnati Daily Commercial,* 7 Apr 1862.
3. Ibid.

4. Ibid.
5. Ibid.
6. II985.
7. Louise Barnett, *Touched by Fire: The Life of George Armstrong Custer,* p. 341.

Chapter 30
1. II856.
2. Alfred Ely, *Journal of Alfred Levy,* pp. 253–57.
3. II856.

Chapter 31
1. II892.

Chapter 32
1. II703, II755.

Chapter 33
1. KK19.

Chapter 34
1. KK182, KK171.
2. William T. Lawler, *The Lawlers, from Ireland to Illinois,* p. 96.

Chapter 35
1. II753.

Chapter 36
1. KK122.

Chapter 37
1. II586.

Chapter 38
1. KK78, KK105, LL2406 folder 1 & 2.

Chapter 39
1. II693.

Chapter 40
1. KK303.

Chapter 41
1. Robert C. Myers, "The Worst Colonel I Ever Saw," *Michigan History Magazine,* January–February 1996, p. 34.
2. Anonymous, "Headquarters Regiment Michigan Infantry," *Niles Inquirer,* 14 May 1862.

Chapter 42
1. KK81.

Chapter 43
1. KK78, KK105.
2. KK78, KK105, KK165.

Chapter 44
1. II809.

Chapter 45
1. KK248.
2. Roy P. Basler, *The Collected Works of Abraham Lincoln*, vol. 8, p. 105.

Chapter 46
1. II835.

Chapter 47
1. KK121.

Chapter 48
1. II604.
2. Dudley T. Cornish, *The Sable Arm,* p. 218.

Chapter 49
1. II838, II831.
2. National Archives RG 393, part 2, entry 2737, volume 57/112.

Epilogue
1. David C. Cole, U.S. Army Center of Military History, personal communication, 1997.
2. Ibid.
3. Robert Girardi, *Madeleine's Ghost,* p. 201.

BIBLIOGRAPHY

BOOKS

Barnett, Louise. *Touched by Fire: The Life of George Armstrong Custer.* New York: Owl Books, Henry Holt, 1996.

Basler, Roy P. *The Collected Works of Abraham Lincoln.* New Brunswick, NJ: Rutger University Press, 1953.

Brand, C. E. *Roman Military Law.* Austin: University of Texas Press, 1968.

Cornish, Dudley T. *The Sable Arm.* New York: Norton, 1956.

DiMona, Joseph. *Great Court-Martial Cases.* New York: Grossett & Dunlap, 1972.

Ely, Alfred. *Journal of Alfred Levy.* New York: Pub. Unknown, 1862.

Ford, Worthington Chauncey. *Journals of the Continental Congress.* Volume 3. Washington, DC: Government Printing Office, 1905.

Frey, Sylvia R. *The British Soldier in America.* Austin: University of Texas Press, 1981.

Girardi, Robert. *Madeleine's Ghost.* New York: Delacorte, 1995.

Kearny, Thomas. *General Philip Kearney.* New York: Putman, 1937.

Lawler, William T. *The Lawlers, from Ireland to Illinois.* Gallatin, TN: Kirby Publishers, 1978.

Meron, Theodore. *Henry's Wars and Shakespeare's Laws.* New York: Oxford University Press, 1993.

McGuffie, T. H. *Rank and File.* London: Hutchinson, 1964.

Neagles, James C. *Summer Soldiers.* Salt Lake City, UT: Ancestry Incorporated, 1986.

Prucha, Francis Paul. *Army Life on the Western Frontier.* Norman: University of Oklahoma Press, 1958.

Warner, Ezra. *Generals in Blue.* Baton Rouge: Louisiana State University Press, 1964.

West, Luthor C. *They Call It Justice.* New York: Viking Press, 1977.

Woodward, E. M. *History of the Third Pennsylvania Reserve.* Philadelphia: Pub. Unknown, 1883.

ARTICLES

Maskin, Meyer H. "Military Psychodynamics—Psychological Factors in the Transition from Civilian to Soldier." *Psychiatry* 6 (August 1943).

Myers, Robert C. "The Worst Colonel I Ever Saw." *Michigan History Magazine* (January–February 1996).
Spindler, G. Dearborn. "American Character as Revealed by the Military." *Psychiatry* 11 (August 1948).
Wheeler, Gerald E. and A. Stuart Pitt. "The 53rd New York: A Zoo-Zoo Tail." *New York History* (October 1956).

MANUSCRIPT COLLECTIONS

Records of the Judge Advocate General's Office (Army), National Archives and Records Administration, Washington, DC.

NEWSPAPERS

Cincinnati Daily Commercial
Los Angeles Times
New York Times
Niles Inquirer

INDEX